Ready-to-Go Lessons

Grade 5

About This Book

Your friends at *The Mailbox®* have done it again! We've combined four previously published books from the Lifesaver Lessons® series for Grade 5 (*Language Arts, Math, Science,* and *Social Studies*) into one comprehensive edition. This new compilation—*Ready-to-Go Lessons, Grade 5*—offers everything you need in one book to supplement all four curriculum areas for your grade level.

What Are Ready-to-Go Lessons?

Just as the name implies, this book includes well-planned, easy-to-implement, curriculum-based lessons that are ready to go in minutes. Each lesson contains a complete materials list, step-by-step instructions, a reproducible activity or pattern, and several extension activities.

How Do I Use a Ready-to-Go Lesson?

Each lesson is designed to decrease your preparation time and increase the amount of quality teaching time with your students. These lessons are great for introducing or reinforcing language arts, math, science, and social studies concepts. They'll even come in handy if you're planning for a substitute, as each lesson is planned and written for you and the materials can be easily gathered in advance. After completing each lesson as described, try one or more of the fun-filled extension activities that are included with each lesson.

What Materials Will I Need?

We've tried to make each lesson as easy to implement as possible, so most of the materials can be easily found right in your classroom. Be sure to read each materials list prior to the activity, as some supplies might need to be gathered from your school library or supply room.

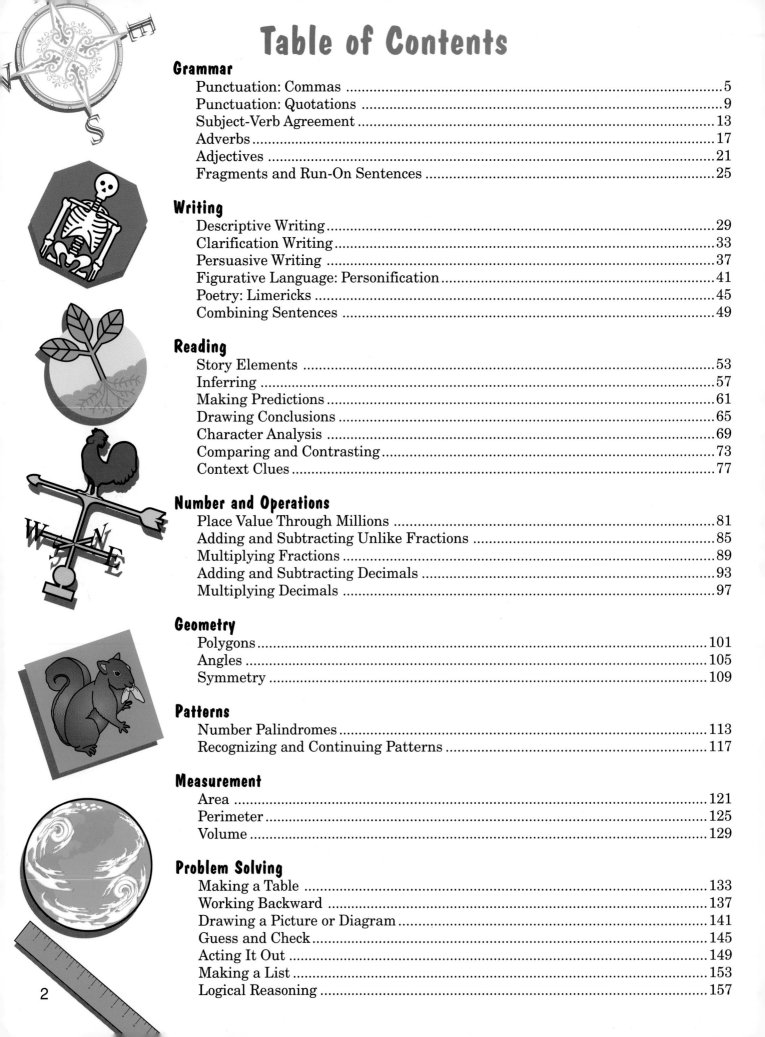

Table of Contents

Graphing, Probability & Statistics

The Scientific Method

Life Science

Physical Science

Earth Science

Map Skills/Geography

U.S. History

Government

Regions

Answer Keys

From Your Friends at The MAILBOX®

Ready-to-Go Lessons

Grade 5

Managing Editor: Scott Lyons
Contributing Writers: Julie Alarie, Marcia Barton, Irving P. Crump, Therese Durhman, Rusty Fischer, Michael Foster, Julie Eick Granchelli, Geri Harris, Elizabeth H. Lindsay, Debra Liverman, Thad McLaurin, Cindy Mondello, Lori Sammartino, Patricia Twohey, David Webb, Stephanie Willett-Smith
Copy Editors: Sylvan Allen, Karen Brewer Grossman, Karen L. Huffman, Amy Kirtley-Hill, Debbie Shoffner
Cover Artists: Nick Greenwood, Clevell Harris
Art Coordinator: Rebecca Saunders
Artists: Pam Crane, Theresa Lewis Goode, Sheila Krill, Clint Moore, Greg D. Rieves, Rebecca Saunders, Barry Slate, Stuart Smith, Donna K. Teal
Typesetters: Lynette Dickerson, Mark Rainey

President, The Mailbox Book Company™: Joseph C. Bucci
Director of Book Planning and Development: Chris Poindexter
Book Development Managers: Elizabeth H. Lindsay, Thad McLaurin, Susan Walker
Curriculum Director: Karen P. Shelton
Traffic Manager: Lisa K. Pitts
Librarian: Dorothy C. McKinney
Editorial and Freelance Management: Karen A. Brudnak
Editorial Training: Irving P. Crump
Editorial Assistants: Terrie Head, Hope Rodgers, Jan E. Witcher

www.themailbox.com

©2002 The Education Center, Inc.
All rights reserved.
ISBN #1-56234-502-8

Manufactured in the United States
10 9 8 7 6 5 4 3 2 1

No Bones About It!

Your students will be comma experts after playing this partner game.

Skill: Using commas correctly in a variety of sentences

Estimated Lesson Time: 45 minutes

Teacher Preparation:
Duplicate one copy of page 7 for each pair of students.

Materials:
1 copy of page 7 for each pair of students
1 die for each pair of students
scissors

Background Information:
- Use a comma to separate items in a list.
  Example: I bought a dog collar, a leash, and a bottle of pet shampoo.

- Use a comma to separate two independent clauses connected by *and, but, or, nor,* or *for.*
  Example: John used to play basketball, but now he plays volleyball.

- Use a comma to set off an introductory word or phrase from the main sentence.
  Examples: When you are finished, check your work with a partner.
  Yes, you can play after you check your work.

- Use a comma to set off the name of the person to whom you are speaking.
  Example: Wendy, can you help me for a minute?

- Use commas with direct quotes.
  Examples: Marilyn asked, "Can you repeat what you just said?"
  "I certainly will," the teacher replied.

Introducing The Lesson:

Begin the lesson by reviewing the five comma rules in "Background Information" on page 5. Share the examples for each rule.

Steps:

1. Pair up students and give each pair a copy of page 7. Provide each pair with scissors and a die.

2. Instruct each student to number a sheet of notebook paper 1–15. Then instruct each pair to cut out each card on page 7.

3. Have each pair shuffle its cards and place them facedown in a pile. To play the game, have one student in each pair turn over a card, then roll the die to determine a point value.

4. Next tell each student to write the point value in the left margin next to the number on his paper that matches the number on the card drawn from the pile. Then instruct each student in the pair to rewrite the sentence from the card next to the matching number on his paper, inserting the missing commas.

5. Have students take turns turning over cards and rolling the die until no cards remain.

6. Have partners switch papers; then as a class go over the correct answers to each card. Tell each partner to circle the point value in front of each *correct* answer. Next have both partners add up the points that were circled. Declare the pair with the most points the winner.

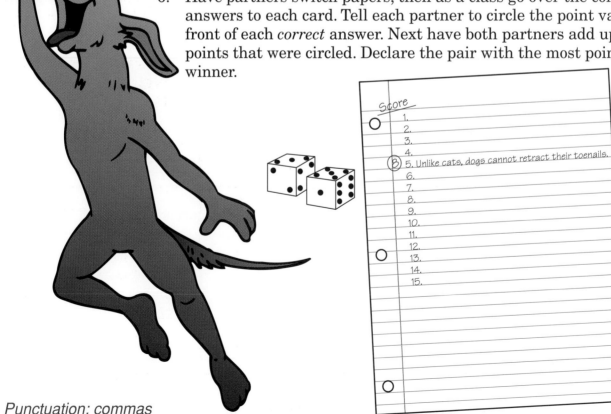

Score
1.
2.
3.
4.
⑧ 5. Unlike cats, dogs cannot retract their toenails.
6.
7.
8.
9.
10.
11.
12.
13.
14.
15.

1.
German shepherds Chihuahuas and basenjis have ears that are pointed and stand straight up.

2.
Kara do you believe that bloodhounds can follow scent trails more than four days old?

3.
Guard hairs fine hairs and tactile hairs are the three basic types of hair in a dog's coat.

4.
At the back of each eye a dog has a mirrorlike structure that helps the animal see in dim light.

5.
Unlike cats dogs cannot retract their toenails.

6.
The vet said "Do not feed your dog any table scraps."

7.
Charleton do you want to go outside for a walk?

8.
A dog's coat may consist of several colors and members of the same breed may have different-colored coats.

9.
Cocker spaniels Labrador retrievers poodles and beagles have long, hanging ears.

10.
Dogs often bury bones or they may simply dig holes.

11.
"Yes the basenji is the only dog that cannot bark" remarked Tisha.

12.
Bone chewing is natural for dogs but it can cause broken teeth.

13.
"The dog" John commented "is an animal that has lived with people as a pet for more than 10,000 years!"

14.
Yes dogs can hear much better than people can.

15.
Some dogs are born with long tails but a veterinarian may dock (cut off) their tails shortly after birth.

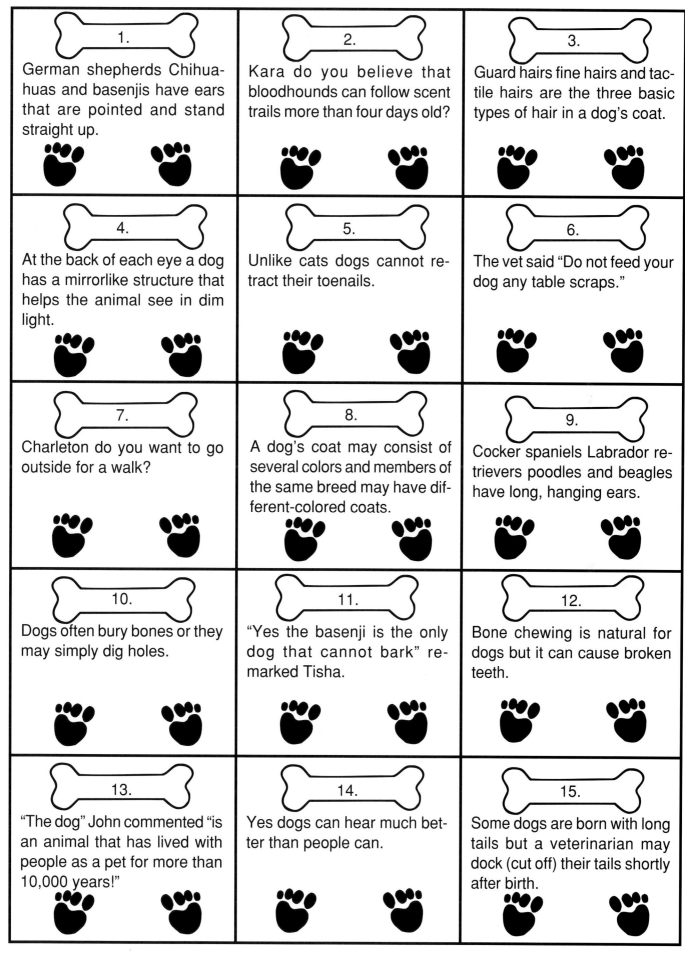

How To Extend The Lesson:

- Have each student write a creative narrative involving a dog. Instruct students to use commas whenever necessary in their writings. On their rough drafts, have students highlight or underline with a colored pen each sentence that contains a comma. Write a variety of the highlighted sentences on overhead transparencies, removing the commas. Use the transparencies to review commas at a later time by having students insert the missing commas.

- Divide the class into groups of five. Have a contest to see how many sentences each group can find using the five comma rules reinforced in this lesson. Instruct each student in each group to choose one of the five comma rules. Tell each student he has 15 minutes to use textbooks, novels, or other written material to find at least two sentences that use the particular comma rule chosen. Each student is responsible for writing down each sentence on a sheet of notebook paper. Reward one point for each correct sentence and declare the team with the most points the winner.

- Challenge students to find commas used in sentences where the five rules from this lesson *don't* apply. Tell students to each record in a journal sentences that use commas in ways other than the five rules discussed in this lesson. After a week, have each student read one or two of his sentences and have the class discuss why the commas were used. Add new comma rules to the list.

Hmm...This sentence doesn't follow the five comma rules. "The jewel thief, who had entered through the window, went directly to the vault."

Conversation Punctuation

Students will definitely have something to talk about after completing this punctuating quotes activity.

Skill: Punctuating direct and divided quotes

Estimated Lesson Time: 45 minutes

Teacher Preparation:
Duplicate one copy of page 11 for each pair of students.

Materials:
1 copy of page 11 for each pair
old magazines
glue
scissors

Background Information:
- Quotation marks are used before and after someone's exact words.
- Periods and commas are always *inside* the quotation marks.
- Question marks and exclamation points go *inside* the quotation marks when punctuating the quote; they are placed *outside* when punctuating the main sentence.
- When writing dialogue, a new paragraph is begun each time a different person speaks.

Introducing The Lesson:

Begin this lesson by having two students carry on a dialogue about lunch in front of the class. After a few sentences, have each student who is sitting down cover his ears. After a few more sentences, stop the conversation and ask the class how they could tell who was speaking—lips moving, hand gestures, body language.

Steps:

1. Next ask students how they know which character in a novel is speaking when they are reading. Explain that quotation marks are used to set off someone's exact words and that the name of the person who is speaking is usually placed before or after the quote.

2. Discuss each of the following situations where quotation marks are needed and how each one is punctuated.

Direct Quotes:

John said, "I can't believe that we have a test today."
"I can't believe that we have a test today," said John.
"Can you believe that we have a test today?" said John.
"I didn't study for the test today!" said John.

Divided Quotes:

"I can't believe," said John, "that we have a test today."
"I can't believe that we have a test today," said John. "I didn't study."

---

3. Assign each child a partner. Give each pair a copy of page 11, an old magazine, scissors, and glue. Instruct them to complete the reproducible after reading the directions.

4. After 15 or 20 minutes, have each pair swap papers with another pair to check for accuracy. Have each pair show its pictures and share its conversations with the rest of the class.

Picture-Perfect Punctuation

If a picture is worth a thousand words, what are they? You decide! With a partner find and cut out from a magazine two different pictures of people. Paste one in each picture frame below. With your partner, create a conversation between the two pictures by taking turns writing sentences on the lines provided. Use quotation marks in each sentence. Look at the conversation below to help you with the punctuation. Use the back of this paper for more space.

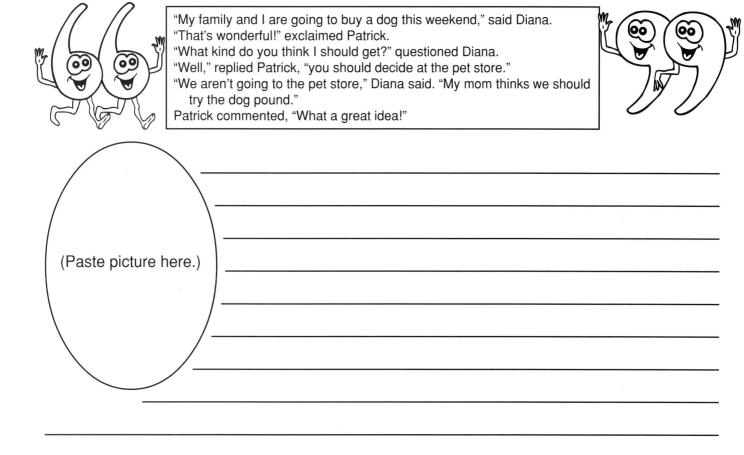

"My family and I are going to buy a dog this weekend," said Diana.
"That's wonderful!" exclaimed Patrick.
"What kind do you think I should get?" questioned Diana.
"Well," replied Patrick, "you should decide at the pet store."
"We aren't going to the pet store," Diana said. "My mom thinks we should try the dog pound."
Patrick commented, "What a great idea!"

(Paste picture here.)

(Paste picture here.)

Bonus Box: Cut another picture from the magazine, this time of an object. On a separate sheet of paper, write a humorous conversation that you would have with this object.

How To Extend The Lesson:

- Have students practice writing quotes while acting as classroom reporters. Divide students into pairs. Instruct each student to spend about ten minutes writing questions for his partner to answer during an interview. Then have the members of each pair take turns interviewing each other. After the interview, have each reporter rewrite the answers to his questions, using appropriate quotation marks in each response.

- Have each student practice punctuating quotes by carrying on a silent conversation with a partner. Have partners take turns writing sentences to each other on a single sheet of notebook paper. Instruct partners to check each other's sentences for correct punctuation.

- Have each student write a fictional story telling about meeting a famous person. Instruct each student to include a dialogue he had with the celebrity.

- Send students out to the lunchroom, playground, or media center to record conversations (with permission) by using a tape recorder. Later have students transcribe their tapes using correct punctuation. Have students check one another's work for accuracy.

Teaming Up With Grammar

Your students will really score while playing this verb agreement card game!

Skill: Using subjects and verbs correctly in sentences

Estimated Lesson Time: 45 minutes

Teacher Preparation:
1. Make one copy of page 15 for each pair of students.
2. Make a transparency of the directions found at the bottom of page 14.

Materials:
1 copy of page 15 for each pair of students
1 pair of scissors for each group
blank transparency

Background Information:
The subject and verb in a sentence must agree in *person* (first, second, or third) and in *number* (singular or plural).

Introducing The Lesson:

Begin the lesson by reading the following paragraph aloud:

> **"Will like to plays on the baseball team. Sometimes he do his homework in the car on the way to practice. Will's mother tell him that if he bring home a poor report card that he will have to quits the team. Will say he studies very hard to get good grades so he can continues to play baseball."**

Ask students to explain what is wrong with the paragraph that you just read.

Steps:

1. Tell students that within a sentence the subject and verb must agree. Explain that a singular noun needs a singular verb and a plural noun needs a plural verb. Demonstrate a few examples of subject and verb agreement for the class.

2. Reread the paragraph above aloud. Stop at the end of each sentence and ask students to replace each incorrect verb with the correct one.

3. Divide students into pairs. Give each pair a copy of page 15 and scissors.

4. Display the transparency of the directions below. Read through the directions with your students; then instruct each pair to begin making and playing the game.

Directions

1. Cut out all the cards and place them facedown in a pile.
2. Take one card off the top of the pile and place it faceup in the center of the playing surface. This card is the lead card.
3. The player with the earliest birthday in the year is Player 1.
4. Player 1 draws a card from the top of the stack.
5. Player 1 places the drawn card next to the lead card so that the subject on the side of one card agrees with a verb on one side of the other card. If the card cannot be placed, Player 1 passes and puts the drawn card at the bottom of the card stack.
6. If the card was placed correctly, Player 1 makes up a sentence using the matching subject and verb from the two cards. The sentence can be silly, but must be grammatically correct.
7. Player 2 then draws a card and the game continues.
8. Players are awarded one point for each correct match and correctly used sentence. If by placing one drawn card a player can make two matches on the same card, he is awarded two points (see the illustration at left). The player with the most points after all the cards have been placed is the winner!

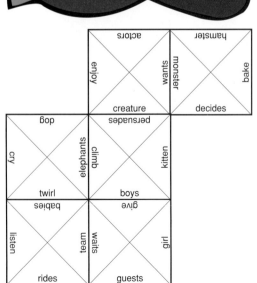

Directions: Carefully cut out each square. Follow the directions posted by your teacher to create and play this matching game.

friends discusses 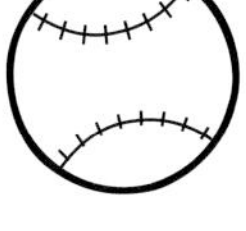 / jogger write	decides bake 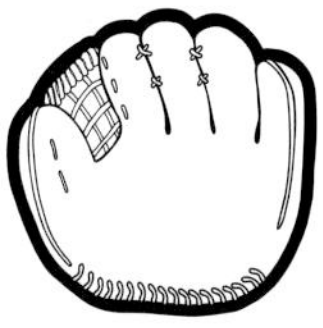 / monster hamsters	kitten persuades 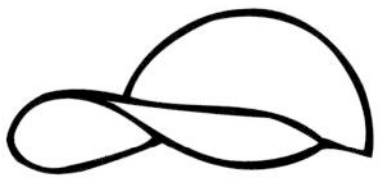 / boys climb	asks student 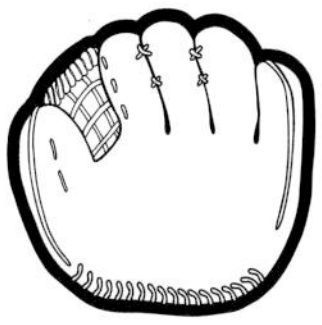 / taste men
wishes bark  / drummer judges	farmers decorates 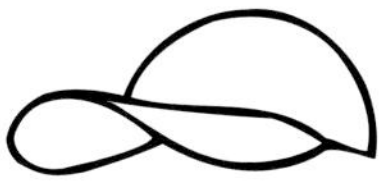 / teacher show	twirls elephants 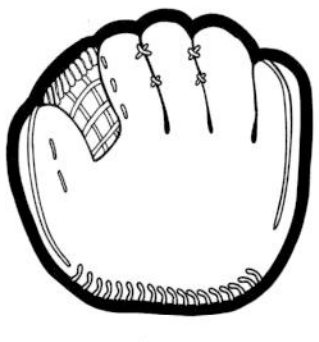 / cry dog	band groups  / participates remain
fly players 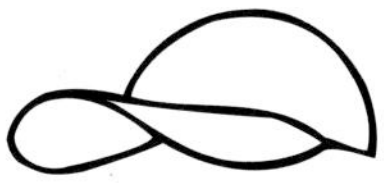 / moose pushes	babies listen  / team rides	people mother  / identifies hurry	aliens dinosaur 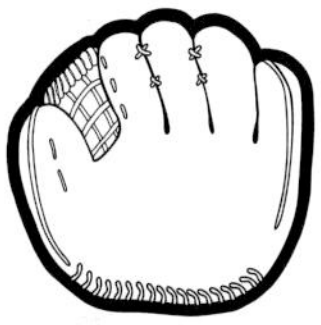 / sail completes
child sheep  / draws scrub	spiders chew 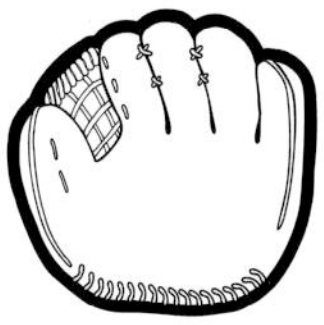 / invents woman	scurry women 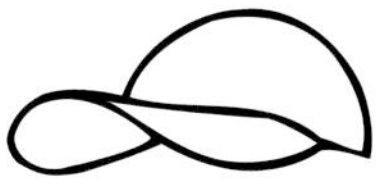 / family blinks	guests girl  / waits give
enjoy creature 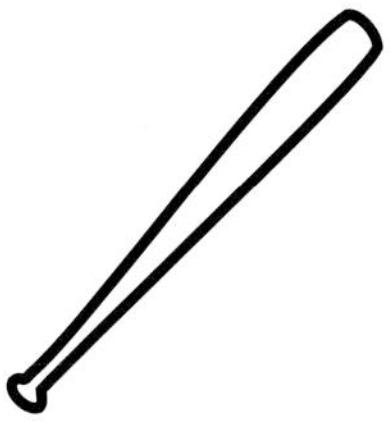 / actors wants	ship promise 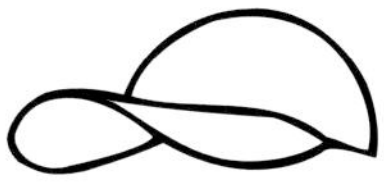 / machines waves	pulls person 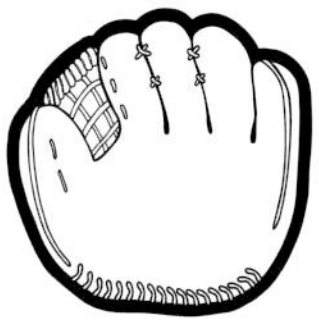 / float doctors	sisters flea 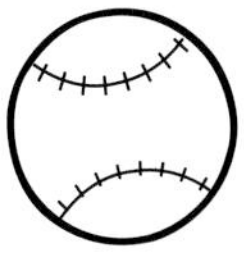 / drinks earn

How To Extend The Lesson:

- Subjects and verbs may agree, but people don't always agree! Help each student reinforce subject and verb agreement by having him write a paragraph explaining something, such as an issue, rule, or law with which he doesn't agree. Instruct the student to underline each subject and verb on the rough draft of his paragraph. Then have students exchange papers to peer edit for correct subject-verb agreement of the underlined words. Have each student write a final copy of his paragraph with the necessary corrections. Display the completed paragraphs on a bulletin board titled "We Disagree!"

- Have students practice matching subjects to correct verb forms with this class game. Divide the class into four groups; then assign each group a type of word—*singular noun, singular verb, plural noun,* or *plural verb.* Give each student in each group a large index card and a piece of tape. Have each student use a marker to write a word on his card and use tape to post the card on his chest. On your signal have each student stand up and try to find a student (from a different group) wearing a word that agrees with his. Instruct students to stand by their matches and be prepared to share a sentence with the class that uses the subject and verb from their cards. After each pair has shared a sentence, signal again to send each student around the room in search of a different match.

Awesome Adverbs

Emphasize the strength of adverbs with this cooperative activity.

Skill: Identifying and using adverbs that modify verbs

Estimated Lesson Time: 45 minutes

Teacher Preparation:
1. Duplicate two copies of page 19 for each cooperative group.
2. Make a transparency of page 19.

Materials:
2 copies of page 19 for each group
transparency of page 19
overhead pens

Background Information:
- An adverb is a word that describes a verb, an adjective, or another adverb.
- Adverbs answer three questions about the verbs they describe—*how, when* and *where.*

Identifying and using adverbs   17

Introducing The Lesson:

Begin the lesson by writing the sentence below on the chalkboard and asking students to identify the verb.

> The bodybuilder exercised.

Steps:

1. Underneath the first sentence, write the following three sentences:

   > The bodybuilder exercised <u>briefly</u>.
   > The bodybuilder exercised <u>outside</u>.
   > The bodybuilder exercised <u>yesterday</u>.

   Show students how adding an adverb to each sentence tells more about each verb.

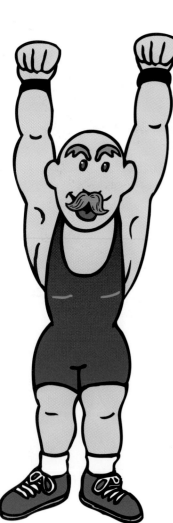

2. Inform students that adverbs are used to provide more information about verbs and can answer three questions about those verbs—*how*, *when*, and *where*. Select students to tell which adverb answers each question in your examples (*How?*—briefly, *When?*—yesterday, *Where?*—outside).

3. Divide students into groups of four, selecting one student from each group to be the recorder. Distribute one copy of page 19 to each group.

4. Tell your students that you will be writing a simple sentence (see the examples below) on the board. Instruct each pair to record the sentence on the line at the bottom of page 19 and list adverbs that tell more about the verb in that sentence. Each adverb should be recorded under the correct heading.

   > The dog barked.
   > The children played.
   > The pig danced.
   > The class ate.

5. After about five minutes, call, "Pencils down." Use the transparency you created to record the adverbs that were found by each group. Each group will receive one point for each adverb it used correctly. Award two points for each adverb that was used by only one group.

6. Distribute a second copy of page 19 to each group, provide them with a different sentence, and play another round.

Name _____

Awesome Adverbs

When?

How?

Where?

How To Extend The Lesson:

- Have students use magazines to find action pictures. Instruct each student to cut out one picture, paste it on a sheet of construction paper, and then write three to five sentences describing the action taking place in the picture. Remind the student to include at least one adverb in each sentence.

- Take students outside to the playground to hunt for adverbs in action. Have each student observe a game that is taking place outside. Instruct each student to write a paragraph describing the action of the game. Remind students to include adverbs in their descriptions.

- Compile a master list of adverbs from the game played in this lesson. Challenge student pairs to write an adventurous story using adverbs correctly.

- Inform students that the three most commonly used adverbs in the English language are *not*, *very,* and *too*. Have each student choose a page at random from a textbook or a novel. Have him estimate the number of times he thinks those three words are used and then count them. As a class figure out the average number of times *not*, *very*, and *too* were found in the books surveyed.

- For some added practice, have students draw pictures to illustrate adverbs modifying verbs. See the illustrations below for examples.

smiling brightly

jumping high

Aiming For Adjectives

Score a bull's-eye with this activity that helps students learn to target and use adjectives.

Skill: Identifying and using adjectives

Estimated Lesson Time: 1 hour

Teacher Preparation:
Duplicate the reproducible on page 23 for each student.

Materials:
1 dictionary for each student
1 timer
chart paper and a marker
1 copy of the reproducible on page 23 for each student

Background Information:
 Adjectives are descriptive words that tell more about a noun or a pronoun. Adjectives can tell which one (this, these, that, those), what kind (blue, square, fluffy), or how many (one, several, many). *A, an,* and *the* are special adjectives called *articles.*

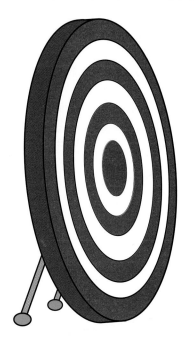

Introducing The Lesson:

Choose an object in the classroom to describe. Give students as many words as possible that describe the object. For example, you might describe a globe as round, light, colorful, smooth, and shiny. Ask your students to guess what the object is, based on the descriptive clues. Explain that a descriptive word that tells *which one, what kind,* or *how many* about a person, place, thing, or idea is an *adjective.*

Steps:

1. Divide students into pairs. Have each pair choose a letter of the alphabet. Then challenge each pair to use a dictionary to find as many adjectives as possible, beginning with its letter, that describe a person. For example, a pair choosing the letter *A* might describe a person as *active, alluring, amiable, angry, antagonistic,* or *athletic.* Set a timer for three minutes. Direct each pair to find its adjectives. When the timer rings, instruct the pairs to stop writing and share their words. Copy the words onto chart paper.

2. Continue the activity by having each pair choose a new letter. Then direct each pair to find other words to describe a place, a thing, or an idea. Add the new words to the list, and hang the list on a wall to use as a reference for future writing.

3. Emphasize how adjectives help improve our speaking and writing by creating detailed and vivid pictures.

4. Give each pair two copies of page 23. Instruct each student to secretly write down the name of a familiar object, such as Roller-blades®, a baseball bat, a slide, or an ice-cream cone, on each arrow. Next tell the student to write an adjective on each level of the target that describes the word. Then have each student share his clues with his partner, starting with the top clue. If his partner guesses the object based on the one adjective clue, the student earns a bull's-eye (25 points). If the partner guesses incorrectly, the student gives the clue on the next level of the target. If the partner guesses correctly, the student earns the point value at that level. Instruct the student to continue giving clues until his partner guesses the object. If the student's partner does not guess the object, the student doesn't earn any points. Partners take turns sharing clues and guessing objects. The goal is to give the best adjective clues possible to earn the most points.

Identifying and using adjectives

Aiming For Adjectives

Directions: On each arrow below, write the name of a familiar object such as Rollerblades®, a baseball bat, or an ice-cream cone. Then on each line of the target, write an adjective that describes the object. Read the first adjective clue to your partner. If your partner guesses the object correctly, you earn a bull's-eye (25 points). If your classmate does not guess the object correctly, read the next clue on the target. If your classmate guesses correctly, you earn the point value at that level. After each correct guess, circle the points you earned. At the end of the game, total your points and record your score at the bottom of the page. (**Hint:** Place your best adjective clue at the center of the target!)

Example:

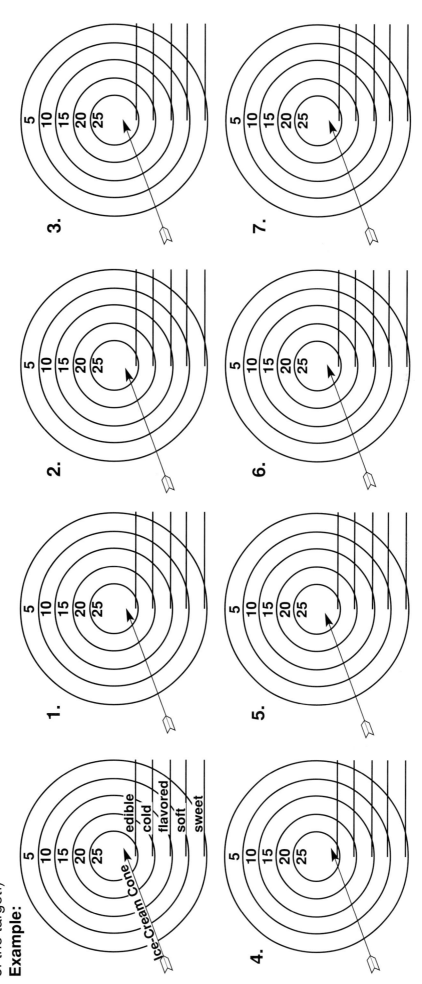

Total Points:

Bonus Box: For each object above, write one sentence on the back of your paper using one or more of the adjectives listed. Be sure to include articles also. Pass your paper to a new partner. Have him underline all of the adjectives in each of your sentences.

©The Education Center, Inc. • *Ready-to-Go Lessons* • TEC1118

How To Extend The Lesson:

It's hard, small, and has buttons. I think it's a...

- Put one mystery object inside each of several small, brown paper bags. Blindfold a student volunteer; then have her pull the object out of one bag. Direct the student to use her senses to describe the object. For example, a student might say the object feels small, is round, has a smooth texture, smells fruity, and tastes sweet (a grape). If the student can then guess the object, invite her to do so. If she cannot, direct her classmates to help her out by giving clues. Stress the importance of using one's senses to aid in the description of a person, place, thing, or an idea.

- Cut out a simple picture from a magazine. Do not let your students see the picture. Direct each student to take out a sheet of blank paper, a pencil, and crayons or markers. Describe the picture, but intentionally leave out some of the details. Tell each student to sketch a drawing of the picture based on your description. After students finish their drawings, show the original picture, and then have each student share his drawing. Have students compare their drawings to the original magazine picture. Then instruct students to point out details you left out that would have been helpful in drawing their pictures. Emphasize the importance of details and descriptive words in creating clear and vivid images.

- Gather several newspapers. Divide students into pairs. Give each pair a different article from a newspaper and four markers (one each of blue, green, orange, and yellow). Instruct each pair to search through the article for adjectives. Direct the pair to underline the adjectives and circle the words that they modify. Next have the pair use markers to color-code each adjective based on its job. (For example, blue = *which one*, green = *what kind*, orange = *how many*, and yellow = *an article*.) Finish the activity by creating a reference list of descriptive words for each type of adjective. Post the list in the classroom and add to it throughout the year.

Cooking Up Complete Sentences

Help your students cook up complete sentences with this activity.

Skill: Identifying and correcting sentence fragments and run-on sentences

Estimated Lesson Time: 45 minutes

Teacher Preparation:
Duplicate page 27 for each student.

Materials:
3 index cards for each student
1 copy of page 27 for each student

Background Information:

A sentence fragment is not a complete sentence because it is missing either a subject or a predicate. For example, "Added pepperoni and mushrooms" is missing a subject. "The chef from Italy" is missing a predicate. To correct a fragment:

1. Add the missing subject.
   The chef added pepperoni and mushrooms.
2. Add the missing predicate.
   The chef from Italy is preparing our pizza.

A run-on sentence is two or more sentences or clauses that run together because there is no punctuation separating or joining them. To correct a run-on sentence, first identify the two separate sentences. For example, "I was hungry I ate a piece of pizza." Then decide how the sentences can be joined:

1. Join the two sentences with a comma and a conjunction.
   I was hungry, so I ate a piece of pizza.
2. Join the two sentences with a semicolon.
   I was hungry; I ate a piece of pizza.
3. Make two separate sentences.
   I was hungry. I ate a piece of pizza.

Introducing The Lesson:

Begin the lesson by sharing the sample sentences found in the Background Information on page 25. Ask your students what is wrong with each sentence. Identify that the first two are sentence fragments, and the other one is a run-on sentence. Show students how to correct sentence fragments and run-on sentences.

Steps:

1. Provide each student with three index cards. Direct the student to label one card with the letter "C," one card with the letter "F," and one card with the letter "R."

2. Read aloud the following types of sentences:
   Complete Sentence: I was thirsty, so I got a drink of water.
   Sentence Fragment: Left the beach early.
   Run-On Sentence: I have a dog and a cat my dog's name is Sandy and my cat's name is Fluffy.

3. Have each class member hold up his "C" card if he hears a complete sentence, his "F" card if he hears a sentence fragment, and his "R" card if he hears a run-on sentence. Announce the answer after students hold up their cards.

4. Instruct each student to correct the sentence fragment on the back of his "F" card and correct the run-on sentence on the back of his "R" card. Then have each student read his corrected sentences.

5. To give students extra practice identifying and correcting sentence fragments and run-on sentences, copy and distribute page 27 to each student.

I left the beach early.

Pick Your Pie, Please!

Chef Pizzoli is new to the country and is learning to speak English. Sometimes his sentences are fragments, and sometimes they are run-on sentences. Read each sentence below. Use the menus to help you decide if each sentence is a complete sentence, a fragment, or a run-on sentence. Then put the number of the sentence on the appropriate pie. Finally, if the sentence is a fragment or a run-on, rewrite the sentence correctly on the back of this sheet.

A fragment is missing either a subject or a predicate. To correct a fragment, add the missing subject or predicate.

1. Example: *Added the pepperoni and the mushrooms.*
   The chef added the pepperoni and the mushrooms.
2. Example: *The chef from Italy.*
   The chef from Italy **is preparing our pizza.**

Pizzoli's

A run-on sentence is two or more sentences that run together because there is no punctuation to join or separate them. Use one of the methods below to correct a run-on sentence.

Example: *I was hungry I ate a piece of pizza.*
1. Join the two sentences with a comma and a conjunction.
   I was hungry, so I ate a piece of pizza.
2. Join the two sentences with a semicolon.
   I was hungry; I ate a piece of pizza.
3. Make two separate sentences.
   I was hungry. I ate a piece of pizza.

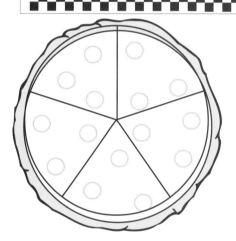

Complete
Sentences

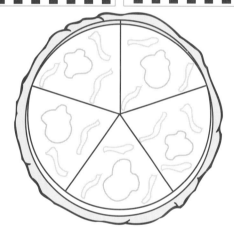

Fragments

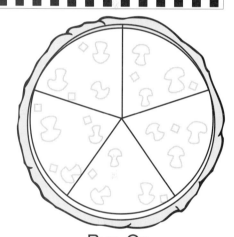

Run-On
Sentences

1. Amy ordered anchovies on her pizza.
2. Spilled his drink.
3. The new waiter.
4. Alexis put a quarter in the jukebox she played her favorite song.
5. Greg ate an order of onion rings.
6. Prepared a fabulous dessert for Jessica.
7. Joseph likes green peppers on his pizza Joshua likes extra cheese.
8. Erin was really hungry she ordered an appetizer before her meal.
9. Joel gave a $2.00 tip to the waitress.
10. Ian paid for his food then he went to the movies.
11. With his fork and knife.
12. Jeff couldn't decide what to eat he ordered a piece of pizza and a bowl of spaghetti.
13. Katie likes the lasagna, so she ordered a large serving.
14. Rachel had her birthday party at the pizza parlor.
15. Tossed the pizza in the air.

How To Extend The Lesson:

- Write several complete sentences on sentence strips—one sentence per strip. Then cut each sentence strip, separating the subject and the predicate. Laminate each strip; then put each strip in a large envelope labeled "Fragments." Then write several run-on sentences on a sheet of writing paper. Laminate the sheet and place it in a large envelope with an overhead marker. Put both envelopes in a center. As a student finishes an assignment, allow her to go to the center. Instruct her to form complete sentences with the fragment pieces, and to use the overhead marker to add the correct punctuation to the run-on sentences. After she has completed the tasks and checked her work, have her mix up the fragments and wipe the laminated page clean for the next student.

- Gather 30 index cards. Divide the deck into two equal stacks. On each card in the first stack, write a subject from the list below. On each card in the second stack, write a predicate from the list below. Shuffle all of the cards. Put the cards at a center. Invite two students at a time to play a game of Fishing For Fragments. Have students follow the same rules used in playing Go Fish. The player who collects the most pairs wins the game.

Subject	Predicate
Mr. Pizzoli	loves to make pizza.
Tony, Sharon, and Kyle	work at Mr. Pizzoli's pizza shop.
The short man wearing the funny hat	owns the pizza shop.
Mr. Pizzoli's menu	includes many different kinds of pizza.
The pizza with anchovies	smells fishy!
Pepperoni and sausage	are served on a meat pizza.
Cheesy pizza	contains five different cheese toppings.
Peppers, onions, and olives	are the three most popular toppings.
One type of pizza on the menu	features twelve different toppings on it.
Mr. Pizzoli's restaurant	was voted the number one pizza shop.
Calzone	tastes like stuffed pizza.
Running a pizza shop	involves a great deal of hard work.
Pizza	is Mr. Pizzoli's favorite food.
Italian music	is played in Mr. Pizzoli's pizza shop.
Nobody	refuses pizza for dinner!

A View To A Skill

Look out a window. What do you see? Help students develop their descriptive writing skills with the following writing and art activity.

Skill: Writing a descriptive paragraph

Estimated Lesson Time: 1 hour

Teacher Preparation:
Duplicate the reproducible on page 31 for each student.

Materials:
1 copy of page 31 for each student
crayons or colored pencils

Background Information:
   A good descriptive paragraph includes an introductory sentence that names the scene to be described. The next three or four sentences describe the scene from left to right or from top to bottom. Specific phrases containing concrete nouns, strong verbs, adjectives, and adverbs make the description more vivid and realistic. Using such words can change a sentence like "The mountains had snow" into "The majestic snow-capped mountains jutted up sharply behind the foothills." Similes and metaphors can also be included. Conclude the paragraph with a short summary statement.

Introducing The Lesson:

Describing a scene so well that a reader can accurately visualize it in his mind takes skill and practice. Begin this lesson by having students close their eyes while you orally describe a favorite room, restaurant, or outside spot. Be very detailed with your description. Have students open their eyes; then call on volunteers to explain how the description enabled them to visualize the scene.

Steps:

1. Give each student one copy of page 31.

2. Inform each student that he has ten minutes to draw a scene he would like to see outside the window that is illustrated on the reproducible. Give suggestions such as a street scene, a mountain landscape, inner-city life, or their backyards. Allow the student to add color if he has time.

3. After ten minutes, have the students stop drawing. Instruct each student to write his name on the back of the reproducible.

4. Instruct each student to spend 25–30 minutes writing a complete, detailed description of his scene on a separate sheet of paper. Remind the student to state the location of the scene in the first sentence, then give specific details using strong nouns, verbs, adjectives, and adverbs.

5. After 30 minutes, collect each student's reproducible and description. Quickly display (temporarily) each reproducible on a wall, bulletin board, or chalk tray.

6. Randomly select a description from the pile to read aloud to the class. Instruct the students to try and match the description to one of the illustrations displayed. Then ask students to give specific details the writer used that were helpful in determining the match.

7. Continue the activity by reading the remaining descriptions and having the students select the matching illustrations.

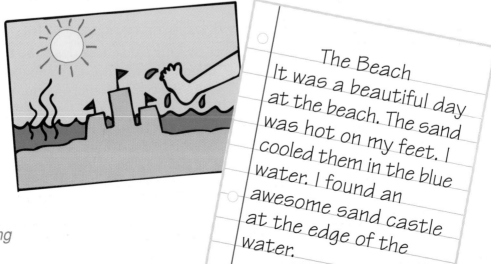

The Beach
It was a beautiful day at the beach. The sand was hot on my feet. I cooled them in the blue water. I found an awesome sand castle at the edge of the water.

A Scenic View

Think of a scene you might see while looking out of the window frame below. It might be your backyard, a mountain landscape, the seashore, or a busy city street. Draw everything you see while looking out of this imaginary window.

Now that you've completed your drawing, describe your scene in writing on a separate sheet of notebook paper. State the location of your scene in the first sentence. Include specific details about the scene in the following sentences. Use strong nouns, verbs, adjectives, and adverbs to make your description as vivid as possible.

Bonus Box: Choose an object or a place to describe, such as a toy or the classroom. Write a paragraph on the back of this page describing the object or place. Remember to use strong nouns, verbs, adjectives, and adverbs in your description.

How To Extend The Lesson:

- Give each student a white sheet of drawing paper and markers or crayons. Then collect each student's written description of his window scene. Next distribute each description to a different student. Instruct each student to read the description, then draw a picture of the scene based on the writer's details. After 15 minutes, have each student read the description he was given, then show his illustration. Next have the original writer/artist show his version of the scene. Have the class discuss why the drawings are very similar or very different.

- Find passages in classroom reading material that contain good descriptions. Have students draw pictures of the scenes, objects, and characters based on the descriptions.

- Display a bowl of popcorn for the class. Tell each student to write a physical description of the popcorn using his five senses—sight, hearing, touch, taste, and smell. End the activity by passing out the popcorn for the students to enjoy while each student reads his description for the rest of the class.

- After students have had practice at writing a descriptive paragraph, challenge them with writing a five-paragraph descriptive paper. The first paragraph consists of an introduction. The next three paragraphs give details about three different aspects of the object or location being described. The final paragraph concludes or summarizes the description.

Supply the classroom with a variety of old magazines. Then give each student one piece of white paper, glue, and scissors. Tell each student to find a picture of an object or location that they want to describe, cut it out, and then glue it to the piece of white paper. Instruct each student to write a five-paragraph descriptive paper about the magazine picture he has selected.

Descriptive Writing Paper

Paragraph 1: Introduction

Paragraph 2: Detail #1

Paragraph 3: Detail #2

Paragraph 4: Detail #3

Paragraph 5: Conclusion/Summary

A Reason For The Season

Use the following prewriting activity to help your students organize their ideas for writing clarification paragraphs.

Skill: Organizing ideas for clarification writing

Estimated Lesson Time: 45–60 minutes

Teacher Preparation:

1. Duplicate page 35 for each student.
2. Make a transparency of page 35.

Materials:

1 copy of page 35 for each student
writing paper
1 transparency of page 35
overhead-projector marker

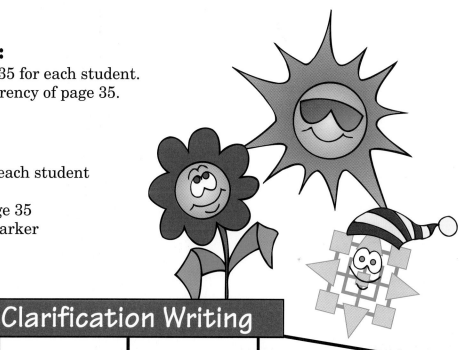

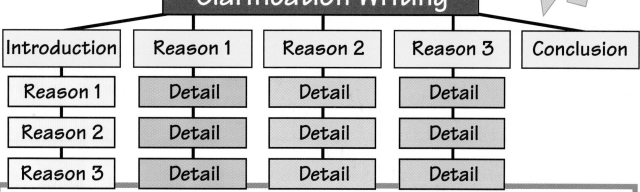

Clarification Writing				
Introduction	Reason 1	Reason 2	Reason 3	Conclusion
Reason 1	Detail	Detail	Detail	
Reason 2	Detail	Detail	Detail	
Reason 3	Detail	Detail	Detail	

Background Information:

A complete clarification writing consists of five paragraphs. It begins with an introductory paragraph that includes a sentence stating why the writer likes or dislikes something. This paragraph also states at least three reasons supporting the writer's opinion. Each subsequent paragraph gives specific details about each reason. The fifth and final paragraph is a short summary statement that repeats the writer's opinion.

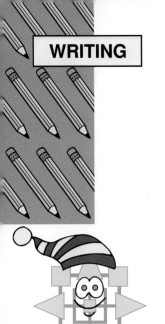

WRITING

Introducing The Lesson:

A student can quickly list his favorite things (television show, toy, food, movie), but ask why these items are his favorites and the response is often much slower. Test this theory by asking each student, "What is your favorite season?" Have several students name their favorite seasons. Then follow up by saying, "Now think of three reasons why the season you selected is your favorite."

Steps:

1. Tell each student that in clarification writing the writer states an opinion, then clarifies it by giving several supporting reasons.

2. Distribute page 35 to each student; then show the transparency of page 35 or quickly draw the chart from page 35 on the board. Tell your students that they will use the reproducible to help organize information about each season.

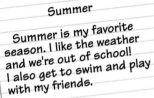

Summer

Summer is my favorite season. I like the weather and we're out of school! I also get to swim and play with my friends.

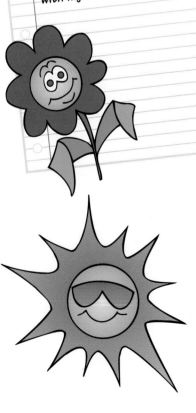

3. Ask students to help you list on the transparency four special events that take place in the fall, such as the beginning of school, Halloween, the school carnival, and election day. Then have the student fill in his own chart. Instruct each student to put a plus sign (+) or a minus sign (−) in the narrow column to the left of each special event to indicate if he likes or dislikes the event.

4. Instruct each student to complete the chart for each season. Then have the student add the plus signs and minus signs for each season.

5. Have each student write a clarification paper—consisting of five paragraphs—about the season with the most plus signs on his chart. Tell the student to follow the outline below for writing each paragraph:
   - **Paragraph 1: Introduction**
     State the name of your favorite season; give three reasons why it's your favorite.
   - **Paragraph 2: Details**
     Give details about and examples of the season's special events.
   - **Paragraph 3: Details**
     Give details about and examples of the season's weather.
   - **Paragraph 4: Details**
     Give details about and examples of typical foods eaten during this season.
   - **Paragraph 5: Conclusion**
     Summarize why the season is your favorite.

6. Instruct the student to summarize or conclude his clarification writing in the last paragraph by briefly restating why the season is his favorite.

A Reason For The Season

Directions: Complete the chart below by naming two or three special events, types of weather, and foods for each season. Use the (+) or (–) column to show which special events, types of weather, and foods you like and dislike for each season.

Season	Special Events	(+) or (–)	Weather	(+) or (–)	Foods	(+) or (–)
 Fall						
 Winter						
 Spring						
 Summer						

After completing the chart, determine your favorite season by counting the number of plus signs for each season. The season with the most plus signs will be your favorite season. Use the information in the chart above and the information below to write a five-paragraph clarification paper on your favorite season.

- **Paragraph 1: Introduction**
  State the name of your favorite season; give three reasons why it's your favorite.
- **Paragraph 2: Details**
  Give details about and examples of the season's special events.
- **Paragraph 3: Details**
  Give details about and examples of the season's weather.
- **Paragraph 4: Details**
  Give details about and examples of typical foods eaten during this season.
- **Paragraph 5: Conclusion**
  Summarize why the season is your favorite.

How To Extend The Lesson:

- For some students, five paragraphs may be overwhelming. Have each of these students work on a four- to five-sentence paragraph that states the name of the season and gives three to five reasons why this season is his favorite. Once this is accomplished, have the student expand his writing by giving more details about each reason.

- Group students according to their favorite seasons. Give each group a large piece of poster board, markers, old magazines, scissors, glue, and various other arts-and-crafts materials. Instruct each group to create a poster about its favorite season. Have each group present its poster to the rest of the class. Throughout the school year, hang each group's poster during the appropriate season.

- Make a chart (similar to the chart on page 35) listing months instead of seasons. Have your students help you add to or change the category titles. Then have each student write a clarification paper about his favorite month.

- Have each student use the reasons listed on her chart to write a poem about her favorite season.

- More clarification writing topics:
  — My Favorite Restaurant
  — My Favorite Place To Vacation
  — My Favorite Movie
  — Why I Like Eating _____ (*Student fills in the blank.*)
  — Why I Dislike _____ (*Student fills in the blank.*)

Month	Special Events	(+) or (−)	Weather	(+) or (−)	Sports	(+) or (−)
January						
February						
March						
April						
May						
June						
July						
August						
September						
October						
November						
December						

The Power Of Persuasion

Encourage your students to take a stand and support their points of view with this powerful lesson.

Skill: Brainstorming, writing, and identifying the elements of persuasive writing

Estimated Lesson Time: 45 minutes

Teacher Preparation:
Duplicate one copy of page 39 for each student.

Materials:
1 copy of page 39 for each student
loose-leaf paper

Background Information:
   In persuasive writing, a writer presents her opinion on a topic. The writer then provides reasons and examples to support her opinion in an effort to get the reader to agree with her point of view. It is helpful for a writer to organize her thoughts prior to writing. Clustering ideas related to a topic is one method of organizing ideas.

WRITING

Introducing The Lesson:

Ask several student volunteers to share occasions in which they tried to convince their parents to let them do something. Have students describe methods they used to attempt to convince their parents to let them do what they wanted. Ask students if they provided reasons or facts to convince their parents the activity would be worthwhile.

Steps:

1. Explain to students that persuasive writing gives a writer's opinion on an issue and provides facts and examples to support that opinion. Tell students that a writer provides the examples in an effort to convince or persuade the reader to agree with his point of view.

2. Write "Students should be allowed to help plan the school menu" in a large rectangle on the board. Direct students to give you several reasons or details to support this opinion. Guide students in providing reasons to support the statement, such as "Less food will be wasted if students get to select what they want," "Children will be happier with their lunch choices if they can help plan the menu," and "More students will buy lunch." Cluster student suggestions in circles around the large rectangle containing the topic.

3. Explain that in order to be successful in writing a persuasive paragraph, a writer must provide examples or reasons to back up his opinion. Then provide each student with a copy of page 39.

4. Instruct each student to follow the directions as written on page 39 to write a persuasive paragraph.

"Students should be allowed to help plan the school menu."

Supporting Details:

Less food will be wasted.

Children will be happier.

More students will buy lunch.

The Power Of Persuasion

Directions: Select a topic from one of the lightbulbs below. Record your opinion on the chosen topic in the rectangle. Use the remaining circles to cluster supporting details and examples to support your opinion. Then use the information to write a persuasive paragraph on a separate sheet of paper, stating your opinion and backing it up with your supporting details.

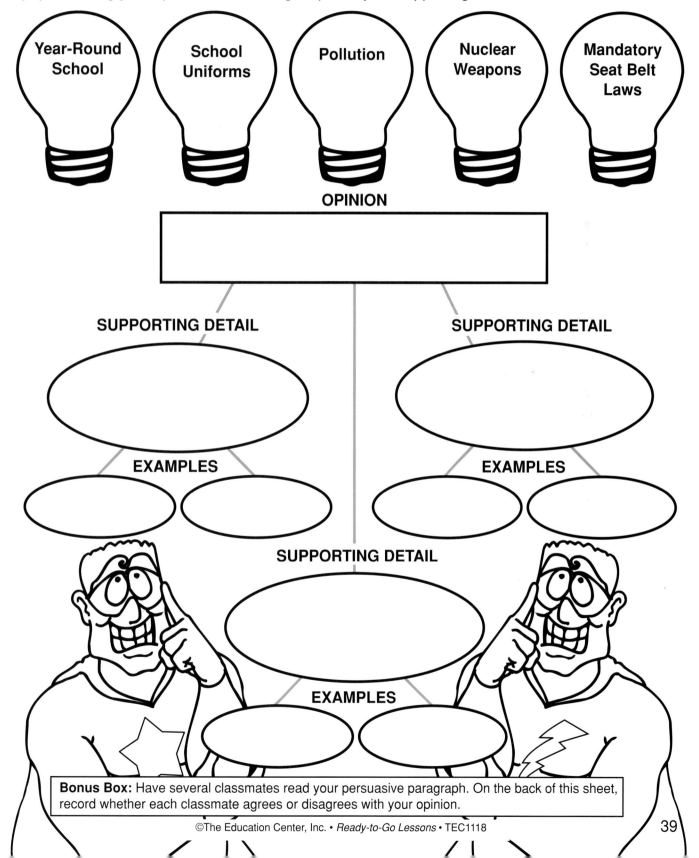

Year-Round School

School Uniforms

Pollution

Nuclear Weapons

Mandatory Seat Belt Laws

OPINION

SUPPORTING DETAIL

SUPPORTING DETAIL

EXAMPLES

EXAMPLES

SUPPORTING DETAIL

EXAMPLES

Bonus Box: Have several classmates read your persuasive paragraph. On the back of this sheet, record whether each classmate agrees or disagrees with your opinion.

How To Extend The Lesson:

- Have students work in pairs to read an editorial you've selected from the newspaper. Ask each pair to define the topic of the article, the author's opinion on the issue, and the facts or reasons the author provides to support his opinion. Then ask each pair to decide whether it agrees or disagrees with the author's viewpoint and state the basis for its decision.

- Direct each student to select something she would really like to change about school. Have her write a letter to you stating her request and backing it up with examples and reasons to support her opinion. Select several letters to read aloud; then have students point out the most persuasive elements in each. For example, a student who says you should not assign homework can attempt to persuade you by pointing out you would have fewer papers to grade if homework was not assigned!

- Challenge each student to write a campaign speech to persuade voters to elect her president of the United States. Remind each student to state her opinion—that she should be elected—and back up the opinion with facts and reasons to convince the voters. Call on student volunteers to share their speeches aloud. Then have students discuss the most persuasive elements of each candidate's speech.

Bring It To Life

Help your students add creativity and interest to their writing with the use of personification.

Skill: Recognizing and using personification in writing

Estimated Lesson Time: 45 minutes

Teacher Preparation:
Duplicate one copy of page 43 for each student.

Materials:
1 copy of page 43 for each student
one 12" x 18" sheet of white construction
    paper for each student
tape

Background Information:
   Personification enables a writer to give human characteristics to things. The following are several suggestions for making an inanimate object appear human:
   1.   Give the object human actions such as *coughing, laughing,* or *crying.*
   2.   Give the object human descriptions such as *intelligent, silly,* or *lazy.*
   3.   Give the object human jobs, friends, food, and hobbies.
   4.   Give the object human emotions such as *happy, sad, angry,* or *giddy.*
   5.   Refer to the object as *he, she, him, her, his, they,* or *them.*

Introducing The Lesson:

Write the following sentences on the board:
• The wind whispered through the trees.
• The car hugged the curb tightly.
• The sun stared down on the sunbathers.
• The rain danced in the streets.
Ask students to explain the meaning of each sentence. Then ask students to identify which thing in each sentence has been given human qualities. Tell your students that giving an object human qualities is a writing technique or literary device called *personification*. Inform your students that personification often lets a writer make a connection between the natural world and human behavior.

Steps:

1. Read the background information on page 41 to your students. Then tell each student to find one object such as a pen, pencil, book, chair, table, eraser, or piece of chalk to personify.

2. Distribute one copy of page 43 to each student. Instruct students to complete the reproducible as directed.

3. Give each student one 12" x 18" sheet of white construction paper. Direct each student to tape his reproducible to the top half of the construction paper, then draw an illustration of his personified object on the bottom half as shown.

4. Have each student show his work to the rest of the class. Then display the illustrations around the classroom for all to enjoy.

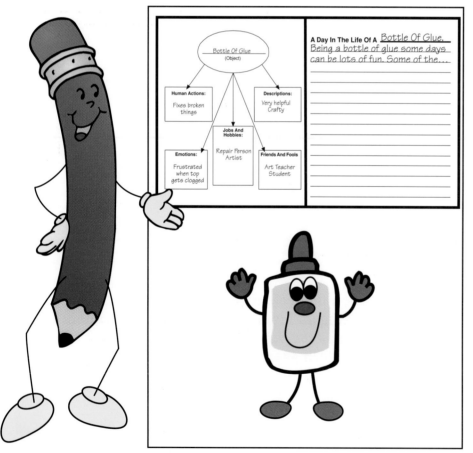

Personify It!

Directions: Choose an object in the room such as a pen, pencil, book, chair, table, eraser, or piece of chalk to personify. Use the left-hand side below to plan out your personification. On the right-hand side, write what a typical day in the life of your object is like. Be sure to incorporate your personification notes from the planning side into your writing.

A Day In The Life Of A _____

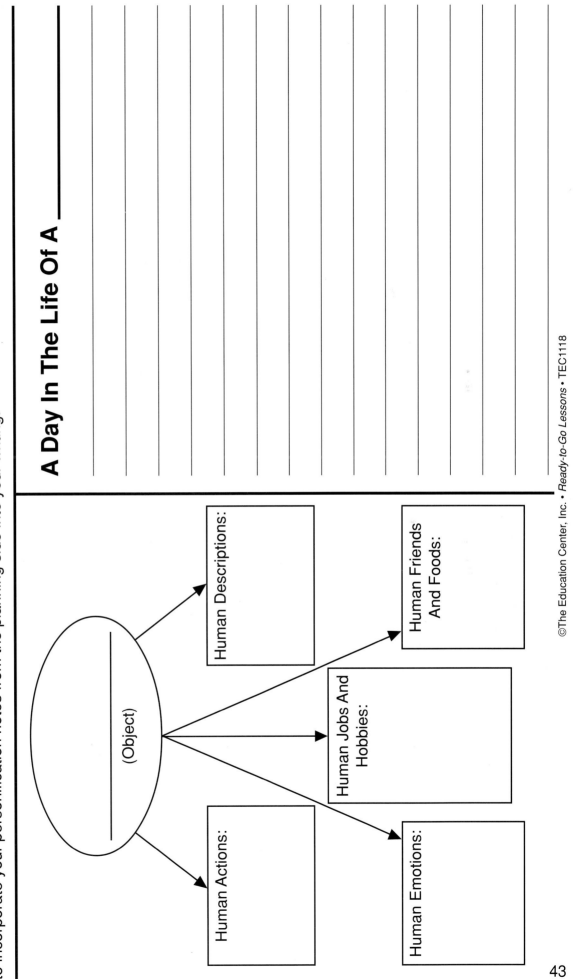

(Object)

Human Descriptions:

Human Friends And Foods:

Human Jobs And Hobbies:

Human Actions:

Human Emotions:

How To Extend The Lesson:

- If you listen carefully, you can hear people use personification every day. Have each student keep a personification log for a week. Instruct the student to carry it with him wherever he goes—the grocery store, the mall, a restaurant. At the end of the week, instruct each student to bring his personification log to school. Have each student read at least one example of personification from his log. Record each response on a large sheet of chart paper. Keep the list in your writing center for students to use as a reference.

- Have each student write a poem about nature. Instruct each student to include personification in his descriptions of the sky, rivers or streams, plants, and animal life.

- *Anthropomorphism* is the personification of animals. Have each student write a short story about the day in the life of his pet or favorite animal. Instruct each student to include anthropomorphism by giving the pet human characteristics, emotions, and actions.

    Listed below are several novels in which the author uses personification and anthropomorphism:
    — *Charlotte's Web* by E. B. White (HarperCollins Children's Books, 1974)
    — *The Mouse And The Motorcycle* by Betsy Byars (Houghton Mifflin Company, 1993)
    — *Mrs. Frisby And The Rats Of NIMH* by Robert C. O'Brien (Simon & Schuster Children's Books, 1986)
    — *Poppy* by Avi (Avon Books, 1995)
    — *Stuart Little* by E. B. White (HarperCollins Children's Books, 1974)

Charlotte's Web

Stuart Little

Poppy

○ **Mrs. Frisby And The Rats Of NIMH** ○

The Mouse And The Motorcycle

A Limerick Picnic

Poetry's a picnic when students write limericks!

Skill: Writing limericks

Estimated Lesson Time: 45 minutes

Teacher Preparation:
Duplicate one copy of page 47 for each student.

Materials:
1 copy of page 47 for each student
decorative paper for final copies of poems

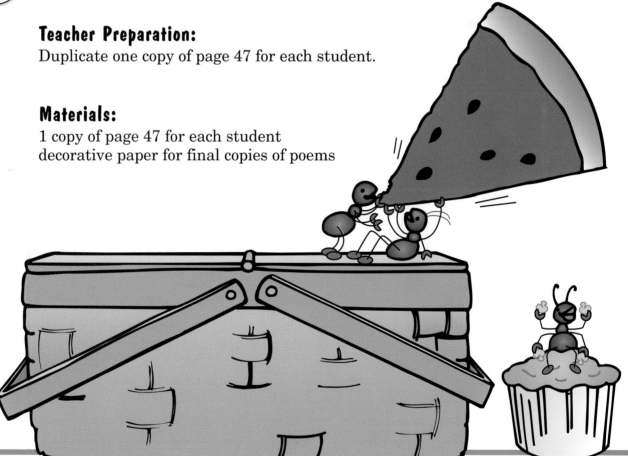

Background Information:
   Limericks are light-hearted poems that are five lines in length. Limericks have a specific rhyme pattern as explained below.

Line 1: 3 stressed syllables (rhymes with lines 2 and 5)
Line 2: 3 stressed syllables (rhymes with lines 1 and 5)
Line 3: 2 stressed syllables (rhymes with line 4)
Line 4: 2 stressed syllables (rhymes with line 3)
Line 5: 3 stressed syllables (rhymes with lines 1 and 2)

Introducing The Lesson:

Begin this lesson by reading aloud the following limerick:

> There once was an ant we called Phil.
>
> Who thought he was king of the hill.
>
> He took a big plunge
>
> And fell in some grunge.
>
> He's no longer the king of the hill.

Steps:

1. Explain to your students that the poem you read is a limerick. Demonstrate the pattern of limericks by counting the stressed syllables in each line of the sample limerick. Next point out which lines rhyme with one another.

2. Write the limerick pattern shown on page 45 on the chalkboard.

3. With help from your students, write a limerick following the specific pattern. Point out again which lines rhyme and the number of syllables in each.

4. Distribute one copy of page 47 to each student.

5. Instruct each student to complete his reproducible as directed.

6. Provide each student with decorative paper on which to write the final copy of his limerick. Have each student also add an illustration to his final copy.

7. Have each student read his limerick to the class. Then collect the limericks and assemble them into a class book.

A Limerick Picnic

The ants are having a picnic—a limerick picnic, that is! Each ant is carrying a group of three rhyming words to the picnic. Choose one group of these rhyming words to help you get started with writing a limerick. Use these three rhyming words for lines 1, 2, and 5 of your limerick. Choose two words from another group for a rhyming pair to use in lines 3 and 4, or use two words of your own. Remember to follow the limerick pattern written in the picnic basket by counting the stressed syllables in each line. Write the final version of your poem on the back of this page.

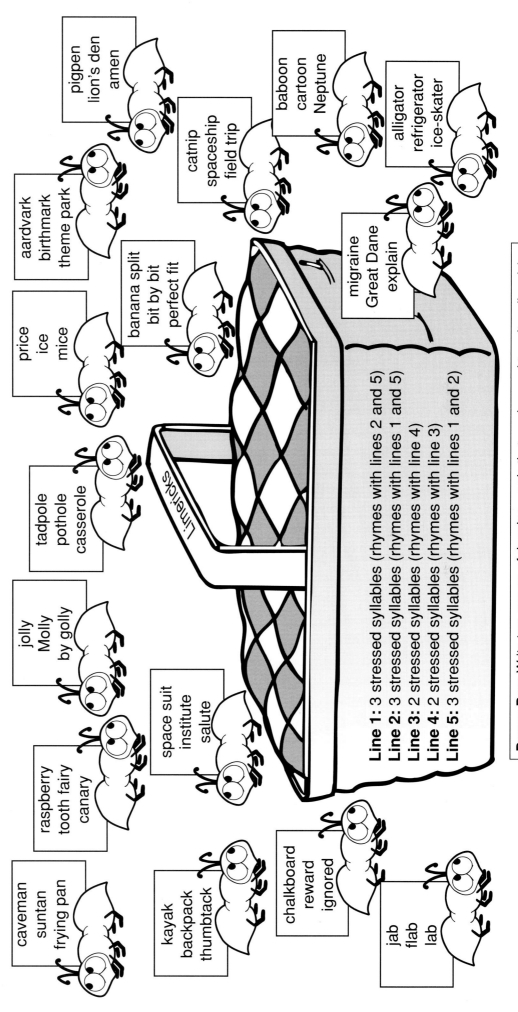

pigpen
lion's den
amen

baboon
cartoon
Neptune

alligator
refrigerator
ice-skater

aardvark
birthmark
theme park

catnip
spaceship
field trip

migraine
Great Dane
explain

price
ice
mice

banana split
bit by bit
perfect fit

tadpole
pothole
casserole

jolly
Molly
by golly

raspberry
tooth fairy
canary

space suit
institute
salute

caveman
suntan
frying pan

kayak
backpack
thumbtack

chalkboard
reward
ignored

jab
flab
lab

Limericks

Line 1: 3 stressed syllables (rhymes with lines 2 and 5)
Line 2: 3 stressed syllables (rhymes with lines 1 and 5)
Line 3: 2 stressed syllables (rhymes with line 4)
Line 4: 2 stressed syllables (rhymes with line 3)
Line 5: 3 stressed syllables (rhymes with lines 1 and 2)

©The Education Center, Inc. • *Ready-to-Go Lessons* • TEC1118

Bonus Box: Write two groups of rhyming words that can be used to write a limerick.

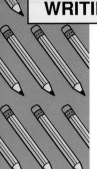

How To Extend The Lesson:

- Provide more practice writing limericks with this group activity. Divide the class into groups of four. Provide one student in each group with a sheet of notebook paper. Read aloud one of the limerick poem starters listed below. Have each student with notebook paper write the poem starter, then add a second line to the limerick. Then direct that student to pass the poem to the student on his left. Have this student add line three. Instruct each student to continue passing the limerick until all five lines have been written. Instruct each group to read its completed limerick aloud.

Poem Starters

1. A scared bear who hid in a cave
2. Whenever I go out to jog
3. I saw a strange sight in my trash can
4. Caesar was just an old barn cat
5. If I found a sack full of money

- Choose from the following list of books containing limericks to share with your class:

  — *There Was An Old Man...A Gallery Of Nonsense Rhymes* by Edward Lear (Morrow Junior Books, 1994)
  — *Walking The Bridge Of Your Nose* by Michael Rosen (Kingfisher, 1995)
  — *Critter Crackers: The ABC Book Of Limericks* by Kathryn Barron (Landmark Editions, Inc.; 1995)
  — *Lots Of Limericks* by Myra Cohn Livingston (Simon & Schuster, 1991)

Come Join The Fun!

Help your students learn to improve the flow of their writings with this lesson on combining sentences.

Skill: Using an appositive, a conjunction, a compound subject, or a compound verb to combine two or more short sentences

Estimated Lesson Time: 45 minutes

Teacher Preparation:
1. Duplicate one copy of page 51 for each student.
2. Create an overhead transparency of the sample sentences found in the background information below.

Materials:
1 copy of page 51 for each student
blank transparency

Background Information:
Combining sentences makes a smoother, more detailed sentence out of two or more shorter sentences.

- **Sentences can be combined by using a compound subject.**
  Example: Nancy found a new hairstyle in a magazine. Betty also found a new hairstyle in a magazine.
  <u>Nancy</u> and <u>Betty</u> found new hairstyles in a magazine.

- **Sentences can be combined by using a compound verb.**
  Example: Pete fell off his bike. He broke his arm.
  Pete <u>fell</u> off his bike and <u>broke</u> his arm.

- **Sentences can be combined by using the conjunctions *and, but, or, nor, for, so,* and *yet*.**
  Example: The rain stopped before the game. The game was canceled because the field was still wet.
  The rain stopped before the game, <u>but</u> it was canceled because the field was still wet.

- **Sentences can be combined by using an appositive phrase.**
  Example: Mrs. Durhman passed out the test papers. Mrs. Durhman is my teacher.
  <u>My teacher</u>, <u>Mrs. Durhman</u>, passed out the test papers.

Introducing The Lesson:

Copy the two sentences below on the chalkboard:

Julie is having her birthday party at the skating rink.
Mary is also having her birthday party at the skating rink.

Read the two sentences aloud; then ask your students to combine the two sentences into one without changing the meaning. *(Julie and Mary are having their birthday parties at the skating rink.)*

Steps:

1. Explain to your students that the new sentence sounds smoother than the two original sentences. Explain further that combining short sentences can improve the flow of writing.

2. Display the transparency of the example sentences from the background information on page 49. Teach your class the four possible ways of combining sentences—*compound subjects, compound verbs, conjunctions,* and *appositive phrases.*

3. Divide students into pairs. Have each student write on a sheet of paper two short sentences that can be combined into one longer sentence using one of the four methods discussed. Direct each student to switch papers with his partner and combine the sentences on the paper he receives. Then have partners check each other's work for accuracy.

4. Distribute one copy of page 51 to each student. Instruct each student to complete his reproducible as directed.

compound subjects

compound verbs

conjunctions

appositive phrases

Come Join The Fun!

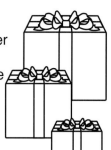

Combining sentences can really help the flow of your writing. Each number below contains two sentences. Use your knowledge of *compound sub-jects, compound verbs, appositive phrases,* and *conjunctions* to combine each pair of sentences into one, more detailed sentence. Remember to insert a comma before using a conjunction. Write each combined sentence on the line provided. The first one has been done for you.

1. Shena is having a birthday party.
   She is going to invite all her classmates.

   Shena is having a birthday party, and she is going to invite all her classmates.

2. Shena needs to decide where to have her birthday party soon.
   She might not have enough time to mail the invitations.

   _____

3. Shena planned the party.
   She sent the invitations to her classmates.

   _____

4. The party will be at Ice Castles.
   Ice Castles is the only ice-skating rink in town.

   _____

5. The boys planned on skating at the party.
   The girls planned on skating, too.

   _____

6. The best skater in the class will be at the party.
   David is the best skater in the class.

   _____

7. Jamie asked her parents if she could go to the party.
   They won't let her go.

   _____

8. Greg listened to the music.
   Greg skated with his friends.

   _____

9. Beverly Cleary sent a birthday card to Shena.
   Beverly Cleary is an author.

   _____

10. John played loud music at the party.
    Tim went home with a headache from the music.

    _____

11. Shena had a great time at the party.
    Her guests had a great time, too.

    _____

Bonus Box: On the back of this page, write a paragraph using each of the 11 combined sentences.

How To Extend The Lesson:

- Divide your class into four groups. Provide each group with magazines or newspapers to cut up, scissors, glue sticks, one paper bag, and one sheet of construction paper for each group member. Have each student look through newspapers and magazines and cut out ten short, simple sentences. Direct each student to place his cut-out sentences in his group's paper bag. Then instruct each group member to randomly choose ten sentences from the paper bag; then combine the ten simple sentences into five sentences. Tell students that their sentences can be silly, but they must not change the meaning from that of the two original sentences. Have each group paste the five pairs of simple sentences on a piece of construction paper; then write each combined sentence underneath the appropriate pair. Students will enjoy reading their sentences to the class.

- Use your class novel to point out several examples where the author used compound subjects, compound verbs, appositives, and conjunctions in his/her writing. Then encourage your students to find similar examples within their classmates' writing while they are peer editing. Set aside a few minutes at the end of the writing workshop for classmates to share the examples that they found.

- Instruct each student to write a paragraph about a time when he went somewhere special with a friend. Have students peer edit each other's papers. Tell students to use what they learned about combining sentences to revise their paragraphs so that each sentence flows smoothly. Display the final writings on a bulletin board for all classmates to read.

Eddie's Birthday Bash
Ted and I went to Eddie's birthday bash. We played games and ate cake and ice cream. We went outside to play, but it began to rain. Mrs. Turner, Eddie's mom, planned a great party.

Map It Out!

Help your students navigate through a story with this marvelous mapping activity!

Skill: Recognizing and analyzing the elements of a story—*setting, characters, plot, events, climax, resolution*

Estimated Lesson Time: 45 minutes

Teacher Preparation:
1. Duplicate page 55 for each pair of students.
2. Select a favorite fairy tale to share with students.

Materials:
1 copy of page 55 for each pair of students

Background Information:
The purpose of storymapping is to help students better understand a story's structure and identify major story elements. The six elements of a story discussed in this lesson are listed below:

- **Setting**—time and place of the story
- **Characters**—main people/animals involved in the story
- **Plot**—main problem or conflict of the story revealed through a series of events that build on one another
- **Events**—situations directly or indirectly related to the story's plot
- **Climax**—most exciting part of the story; usually in the middle of a story, but can also be found at the beginning or end
- **Resolution**—how the problem or conflict is solved or resolved

Setting
Characters
Plot
Events
Climax
Resolution

Introducing The Lesson:

Ask your students the following questions:
- "Where does your favorite story take place?"
- "Is your favorite story about one person or several people?"
- "What is the conflict or problem your favorite story is centered around?"
- "What was the most exciting part of your favorite story?"
- "Did certain things occur before this exciting part happened?"
- "How does your favorite story end?"

Call on several students to answer each question; then reveal to your students that they have just shared the major elements of a story—setting, characters, plot, events, climax, and resolution.

Steps:

1. Write the six elements of a story on the board—setting, characters, plot, events, climax, and resolution.

2. Tell your students that you are going to read aloud one of your favorite fairy tales. Instruct each student to listen carefully for examples of each story element listed on the board.

3. Read the fairy tale; then divide the students into pairs.

4. Distribute page 55 to each pair of students. Inform the class that each pair has just received a storymap. Tell each pair that a storymap is a quick-and-easy way to identify and record each major element of a story.

5. Instruct each pair to complete a storymap of the fairy tale.

6. Give each pair about 20 minutes to complete its storymap; then have each pair share its map.

7. After each pair has shared its storymap, discuss why each pair's storymap may have had slightly different information for each element. Discuss with your students how each pair can have a slightly different interpretation of the same story, and explain that that's to be expected.

setting   characters   plot   events   climax   resolution

Mapping It Out

Listen carefully to your teacher read a story. After hearing the story, complete each section of the storymap below.

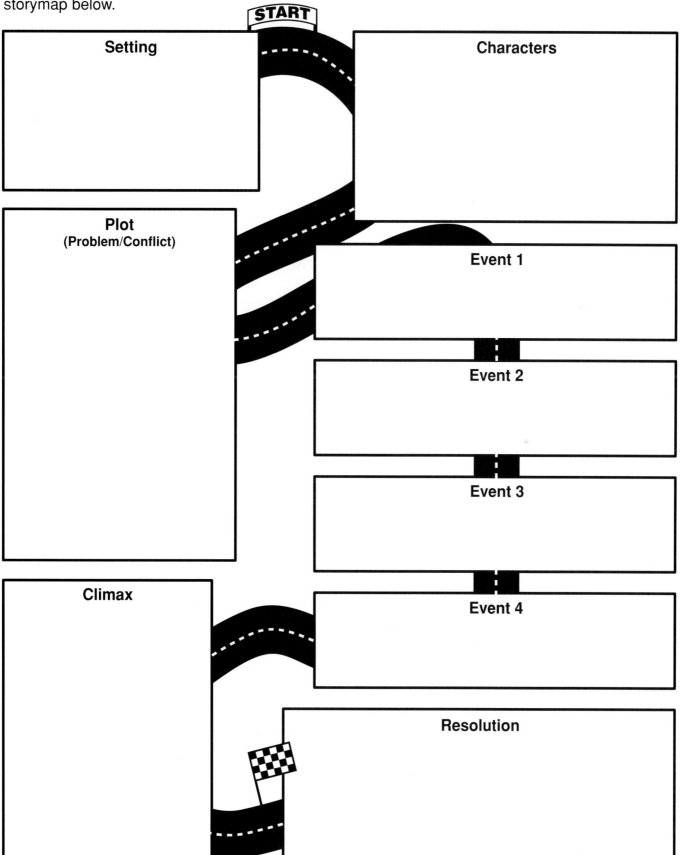

START

Setting

Characters

Plot
(Problem/Conflict)

Event 1

Event 2

Event 3

Climax

Event 4

Resolution

How To Extend The Lesson:

- Divide the students into groups of three or four; then give each group a different fairy tale. Select one student in each group to quietly read his group's fairy tale to the other members of his group. Then instruct each group to change the setting, plot, climax, and resolution of its fairy tale. Also have each group change the names and physical characteristics of the major characters. Give each group a piece of chart paper; then direct each group to write a short summary of its altered fairy tale. Have each group read its new version to the rest of the class and see if anyone can guess the name of the original tale.

- Select a familiar story or fairy tale to tell your students. This time, however, tell it backwards by starting with the story's resolution and working your way back through the story's plot. See how quickly your students can recognize the story. Instruct students to raise their hands if they think they know the name of the story. Call on a student and record his guess on the board. Continue telling the story, calling on students and recording guesses until you have finished the story. Then reveal the story's name and see how many students were correct.

- Divide the students into six groups. Assign each group a different story element—setting, characters, plot, events, climax, or resolution. Give each group a piece of poster board and a supply of colorful markers. Instruct each group to design a poster explaining its assigned story element. Direct each group to define its element, give an example, and include an illustration. Have each group present its story element poster to the rest of the class. Display the posters in the correct order on a wall or bulletin board in your classroom.

Setting
time and place of the story
the Kansas prairie, 1867

Get The Hint?

Help students understand and enjoy what they read by teaching them to "read between the lines."

Skill: Making inferences

Estimated Lesson Time: 45 minutes

Teacher Preparation:
Duplicate one copy of page 59 for each student.

Materials:
1 copy of page 59 for each student

Background Information:
   Making inferences helps provide understanding as a child reads. To make an inference, students should look for clues in the story and think about related personal experiences.

Introducing The Lesson:

Authors don't always tell you everything they want you to know about a story. Demonstrate this by reading the following passage to the class. Tell your students to listen carefully because you will be asking them some questions.

When Lori and Mark spotted the headlights drawing nearer, they knew they would survive. They had spent five hours stranded on the side of that deserted road hoping someone would drive by. Finally a truck that was clearing the road of its white blanket passed their car. The nightmare was finally over!

During that time spent in the car, Lori regretted trying to take the shortcut to her mom's house. They shouldn't have attempted to get there at all. Every year at this time the family got together to celebrate. Lori and Mark didn't want to miss out, so they risked traveling in the dangerous weather.

Now everything was ruined. They wouldn't be able to get their car back until the storm was over, they were late for dinner again, and on top of everything there wasn't enough room in the truck to bring their luggage. No luggage meant no presents. However, once Lori saw the look on her mother's face, she began to feel better.

Steps:

1. After reading the entire selection, read each of the questions below. Select a student to answer the question and tell what clues or hints helped him figure out the answer.

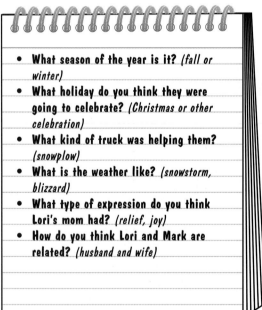

- **What season of the year is it?** *(fall or winter)*
- **What holiday do you think they were going to celebrate?** *(Christmas or other celebration)*
- **What kind of truck was helping them?** *(snowplow)*
- **What is the weather like?** *(snowstorm, blizzard)*
- **What type of expression do you think Lori's mom had?** *(relief, joy)*
- **How do you think Lori and Mark are related?** *(husband and wife)*

2. Inform students that they are using inferences—clues and personal experiences—to answer the questions. At times there can be more than one answer to fit the situation. Have students point out questions that have more than one possible answer.

3. Have each student practice making inferences by completing the reproducible on page 59.

Sleuthing For Clues

An author often puts descriptive words and details into a story as clues to help you make inferences. In each situation below, there are hints or clues to help you answer each question. Write your answer on the line of each magnifying-glass handle. Then underline the word or words from the paragraph that led you to your answer. Good luck, Detective!

The boys packed up their bags and headed back down toward the campsite. Their leader said they'd have to earn that patch another weekend.

1. What type of group or club might the boys belong to?

(answer)

The list of people who made the team was posted at 8:00 the next morning. Not one girl who was on the court that day slept a wink.

2. What took place on the court that day?

(answer)

Patrick walked into the classroom and he knew his cast would stir up questions. If only he hadn't climbed that tree.

3. What happened to Patrick?

(answer)

Even though Kathleen is in eighth grade, she stills gets nervous when the teacher asks the students to clear their desks and begins passing out the papers.

4. What makes Kathleen nervous at school?

(answer)

For the third day in a row, it rained. Josh's teacher found a game for the class to play inside, but it just wasn't the same.

5. What is Josh's class missing because of rain?

(answer)

Bonus Box: Now it's your turn. Write a paragraph of your own to try out on a friend. Remember to leave something out for your reader to figure out. Don't forget to leave him or her clues.

How To Extend The Lesson:

- Using the novel you are currently reading, point out instances where the author expects the reader to infer. Discuss why the author might have chosen this method to relay information, rather than telling the reader directly.

- Bring in a collection of various types of shoes—slippers, worn shoes, ballet shoes, cleats, high heels, work boots. Show the shoes one at a time to the class. Have each student infer what life is like for the person who wears that shoe.

- Students can also make inferences with pictures. Divide the class into groups. Give each group a picture book that does not have any text. Have each group create text to go along with each page of its book, based on what it infers from the picture. Allow each group to read its book while showing the pictures. Variation: Try using a magazine or art print and have students infer what is taking place in the picture.

- Have students use the sense of touch to make inferences. Place an object in a brown paper bag. Have a student try to guess what the object is by placing his hand in the bag and touching it. Create several of these bags to pass around to each student. Use some unique objects for a real challenge.

Foreseeing The Future

Create some soothsayers in your classroom with this lesson on predicting outcomes.

Skill: Using text and prior knowledge to predict outcomes

Estimated Lesson Time: 30 minutes

Teacher Preparation:
Duplicate one copy of page 63 for each student.

Materials:
1 copy of page 63 for each student

Background Information:
   Predicting outcomes involves looking for clues in a story and using prior knowledge to make a guess about what is going to happen.

What Will Happen Next?

Introducing The Lesson:

Begin by instructing students to carefully watch what you are doing. Without talking, act out a familiar task that the students are used to seeing you do. For example, open the closet door, get the playground balls out, put on your coat, and stand by the classroom door. Ask students to predict what you will do next *(line up the class to go outside)*.

Steps:

1. Ask students how they determined what you were going to do next. Guide students to realize that they saw what you did and related it to past experiences in the classroom.

2. Explain to students that while reading, they should use the same strategy to predict what might happen next. Predicting outcomes involves looking for clues in a story and using prior knowledge to make a guess about what is going to happen.

3. Give each student a copy of page 63. Have students follow the directions to complete the activity.

4. Conclude the activity by having student volunteers share their predictions with the class. Instruct the class to determine whether or not each prediction is logical.

It's Crystal Clear

Do you ever wonder what the future holds? Read each numbered paragraph. Then write your prediction of what will happen next in the base of each crystal ball. Underline the words in each paragraph that helped you make your prediction.

1. Rasheeda couldn't wait to go to the beach. She and her family were planning to leave the next morning at 5:00 A.M. Rasheeda woke up at 7:00 A.M. to the sound of raindrops. She ran into her parents' room and saw her mother unpacking the suitcase.

Prediction

2. Matt was so excited when his teacher said, "Anyone interested in trying out for the school play should meet after school." Matt was not a very good actor, but hardly anyone showed up at last year's meeting. When Matt walked into the room after school, he couldn't even find a place to sit!

Prediction

3. Maurice is not allowed to have friends in the house when he is home alone. The doorbell rang and Maurice saw that it was his friend Nick with a new video game. Maurice remembered that he got in trouble the last time he let a friend in the house when he was home alone.

Prediction

4. When Fiona woke up in the morning for school, she looked outside to see the ground covered in a blanket of white. She couldn't even see the road! Fiona quickly turned on the radio and listened.

Prediction

5. Kathleen always did what her mother told her. Kathleen's friend Donna wanted to sneak into a movie that Kathleen was not allowed to see. Donna said to Kathleen, "I won't go to your slumber party unless you go to the movie with me."

Prediction

6. Tara always fed her dog, Rex, before she ate her own lunch. Today she was just too hungry to wait. Tara made her sandwich and put it on the table. Rex started begging, so she gave him a small piece of bread. The phone rang and Tara left the room to answer it.

Prediction

Bonus Box: On the back of this sheet, write a story using the topic from one of the paragraphs you just read. Your story should include a beginning, a well-developed middle, and an ending.

How To Extend The Lesson:

- Show students a series of pages from a picture book; then have them predict what they think will happen next in the story. Have students justify their answers by explaining the clues they used to make their predictions. Show the final few pictures from the story so students can check the accuracy of their predictions.

- Begin reading a story to the class; then stop reading at an exciting part. Have each student create a newspaper headline predicting what will happen next. Instruct each student to write an article to accompany her headline. Allow students to share their articles; then finish reading the story. Have students check the accuracy of their predictions.

- Before reading a story, make an overhead transparency of the book's cover art. Place the picture on an overhead projector for students to view. Have each student write a paragraph predicting what the book is about. Tell students to look carefully at the title and the details of the illustration. Collect the paragraphs. After finishing the story, return the paragraphs to the students to check their predictions.

- Enlarge and duplicate the pattern below for each student. Read part of a short story to your students; then stop reading and have each student make an illustrated prediction in his crystal-ball pattern about what will happen next. Have each student share her prediction with the class. Continue reading the story so students can check their predictions.

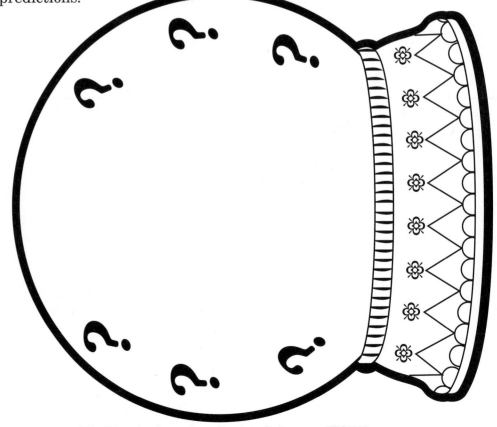

Jumping To Conclusions!

Your students will leap enthusiastically into logical conclusions with this lesson.

Skills: Analyzing information; making inferences; drawing logical conclusions

Estimated Lesson Time: 45 minutes

Teacher Preparation:
1. Duplicate one copy of page 67 for each student.
2. Gather two gifts (items found in your classroom).
3. Wrap each gift in decorative paper.

Materials:
1 copy of page 67 for each student
2 gifts (items found in the classroom)
wrapping paper

Background Information:
Conclusions can be reached by using inductive or deductive reasoning. Inductive reasoning involves looking at clues to come up with several probabilities. Deductive reasoning involves analyzing clues to come up with one particular conclusion.

Introducing The Lesson:

Begin by asking your students to explain what the phrase "look before you leap" means. Explain that when drawing conclusions, it is important to observe that piece of advice. Then discuss with students the importance of examining available information carefully so that when they make that jump, it's to the right, or logical, conclusion.

Steps:

1. Show your class one of the wrapped gift boxes. Pass the box around the room. Then challenge your students to write down what they think is in the box.

2. Ask student volunteers to share their guesses. Have each volunteer explain what information he based his decision on. Guide volunteers in mentioning the size, shape, and weight of the gift as factors in the conclusion-drawing process.

3. Provide students with additional clues and details related to the gift. Include information on a possible recipient of the gift as well as the possible uses for the gift. Also mention information such as the item's price and where it can be purchased.

4. Direct each student to reconsider his original conclusion about the gift based on the additional information. Open the package and show its contents. Discuss how examining details or clues helps a person to draw a more accurate conclusion. Explain that this method of drawing a conclusion is an example of deductive reasoning.

5. Ask a student volunteer to open the second package and show the class the gift inside. Then have your students brainstorm possible recipients for the gift. Guide your students in generating a list of several logical recipients for such a gift. Explain that this method of developing several probabilities is an example of inductive reasoning.

6. Provide each student with a copy of page 67. Instruct him to complete the reproducible as directed.

Name_____ *Drawing conclusions*

Look Before You Leap!

Felix Frog's birthday is tomorrow and just about every frog in Placid Pond is going to the party. Each frog is hoping to have found the perfect gift. Examine the thoughts of each frog below. Then use that information to draw a logical conclusion about what he or she will give Felix. Draw and label each gift in the giver's box. Be ready to explain why you selected each item.

I'm Felix's mom. I want to give him something that reminds him of his childhood.

I'm Felix's best friend, Franklin. I want to give him a game we can play together.

I'm the pond bully. I'm giving Felix something to make him jump out of his skin!

Felix is a big football fan. His favorite team is the Amphibians. I know exactly what I'll get him.

I'm Felix's grandmother. I think I'll prepare Felix a special treat to eat.

I'm Felix's girlfriend, Fluffy. I want to give him something romantic for his birthday.

I got Felix a gift from the Frogtown Furniture Factory where I work.

I am Felix's soccer coach. I want to give him something he can use in a game.

Felix loves to read. I know exactly what to give him!

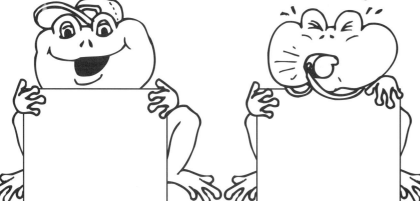

Bonus Box: On the back of this sheet, record an additional clue from Felix's musician friend, Fabio, concerning what he plans on giving Felix for his birthday.

©The Education Center, Inc. • *Ready-to-Go Lessons* • TEC1118

67

How To Extend The Lesson:

- Select a short story to read to your class, omitting the ending. Then divide your class into groups of three or four students. Direct each group to develop a logical conclusion for the story. Direct each group to use the details in the story to justify its conclusions. Have each group read its conclusion to the rest of the class.

- Direct each student in your class to select a famous actor or politician. Explain to each student that she will need to think of the perfect gift for her celebrity. Instruct each student to choose the gift carefully and list the reasons why she selected this particular gift. Have each student present her gift idea, the recipient's name, and the reasoning behind selecting the gift to the rest of the class.

- Cut several comic strips from the newspaper. Remove the final frame from each strip and place it in an individually numbered envelope. Next glue each comic strip (minus the last frame) to a separate sheet of construction paper. Number each mounted comic strip with the same number as the envelope featuring the strip's final frame. Place these sheets and envelopes in a center in your room. Challenge each student who visits the center to select one of the sheets of construction paper. Then have her literally draw her conclusions about the events of the missing final frame on a piece of paper. Direct each student to check the envelope of the same number to compare the concluding frame she created to that generated by the actual cartoonist.

Character Creations

Help students analyze and identify character traits with this fun activity.

Skill: Identifying character traits

Estimated Lesson Time: 1 hour

Teacher Preparation:
1. Choose a passage from a popular children's book that details a character's thoughts, words, and actions.
2. Cut small strips of paper and label each one with a character trait.
3. Duplicate page 71 for each student.

Materials:
small strips of paper (one for each student)
paper bag
crayons
1 copy of page 71 for each student

Background Information:
To help a reader better understand a character, an author tries to create a mental picture of him or her. The author does this by describing how a character looks, speaks, thinks, and acts. The character's traits may be revealed directly, or the author may leave it up to the reader to draw her own conclusions.

Introducing The Lesson:

Ask your students to close their eyes and listen carefully to what you are about to describe. Then read a description of a character from a popular book. Tell your students to open their eyes; then ask them to tell you about the character you described.

Steps:

1. Explain to students that an author tries to create a mental picture of a character. The author reveals the character's traits through the character's thoughts, words, and actions. Tell students that these traits are sometimes stated and sometimes implied by the author. Readers often have to draw their own conclusions based on the author's descriptions. Ask each student to list the character traits revealed in the passage. Create a character web on the chalkboard that includes specific examples from each student.

2. Brainstorm with your students a list of character traits such as honesty, courage, and laziness. Write each character trait on a small strip of paper (one strip for each student). Place the strips in a small paper bag labeled "character traits." Direct each of your students to pick one strip from the bag.

3. Instruct the student to write three sentences that describe a character with the trait that was drawn—without using the word written on her strip. Have the student write one sentence each about what the character thinks, says, and does. For example, if a student drew the trait *responsible,* she would write the following types of sentences:
   • The character thought that she needed to complete her homework before evening basketball practice.
   • The character told her friend, "I'll pay for your necklace since I broke it."
   • The character baby-sat her little sister while their mother went grocery shopping.

4. Direct each student to read her sentences to another student to see if he can guess the character trait based on the descriptions.

5. Duplicate page 71 for each student. Distribute the reproducible and crayons; then direct each student to either use the character trait she picked from the bag or choose one of her own to complete the activity. Emphasize that a character's traits reveal his personality. After all students have completed the activity, have each student show her character to the rest of the class.

courage

honesty

laziness

Character Creation

Character traits reveal a character's personality. He or she might be caring, intelligent, creative, and athletic. An author reveals these traits through the character's thoughts, words, and actions.

Directions: Choose a character trait. Name your character based on the trait such as "Intelligent Ingrid" or "Caring Carl." Next decide what your character looks like. Draw and color your character's physical features and clothing on the pattern below. Then decide what kinds of things your character would think, say, and do. Add the thoughts and words to the bubbles. Draw props and a setting around your character to express your character's actions. For example, Intelligent Ingrid could be drawn in a library surrounded by books and a computer.

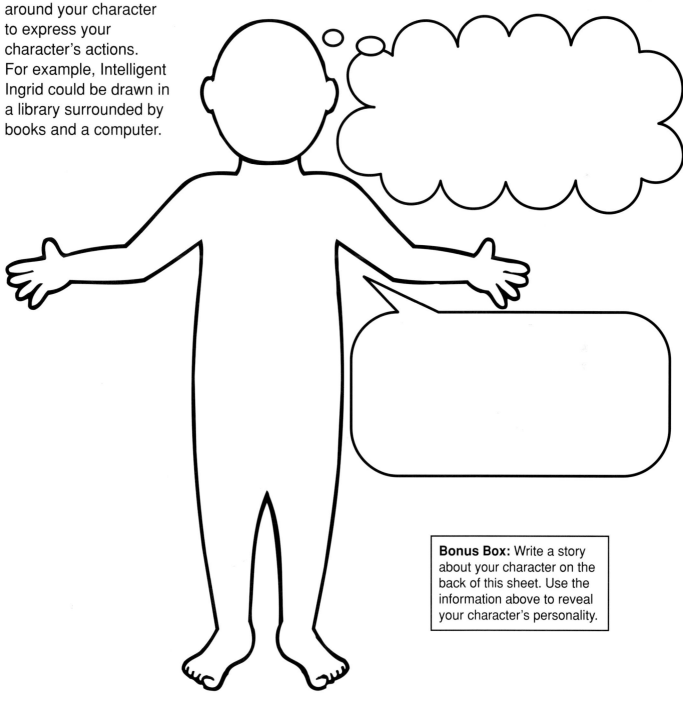

Bonus Box: Write a story about your character on the back of this sheet. Use the information above to reveal your character's personality.

character's name

©The Education Center, Inc. • *Ready-to-Go Lessons* • TEC1118

How To Extend The Lesson:

- As students read their favorite stories, have them create character clusters based on a character's physical traits, thoughts, words, and actions.

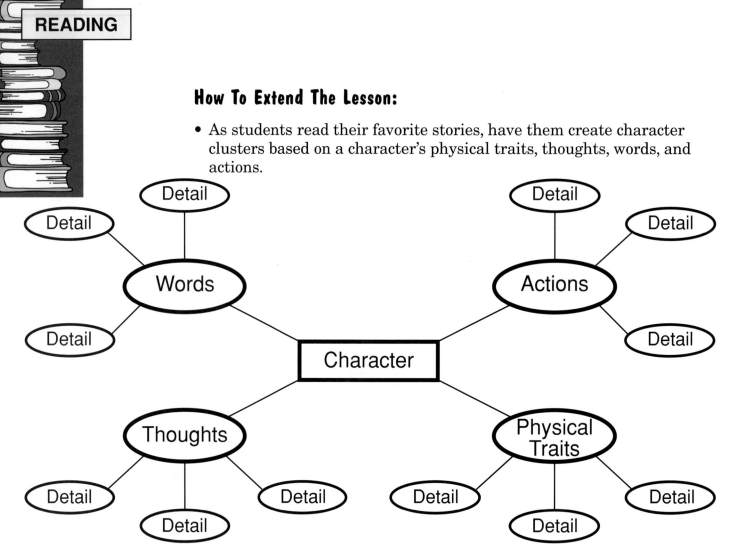

- Have each student cut out a picture of a famous person from a newspaper or magazine. Direct the student to identify traits that he feels reflect the person's character. Then tell the student to support his listed traits with examples of the person's thoughts, words, and actions.

- Brainstorm with your students a list of admirable character traits such as honesty, dependability, and caring. Direct each student to set a goal in which he works to develop one of the traits. Then have the student write a journal entry describing the various ways (thoughts, words, and actions) he can achieve this.

- Have each student create a thank-you card for someone in her life who she believes shows good character. Instruct the student to write a message to the person in the form of a poem, song, or letter on the inside of the card. Direct the student to describe the person's admirable traits in her message. Then have the student draw a picture that illustrates the person expressing one of these good character traits on the outside of the card. Finally have the student sign and deliver her card.

A Perfect Pair

Guide your students in the skill of comparing and contrasting with the following activity.

Skill: Comparing and contrasting information

Estimated Lesson Time: 45 minutes

Teacher Preparation:
1. Duplicate one copy of page 75 for each student.
2. Find pictures of two animals, such as a cat and a dog.

Materials:
1 copy of page 75 for each child
pictures of two animals to be compared, such as a cat and a dog

Background Information:
Comparison involves looking at two items to find common characteristics. *Contrasting* involves looking at items to find their differences. Information about similarities and differences between two items is often organized in a chart called a *Venn diagram.*

Certain words and phrases are used to indicate when items are being compared or contrasted. Words and phrases such as *in the same way, also, likewise, like, as,* and *similarly* are often used to compare items. Words such as *yet, but, however, on the other hand, still, otherwise, although,* and *even though* are used to contrast items.

Introducing The Lesson:

Write the names of two popular television shows on the board. Then ask your students to explain how the two shows are alike and how the two shows are different. List their responses on the board. Tell your students that they have just used the skills of comparing and contrasting.

Steps:

1. Display the pictures of the cat and dog, or two other animals you've selected. Draw a chart like the one below on the board. Have your students help you create a list of similarities and differences between the two animals. Record this information on the chart in the appropriate columns.

Cats and Dogs		
Cats	Both	Dogs

2. Next guide your students in a similar comparison of fourth and fifth grade. Draw a chart like the one below on your board.

Fourth Grade and Fifth Grade		
Fourth Grade	Both	Fifth Grade

3. Then show students how the same information can be displayed in a Venn diagram like the one shown below.

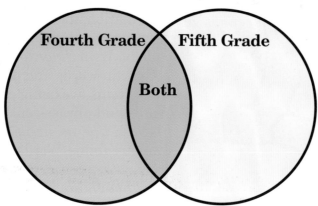

4. Provide each student with a copy of the reproducible on page 75. Direct each student to complete the reproducible as directed.

Name _____

A Perfect Pair!

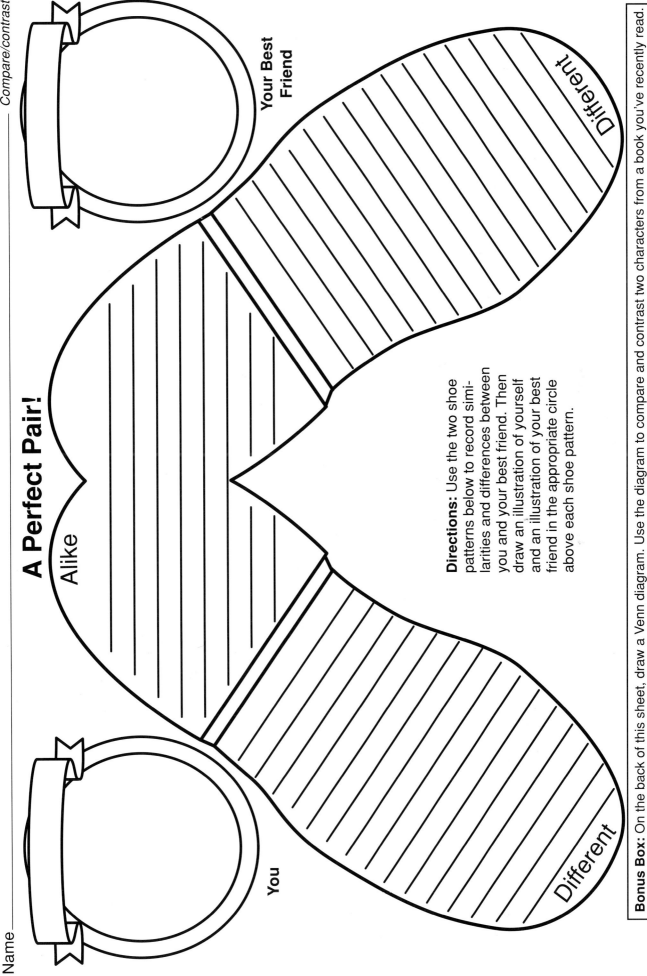

Alike

You

Your Best Friend

Different

Different

Directions: Use the two shoe patterns below to record similarities and differences between you and your best friend. Then draw an illustration of yourself and an illustration of your best friend in the appropriate circle above each shoe pattern.

©The Education Center, Inc. • *Ready-to-Go Lessons* • TEC1118

Bonus Box: On the back of this sheet, draw a Venn diagram. Use the diagram to compare and contrast two characters from a book you've recently read.

75

How To Extend The Lesson:

• Explain to your students that Venn diagrams are helpful tools in organizing information for writing. Use the cat and dog comparison and contrast chart as the basis for a writing assignment. Direct each student to write a paragraph describing the ways in which cats and dogs are similar and different.

• Challenge each student to use the information he recorded about his best friend and himself to write a poem entitled "My Best Friend And I: A Perfect Pair."

• Extend the concept of comparing and contrasting into another curricular area such as social studies. Have each student select two historical figures. Then direct the student to research both individuals and record his findings in a Venn diagram or similar graphic organizer. Have each student present his findings to the rest of the class.

Abraham Lincoln

• Wrote the Emancipation Proclamation which formally freed the slaves.
• Wrote the Gettysburg Address.
• The Civil War
• First president to wear a beard in office.

• Both were U.S. presidents.
• Both died in office.

John F. Kennedy

• Youngest man ever elected president.
• "Ask not what your country can do for you. Ask what you can do for your country."— famous quote from inaugural address.
• The Cold War
• First president to have been a Boy Scout.

76   *Comparing and contrasting information*

Cue Into Context Clues

Help your students use context clues to cue into word meanings.

Skill: Identifying and using context clues

Estimated Lesson Time: 1 hour

Teacher Preparation:
Duplicate page 79 for each student.

Materials:
1 copy of page 79 for each student
1 blue, one yellow, and one green crayon
   for each student
paper and pencil for each student

Background Information:
Context clues help a reader to define unfamiliar words. The clues may be words or phrases that come before or after an unfamiliar word, and may be in the same sentence or in surrounding sentences. The clues may define the word in several ways:

1. **A context clue may describe the unfamiliar word.**
   "Joe's favorite indoor game is *billiards*. It is played on a rectangular table with openings called pockets."
2. **A context clue may restate the idea.**
   "The *cue,* a long tapered stick, is used to hit plastic balls into the pockets of the table."
3. **A context clue may compare the unfamiliar word with another word.**
   "Players try to *sink* the balls, but sometimes they miss the pockets completely."

Using context clues helps make readers more independent. Students learn how to find the meanings of new words in the context of a passage or story.

Describe

Restate

Compare

Introducing The Lesson:

Write an unusual word on the board such as *gobbledygook*. Ask your students to tell you the meaning of the word. If they cannot, write a sentence on the board and tell them that there are clues within the sentence that will help them define the meaning of the word. For example, "The boy received a letter from his three-year-old nephew that was gobbledygook; he couldn't understand a word of the young boy's message."

Steps:

1. Explain to students that context clues are words or phrases within a sentence or paragraph that help define unfamiliar words. The clues may *describe* the unfamiliar word, *restate* the unfamiliar word, or *compare* the unfamiliar word with another word.

2. Using the sentence in the introduction above, ask students to tell you what word or words within the sentence are clues to the meaning of *gobbledygook* (the boy couldn't understand a word of it; it's from a three year old). Then ask students if the clue describes the word, restates the word, or compares the word to another word. (It describes the word.)

3. Copy and distribute the reproducible on page 79 to each student. Have the student follow the directions on the page to discover the meanings of the unfamiliar words. After your students complete the work, wrap up the lesson by emphasizing how context clues help readers figure out the meanings of unfamiliar words, or help them learn new meanings of familiar words.

4. Challenge each of your students to make up a nonsense word. Have each student write three sentences with context clues that give the word three different meanings. For each sentence the student should vary the purpose of each clue (to describe, restate, and compare). Then have each student exchange papers with a partner. Direct the partner to underline the clues and identify the intended meanings of the word from its context.

Cue Into Context Clues

To figure out the meaning of an unfamiliar word, look at other words or phrases around that word. They can be in the same sentence or a surrounding sentence. Use the examples below to help you.

(1.) **Context clues describe:** A phrase or sentence following the word gives more information.
"Joe's favorite indoor game is *billiards*. It is played on a rectangular table with openings called pockets."

(2.) **Context clues restate:** A short definition set off by commas follows the unfamiliar word.
"The *cue,* a long tapered stick, is used to hit plastic balls into the pockets of the table."

(3.) **Context clues compare:** The unfamiliar word is compared to its action or purpose. It may also be compared to something similar or very different.
"Players try to *sink* the balls, but sometimes they miss the pockets completely."

Directions: Read each sentence below. Circle the context clues that help you determine the meaning of each boldface word. Then identify the type of clue used in each sentence by coloring the numbered cue ball at the beginning of each sentence. Use the code below:
• **Describes** = blue   • **Restates** = yellow   • **Compares** = green

1. In croquet a point is scored when a ball is hit through a **wicket,** or narrow arch.

2. The next player picked up a croquet **mallet.** He used the long, wooden, hammerlike stick to hit the ball.

3. The **jai alai** game was uneventful, although it is usually fast and dangerous.

4. The jai alai **pelota** is a ball slightly smaller than a baseball.

5. In order to win the game, the table-tennis player **killed** the ball by hitting it as hard as he could.

6. The **rally** of the ball continued for five minutes until the ball was hit out of bounds.

7. Polo ponies don't have to be a special breed, although three-quarter **thoroughbreds** are the most acceptable.

8. There are four **chukkers,** or seven-minute periods, in polo.

9. **Cricket,** a game played with bats and a ball, is popular in England.

10. One of the **batsmen** on Tom's team hit the ball and won the cricket game.

How To Extend The Lesson:

• Cut out an article from a local newspaper. White-out 10–15 key words from the section after writing a list of these words on the board in random order. Next duplicate a copy of the article for each student; then distribute the copies. Direct each student to use the context clues within the article to fill in each blank with an appropriate word from the word list.

• Choose 12–15 words that you know will be unfamiliar to your students. Write each word and its definition on a sentence strip. Then, on separate index cards, write two or three clues for each word. Make duplicate clue cards so each student will have one. (Be sure the clue-card words are not part of the definitions on the sentence strips.) For example, for the word *parka* (a jacket), write "zipped" and "hood" as clue words.

Distribute one clue card to each student. Then post one sentence strip containing an unfamiliar word and its definition on the board. Read the unfamiliar word and the definition to your class. Then instruct each student to look at his clue card. If he feels his card could be used as a clue to the unfamiliar word, direct him to hold up the card. Have the class discuss which of the raised cards best describes the unfamiliar word.

After each unfamiliar word has been matched with its clues, divide the students into 12–15 groups. Assign each group one of the unfamiliar words and instruct group members to write a sentence that uses the unfamiliar word and the clue-card words as context clues. For example, "Michael zipped his parka and pulled up the hood." Finally have each group read its sentence to the other groups.

• Have each student find ten unfamiliar words from a book he is currently reading. Instruct the student to identify the context clues and use them to define the words.

Unfamiliar Word	Clues	Definition
conduct	orchestra	to direct an orchestra

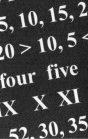

Putting Numbers In Their Place

Reinforce place value through millions with this exciting whole-class game.

Skill: Place value through millions

Estimated Lesson Time: 45 minutes

Teacher Preparation:
1. Duplicate one copy of page 83 for each student.
2. Label two paper bags "blue bag" and two paper bags "red bag."
3. Label 20 index cards with the numbers 0–9 (two cards per number).
4. Attach a strip of magnetic tape to the back of each labeled index card.
5. Place one set of the index cards numbered 0–4 in each red bag.
6. Place one set of the index cards numbered 5–9 in each blue bag.

Materials:
1 copy of page 83 for each student
4 paper lunch bags
20 index cards
magnetic tape

Background Information:
The value of each digit is determined by its place in the number.

MILLIONS			THOUSANDS			ONES		
hundreds	tens	ones	hundreds	tens	ones	hundreds	tens	ones
4	**3**	**7,**	**2**	**1**	**8,**	**6**	**4**	**2**

400,000,000   10,000   40

Numbers are separated by commas into groups of three digits called *periods*.

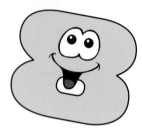

Introducing The Lesson:

Begin the lesson by drawing a place-value chart through millions on the chalkboard. Call out a large number and have a student come to the board and place its digits in the correct columns of the chart. Repeat this process with two other large numbers. Do not erase any of the digits from the three numbers. Discuss which number is the largest, which is the smallest, and how you can tell.

Steps:

1. Erase the work from the board and then draw two identical place-value charts like those on the reproducible on page 83. Then draw a point-tally column for each team as shown.

Millions	Hundred Thousands	Ten Thousands	Thousands	Hundreds	Tens	Ones	Team One's Points
,			,				

2. Divide the class into two teams, giving each group one red and one blue bag. Give each student a copy of the reproducible on page 83. Instruct students not to solve the problems.

3. Assign each student in Team 1 a different number. Assign each student in Team 2 a corresponding number from Team 1. Tell each student he has one minute to solve problem number 1 in Round 1 on his reproducible.

4. When one minute is up, check the answers of the two students who were given number 1. If a student's answer is correct, have him draw a card from his team's *blue bag* and place it anywhere on his team's place-value chart. If his answer is incorrect, have him draw a card from his team's *red bag* and write it anywhere on his team's place-value chart. Have each team member record the number in the appropriate section on his own sheet. Tell students that their goal is to create a larger number than the other team.

5. Randomly select another student from each team and check his answer to problem number 1. If the answer is correct, award his team one point. Continue play with problems 2–6. At the end of each round, allow the team with the most points the option of switching two numbers on its place-value chart. The team that creates the largest number is the winner of Round 1. Repeat the process for Round 2 and Round 3.

Grab-Bag Math

Round 1

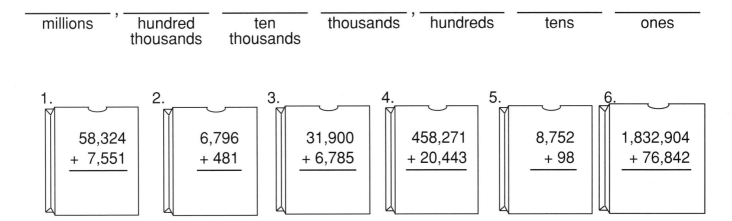

_____ , _____ _____ _____ , _____ _____ _____
millions   hundred   ten   thousands   hundreds   tens   ones
thousands   thousands

1.
58,324
+ 7,551

2.
6,796
+ 481

3.
31,900
+ 6,785

4.
458,271
+ 20,443

5.
8,752
+ 98

6.
1,832,904
+ 76,842

Round 2

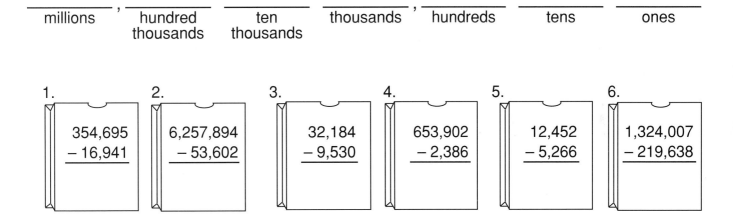

_____ , _____ _____ _____ , _____ _____ _____
millions   hundred   ten   thousands   hundreds   tens   ones
thousands   thousands

1.
354,695
− 16,941

2.
6,257,894
− 53,602

3.
32,184
− 9,530

4.
653,902
− 2,386

5.
12,452
− 5,266

6.
1,324,007
− 219,638

Round 3

_____ , _____ _____ _____ , _____ _____ _____
millions   hundred   ten   thousands   hundreds   tens   ones
thousands   thousands

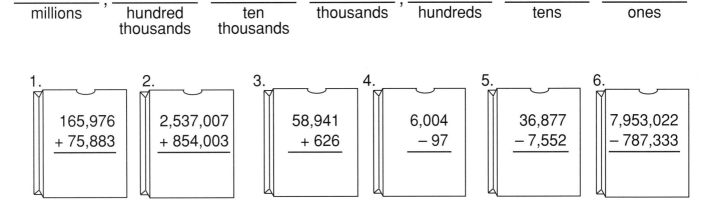

1.
165,976
+ 75,883

2.
2,537,007
+ 854,003

3.
58,941
+ 626

4.
6,004
− 97

5.
36,877
− 7,552

6.
7,953,022
− 787,333

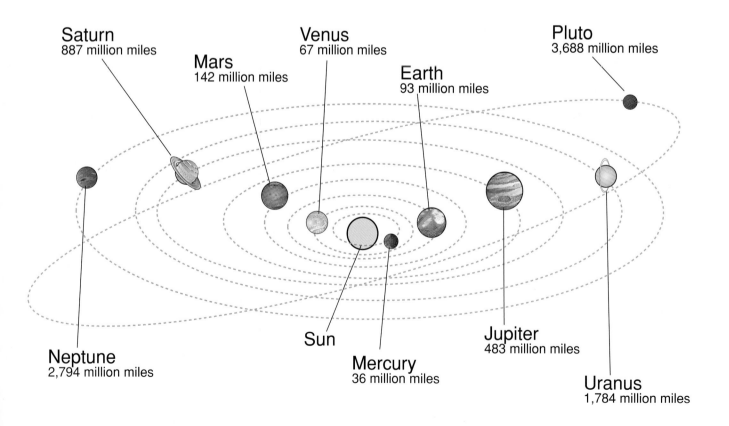

How To Extend The Lesson:

- Have students look for examples of large numbers being used in real-world situations. Give each student a newspaper. Challenge him to find numbers with digits in the thousands or millions place. Have him write down the number, along with the information that accompanied the number. Have each student present his findings to the rest of the class.

- Divide your class into small groups. Provide each group with a world almanac. Instruct each group to find ten cities with populations of one million people or more. Instruct each group to write ten facts about the differences in population among the ten cities, then share its findings with the class.

- Divide your students into pairs. Provide each pair with a copy the information shown below on the distance of each planet from the sun. Direct students to create three word problems using the information. Collect each pair's problems and redistribute them so that no pair receives its own work. Instruct students to work together to solve the three problems that they receive. Have the original writers of each set of word problems check the solutions for accuracy.

Saturn
887 million miles

Mars
142 million miles

Venus
67 million miles

Earth
93 million miles

Pluto
3,688 million miles

Neptune
2,794 million miles

Sun

Mercury
36 million miles

Jupiter
483 million miles

Uranus
1,784 million miles

"A-maze-ing" Fractions!

Help students find their way through addition and subtraction of unlike fractions with the following activity.

Skill: Adding and subtracting unlike fractions

Estimated Lesson Time: 1 hour

Teacher Preparation:
1. Duplicate two copies of "Fraction Strips" on page 87 for each student.
2. Duplicate one copy of "Fraction Maze" on page 87 for each student.

Materials:
2 "Fraction Strips" reproducibles (page 87) for each student
1 "Fraction Maze" reproducible (page 87) for each student
scissors
crayons
glue or tape

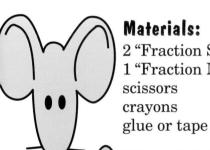

Background Information:

Before beginning adding and subtracting unlike fractions, students should have mastered equivalent fractions. To add unlike fractions, follow these simple steps:

Step 1: Find the lowest common denominator. Stress that finding the lowest common denominator will simplify the last step of reducing the fraction to its lowest terms.
Example:
$5/8 + 1/4$
Eight is the lowest common denominator because it is the smallest number divisible by both denominators.

Step 2: Rewrite the fractions as equivalent fractions.
Example:
$5/8 = 5/8$
$1/4 \times 2/2 = 2/8$

Step 3: Add the numerators. Put the sum over the common denominator. (Be sure the answer is in lowest terms.)
Example:
$5/8 + 2/8 = 7/8$

I ran the MAZE!

Introducing The Lesson:

Tell students that adding and subtracting like fractions is fairly easy because the denominators are the same. You simply add or subtract the two numerators and place the sum or difference over the denominator. Inform students that adding and subtracting unlike fractions is easy too. You just have a few extra steps to complete.

Steps:

1. Supply each student with two copies of "Fraction Strips" (page 87), scissors, and crayons. Instruct each student to lightly color each fraction strip on one of the sheets a different color. Then direct each student to cut each colored strip into fraction pieces as marked. Inform students that the uncolored and uncut sheet will be used as a template or workmat.

2. Guide each student to use his fraction pieces to show $2/4 + 1/4$ by first placing two $1/4$ pieces and one $1/4$ piece on the fourths strip of the template sheet. Have each student identify the sum of the three fraction pieces $(2/4 + 1/4 = 3/4)$.

3. Next have each student find which fraction strips will fit inside (equally) other fraction strips, such as:
   - *two $1/8$ pieces equal one $1/4$ piece*
   - *two $1/4$ pieces equal one $1/2$ piece*
   - *two $1/2$ pieces equal one whole strip*

   Then ask students what common denominators they recognize.
   (Students will recognize 2, 4, and 8 using halves, fourths, and eighths; 3, 6, and 12 using thirds, sixths, and twelfths; 2, 6, and 12 using halves, sixths, and twelfths; and 5 and 10 using fifths and tenths.)

4. Instruct each student to use his fraction pieces and template to show $3/8 + 1/4$. Instruct the student to find one fraction strip on the template that three $1/8$ pieces and one $1/4$ piece will fit into equally. *(The four pieces will fit into the eighths strip.)* Have each student name the new fraction *($5/8$)*. Have students repeat the process to solve the following problems:
   - $1/4 + 1/2 = (3/4)$
   - $1/3 + 1/2 = (5/6)$
   - $3/10 + 2/5 = (7/10)$
   - $5/12 + 1/3 = (9/12)$ *or* $(3/4)$

5. Ask students what pattern they notice about the denominators in each equation. *(The sum's denominator is a multiple of the other denominators.)* Explain to students that when adding or subtracting fractions, the denominators must be the same.

6. Discuss the steps for adding (and subtracting) fractions with unlike denominators as shown in the "Background Information" on page 85.

7. Distribute one copy of "Fraction Maze" on page 87, scissors, and glue or tape to each student to complete as an independent assignment.

Name _____

Fraction Maze

Use your knowledge of adding and subtracting unlike fractions to complete the maze below.

Directions: Beginning at "Start," solve each problem. When you've solved the problem, find the answer below, cut it out, and glue or tape it in the appropriate box on the maze.

Steps For Adding/Subtracting Unlike Fractions:

Step 1: Find the lowest common denominator (LCD).

Step 2: Rewrite each fraction as an equivalent fraction using the LCD.

Step 3: Add or subtract the numerators. Then put the sum or difference over the LCD. Be sure the fraction is in lowest terms.

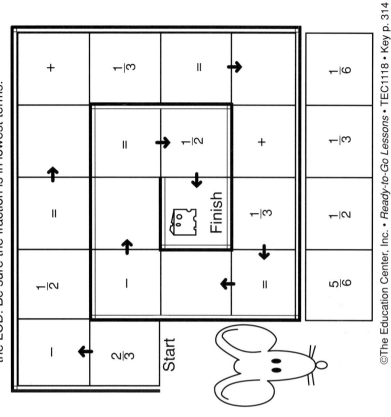

©The Education Center, Inc. • Ready-to-Go Lessons • TEC1118 • Key p. 314

Note To The Teacher: Duplicate two copies of "Fraction Strips" for each student to use with the lesson explained on page 86. Duplicate one copy of "Fraction Maze" for each student to complete independently.

1				
$\frac{1}{2}$			$\frac{1}{2}$	
$\frac{1}{3}$		$\frac{1}{3}$		$\frac{1}{3}$
$\frac{1}{4}$		$\frac{1}{4}$	$\frac{1}{4}$	$\frac{1}{4}$
$\frac{1}{5}$	$\frac{1}{5}$	$\frac{1}{5}$	$\frac{1}{5}$	$\frac{1}{5}$
$\frac{1}{6}$	$\frac{1}{6}$	$\frac{1}{6}$	$\frac{1}{6}$	$\frac{1}{6}$ $\frac{1}{6}$
$\frac{1}{8}$ $\frac{1}{8}$	$\frac{1}{8}$	$\frac{1}{8}$	$\frac{1}{8}$ $\frac{1}{8}$	$\frac{1}{8}$ $\frac{1}{8}$
$\frac{1}{10}$ $\frac{1}{10}$ $\frac{1}{10}$	$\frac{1}{10}$ $\frac{1}{10}$	$\frac{1}{10}$ $\frac{1}{10}$	$\frac{1}{10}$ $\frac{1}{10}$	$\frac{1}{10}$
$\frac{1}{12}$ $\frac{1}{12}$ $\frac{1}{12}$	$\frac{1}{12}$ $\frac{1}{12}$ $\frac{1}{12}$	$\frac{1}{12}$ $\frac{1}{12}$	$\frac{1}{12}$ $\frac{1}{12}$ $\frac{1}{12}$	$\frac{1}{12}$

Fraction Strips

Directions: Make sure that your teacher has given you two copies of these strips. Lightly color each fraction strip on one set a different color. Then carefully cut out each colored, labeled fraction piece. Do not color or cut the second set. The second set will be used as a template or workmat. Listen carefully as your teacher explains how to use your fraction piece cutouts and template.

How To Extend The Lesson:

- Label 20 index cards with one unlike fraction on each card. Shuffle the cards and place them at a center along with paper and pencils. Invite two students at a time to the center. Instruct the pair to spread out the cards facedown on the table. Then direct one student at a time to turn over two cards. Have the student (if possible) announce a lowest common denominator, rewrite the fractions as equivalent fractions, and add the two fractions on a piece of paper. If the student adds correctly, tell her to keep the cards. If she does not add correctly, tell her to put the cards back facedown in their original places. After all cards have been collected, have each student count her cards. The student with the most cards wins.

- Supply students with various magazines that contain seasonal recipes. Next give each student an index card. Instruct the student to find and cut out a favorite seasonal recipe. Then direct the student to rewrite the recipe, adding a 1/2, 1/3, or 1/4 to or subtracting a 1/2, 1/3, or 1/4 from each measured ingredient. Instruct the student to show his work on the card. Finally have the student decorate the recipe card. Check the cards and display them on a bulletin board titled "What's Cooking!"

- Cut out action pictures from various magazines. Divide students into groups of three, and give each group a magazine picture, a sheet of 9" x 12" construction paper, and glue. Direct the group to create a word problem using the information that is presented in the picture. Tell the group that the problem must involve adding or subtracting unlike fractions. Instruct the group to glue its picture to the top of the paper, write its problem at the bottom, and write its answer on the back. Collect the papers; then distribute a different one to each group. Have each group solve its new problem and check the answer.

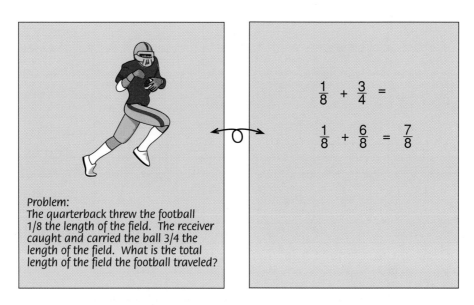

Problem:
The quarterback threw the football 1/8 the length of the field. The receiver caught and carried the ball 3/4 the length of the field. What is the total length of the field the football traveled?

$$\frac{1}{8} + \frac{3}{4} =$$

$$\frac{1}{8} + \frac{6}{8} = \frac{7}{8}$$

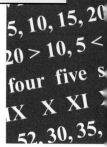
Nail Down Fractions

Nail down your students' understanding of multiplying fractions with the following hands-on activities!

Skill: Multiplying fractions

Estimated Lesson Time: 1 hour

Teacher Preparation:

1. Copy the steps for multiplying fractions onto a sheet of chart paper.
2. Duplicate page 91 for each student.

Materials:

1 sheet of chart paper
1 copy of page 91 for each student
1 sheet of 8 1/2" x 11" paper for each student
2 crayons or colored pencils for each student:
    1 red and 1 blue
1 ruler for each student

Background Information:

When having students multiply fractions to find a product, instruct them to use the steps outlined below. Stress that students should align the fractions as shown, and be sure to simplify all answers.

Step 1: Write the fractions with the numerators and denominators lined up as shown.

numerators $\dfrac{1}{3}$ **x** $\dfrac{3}{4}$

denominators

Step 2: Multiply the numerators; then multiply the denominators.

$$\frac{1}{3} \times \frac{3}{4} = \frac{3}{12}$$

Step 3: Simplify the answer.
The greatest common factor of the numerator 3 and the denominator 12 is 3. Divide the numerator and the denominator by 3.

$$\frac{3}{12} \div \frac{3}{3} = \frac{1}{4}$$

Introducing The Lesson:

Help students understand the concept of multiplying fractions by looking at patterns in the products of whole numbers. Write the following equations on the board: 6 x 3 = ?, 6 x 2 = ?, and 6 x 1 = ? Have students find the products *(18, 12, 6)*. Then ask students what pattern they see in the products. *(The product becomes smaller as the factors become smaller.)* Next ask students what they think the product would be if the 6 were multiplied by a fraction *(less than 6)*. Guide students to recognize that if a number were multiplied by a fraction, the product would be less than the number; and if two fractions were multiplied, the product would be less than either of the two fractions.

Steps:

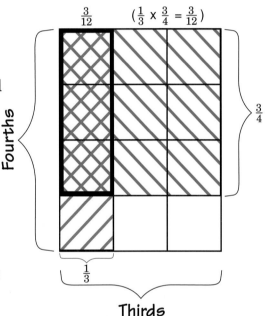

1. Supply each student with one 8 1/2" x 11" sheet of paper, a ruler, and a red and a blue crayon or colored pencil. Using the diagram shown as a guide, direct each student to use the ruler and a pencil to divide his paper into thirds, and use a blue crayon to shade in the area that represents $\frac{1}{3}$. Again using the diagram below as a guide, have each student use the ruler and pencil to divide his paper into fourths. Direct each student to use a red crayon to shade in $\frac{3}{4}$ of his paper.

2. Next write the equation $\frac{1}{3}$ x $\frac{3}{4}$ = ? on the chalkboard. Have each student count the spaces that are shaded with both colors *(3 spaces)*, then count the total number of spaces *(12 spaces)*. Write the number of spaces on the board as a fraction: the first number as the numerator (it represents a fractional part), and the second number as the denominator (it represents the total number of spaces).

3. Next explain to students that when they are asked to find a fraction of something, the "of" is a clue to multiply. So $\frac{1}{3}$ of $\frac{3}{4}$ is the same as $\frac{1}{3}$ x $\frac{3}{4}$.

4. Explain the steps in multiplying two fractions using the chart that you previously programmed.

5. For additional practice multiplying fractions, give each student a copy of page 91. Pair students; then have each pair complete the reproducible as directed. After each pair completes the activity, discuss the answers as a class.

Nail Down Fractions!

Like building a house, multiplying fractions takes several important steps! Use the steps listed on the toolbox to help Cal construct the correct answer for each of the problems below. First work out the problem on the back of this sheet; then write the letter from the hammer that matches your answer on the blank next to each number.

Step 1: Write the fractions with the numerators and denominators lined up.

numerators ➜ $\dfrac{1}{3}$ x $\dfrac{3}{4}$
denominators ➜

Step 2: Multiply the numerators; then multiply the denominators.

$$\frac{1}{3} \times \frac{3}{4} = \frac{3}{12}$$

Step 3: Simplify the answer.

$$\frac{3}{12} \div \frac{3}{3} = \frac{1}{4}$$

A. $\frac{1}{16}$

B. $\frac{3}{8}$

C. $\frac{1}{10}$

D. $\frac{3}{10}$

E. $\frac{5}{24}$

F. $\frac{1}{18}$

G. $\frac{3}{14}$

H. $\frac{5}{36}$

I. $\frac{5}{16}$

J. $\frac{6}{35}$

K. $\frac{3}{16}$

L. $\frac{1}{5}$

M. $\frac{7}{30}$

N. $\frac{3}{5}$

O. $\frac{2}{5}$

_____ 1. $\frac{2}{3}$ x $\frac{3}{5}$

_____ 2. $\frac{7}{10}$ x $\frac{1}{3}$

_____ 3. $\frac{3}{4}$ x $\frac{1}{4}$

_____ 4. $\frac{5}{6}$ x $\frac{1}{4}$

_____ 5. $\frac{1}{2}$ x $\frac{5}{8}$

_____ 6. $\frac{6}{7}$ x $\frac{1}{4}$

_____ 7. $\frac{3}{5}$ x $\frac{1}{2}$

_____ 8. $\frac{9}{10}$ x $\frac{2}{3}$

_____ 9. $\frac{5}{12}$ x $\frac{1}{3}$

_____ 10. $\frac{1}{8}$ x $\frac{4}{5}$

_____ 11. $\frac{1}{2}$ of $\frac{3}{4}$

_____ 12. $\frac{1}{4}$ of $\frac{4}{5}$

_____ 13. $\frac{2}{7}$ of $\frac{3}{5}$

_____ 14. Cal opened up a box of nails. 1/2 of the nails were four inches long and 1/2 were two inches long. 1/8 of the four-inch nails were rusted. How many of the nails were rusted?

_____ 15. Candy took a break from hammering to eat a small pizza. 1/3 of her pizza had cheese. 1/4 of the cheese was American, and another 1/6 was mozzarella. How much of her pizza had mozzarella on it?

Bonus Box: Write the letters *A* to *Z* on a separate sheet of paper. Write a pizza topping beginning with each letter. How about anchovies, bananas, and caramel?

How To Extend The Lesson:

- Obtain two index cards for each student. Label each card with a fraction. Direct each student to choose two of the fraction cards. Then provide each student with a 9" x 12" sheet of white paper and two light-colored crayons or colored pencils. Have the student use the fractions on his cards to write a multiplication problem on one side of his paper, then draw a diagram on the other side that represents the equation and its product. (See the example in Step 1 on page 90.) After students complete their pictures, number each one; then display them on a wall or bulletin board. Then instruct each student to determine the problem represented by each picture, and find the product of each problem. Finally, after all students have completed the activity, instruct volunteers to record their equations and answers on the chalkboard. Have each author determine if the problem and answer to his picture are correct.

Ben

$$\frac{2}{3} \times \frac{1}{3} = \frac{2}{9}$$

$\frac{2}{3}$ $\frac{1}{3}$

- Divide students into groups of three and give each group a deck of playing cards. Direct each member of the group to turn over four cards. Then have each student write two fractions with the cards' numbers—using the lower-numbered cards as the numerators and the higher-numbered cards as the denominators (face cards represent the number 10 and aces represent the number 1). Next instruct each member to multiply her fractions. Have members check one another's answers. The member with the largest fraction gets to keep all the members' cards. Have students continue playing until there aren't enough cards for a turn. The member with the most cards at the end of the game wins.

- Bring in several copies of newspaper store ads and catalogs. Direct each student to choose five items that are priced at whole-dollar values (not dollars and cents) and write these items on a sheet of paper. Then tell the class that the store is having a sale. Each item can be purchased at a reduced price: $\frac{1}{2}$, $\frac{1}{3}$, $\frac{1}{4}$, $\frac{1}{5}$, and $\frac{1}{6}$ off, respectively. Direct each student to find the reduced amount for each item, then determine the new price for each one.

HARDWARE SALE!

Three Little Shopping Pigs

Revisit The Three Little Pigs *with this lesson on addition and subtraction of decimals.*

Skill: Adding and subtracting decimals

Estimated Lesson Time: 1 hour

Teacher Preparation:

1. Duplicate one copy of page 95 for each student.
2. Obtain a catalog or sales flyer for each pair of students.

Materials:

1 copy of page 95 for each student
1 catalog or sales flyer for each pair of students
1 copy of *The Three Little Pigs* (optional)

Background Information:

To add or subtract decimals, first align the decimal points of all the decimals. Then add or subtract the decimals as if they were whole numbers. Finally align the decimal point in the sum or difference.

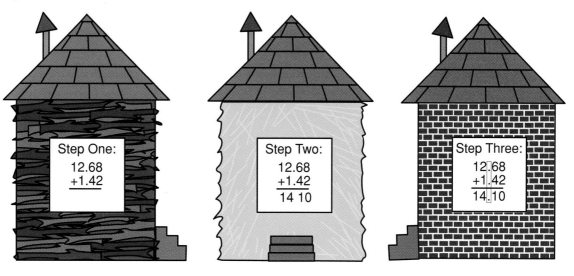

Step One:

```
 12.68
+ 1.42
```

Step Two:

```
 12.68
+ 1.42
 14 10
```

Step Three:

```
 12.68
+ 1.42
 14.10
```

Introducing The Lesson:

Use the background information and the problems below to demonstrate how to add and subtract decimals. Point out that the decimal points need to be lined up in order to solve the problem correctly.

$$\begin{array}{r} \$25.99 + \$1.25 = \$25.99 \\ + \$1.25 \\ \hline \$27.24 \end{array} \qquad \begin{array}{r} 40.5 - 1.2 = 40.5 \\ - 1.2 \\ \hline 39.3 \end{array}$$

Steps:

1. Have each student solve the five problems below. Circulate the room to assess each student's mastery; then go over the correct answer to each problem.

   $14.67 + $0.89 = ($15.56)
   45.8 + 5.8 = (51.6)
   8.34 − 1.23 = (7.11)
   76.5 − 1.2 = (75.3)
   1.34 + 6.3 + 5.2 = (12.84)

2. Read aloud *The Three Little Pigs* or refresh your students' memories of this story.

3. Discuss the personality of each pig. Guide students to recognize that the first two pigs seemed more carefree, more fun-loving, and less conscientious than their brother who built the brick house.

4. Ask students what types of items the first two pigs might buy for their houses, using what they know about the two pigs' personalities—things such as games, radios, or televisions.

5. Next ask students what the third pig might buy for his brick house, using what they know about his personality—items like tools, dishes, or a smoke detector.

6. Pair your students, and give each student a copy of page 95 and each pair a sales flyer or catalog.

7. Instruct each pair to complete the page as directed.

Three Little Shopping Pigs

The three little pigs have built their houses and are ready to furnish the insides. The first and second pig brothers managed to save a total of $400 to split between the two of them. Not surprisingly, the third pig saved $400 all by himself.

Look through a sales flyer or catalog and choose items that you think the pig brothers might purchase for their new houses. Record the name of each item and its price in the correct house below. Each time you write down an item for the first two pigs, add the price to the current total. Each time you record an item for the third pig, subtract the price from the current total. Remember you only have $400 to spend on a total of eight items for each set of pigs. Happy spending!

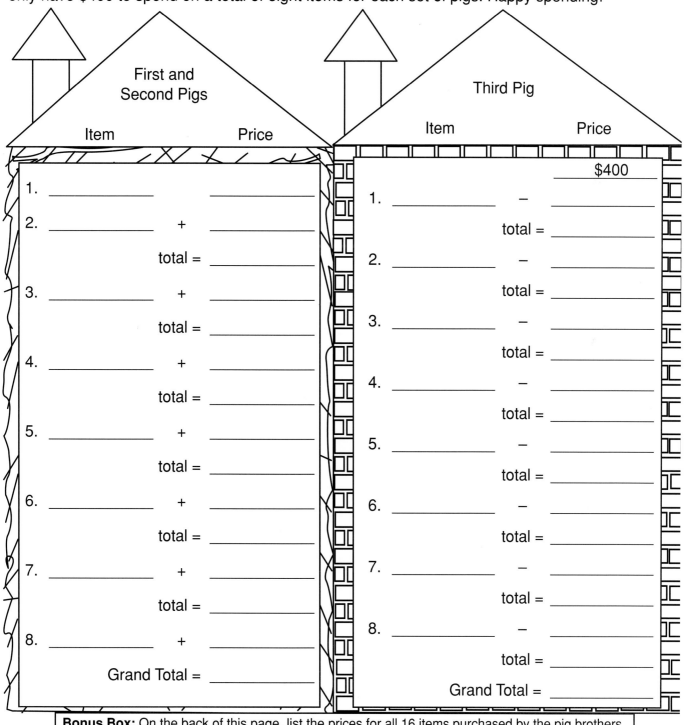

First and Second Pigs

Item	Price
1. _____	_____
2. _____	+ _____
	total = _____
3. _____	+ _____
	total = _____
4. _____	+ _____
	total = _____
5. _____	+ _____
	total = _____
6. _____	+ _____
	total = _____
7. _____	+ _____
	total = _____
8. _____	+ _____
	Grand Total = _____

Third Pig

Item	Price
	$400 _____
1. _____	– _____
	total = _____
2. _____	– _____
	total = _____
3. _____	– _____
	total = _____
4. _____	– _____
	total = _____
5. _____	– _____
	total = _____
6. _____	– _____
	total = _____
7. _____	– _____
	total = _____
8. _____	– _____
	total = _____
	Grand Total = _____

Bonus Box: On the back of this page, list the prices for all 16 items purchased by the pig brothers in order from least to greatest.

How To Extend The Lesson:

- Pair your students; then have each pair peruse a grocery-store flyer to plan a party for ten friends. Explain that each pair has a total of $50 to spend on anything in the store flyer. Instruct each pair to create a store receipt to show what it purchased and the cost of its total bill.

- Place a collection of local-restaurant menus in your math learning center. Invite each student to visit the center to treat herself and three friends to lunch at one of the restaurants. Explain that she should choose a beverage, an entree, and a dessert for each person and then create a restaurant bill to determine the total cost of the lunch.

- Place a variety of sales flyers in your math learning center. Challenge each student to visit the center and buy as many items as he can from one of the flyers for a total purchase price of $100. Explain that he can only buy one of each item. Then have him list each item that he is purchasing along with its price. Instruct each student to total his purchases, then add or delete items to reach the $100 goal.

Diving Into Decimals

You'll obtain a seal of approval for this multiplying-decimals lesson!

Skill: Multiplying decimals

Estimated Lesson Time: 45 minutes

Teacher Preparation:
Duplicate one copy of page 99 for each student.

Materials:
1 copy of page 99 for each student
1 crayon for each student

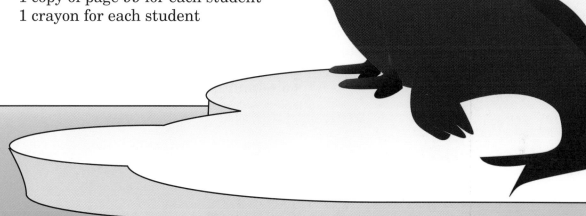

Background Information:
To multiply decimals, ignore the decimal points and multiply as if they were whole numbers. Then count the number of places to the right of the decimal point in the multiplicand and in the multiplier. Finally insert the decimal point in the product by counting over from the right the same number of places that were in the multiplicand and the multiplier.

Example:

$$
\begin{array}{r} 5.3 \\ \times\ 0.2 \\ \hline 106 \end{array}
\qquad
\begin{array}{r} 5.③ \\ \times\ 0.② \\ \hline 106 \end{array}
\qquad
\begin{array}{l} \text{multiplicand = 1 place} \\ \underline{\text{multiplier = 1 place}} \\ \text{total \# of places = 2} \end{array}
\qquad
\begin{array}{r} 5.③ \\ \times\ 0.② \\ \hline 1.06 \end{array}
\ \text{(Count over 2 places from the right.)}
$$

Introducing The Lesson:

Begin this lesson by writing the following multiplication problem on the board. Have a student volunteer solve the problem, explaining each step to the class.

$$\begin{array}{r} 681 \\ \times\ 6 \\ \hline \end{array}$$

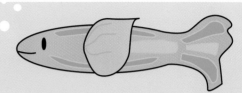

Steps:

1. Write the same multiplication problem again on the board, this time inserting a decimal point between the six and the eight. Explain that multiplying decimals is the same process as multiplying whole numbers except you need to insert the decimal point in the product.

2. Multiply the problem; then demonstrate how to count the number of places after the decimal point in the multiplicand and the multiplier. Circle the numeral(s) that is in each of those places (see the illustration).

    $$\begin{array}{r} 6.\text{⑧①} \leftarrow \text{multiplican} \\ \underline{\times\ 6} \leftarrow \text{multiplier} \\ 4086 \end{array}$$

3. Show students how to insert the decimal point the correct number of places from the right.

    $$\begin{array}{r} 6.\text{⑧①} \\ \underline{\times\ 6} \\ 40.86 \end{array}$$ (Count over two places from the right.)

4. Demonstrate a few other examples (see the problems below), each time circling the places after the decimal point in the multiplicand and the multiplier to determine the correct placement of the decimal point in the product.

    $$\begin{array}{r} 4.\text{⑥} \\ \underline{\times\ 1\text{②}} \\ 92 \\ \underline{460} \\ 5.52 \end{array} \qquad \begin{array}{r} 6.\text{①②} \\ \underline{\times\ 3.\text{①}} \\ 612 \\ \underline{18360} \\ 18.972 \end{array}$$

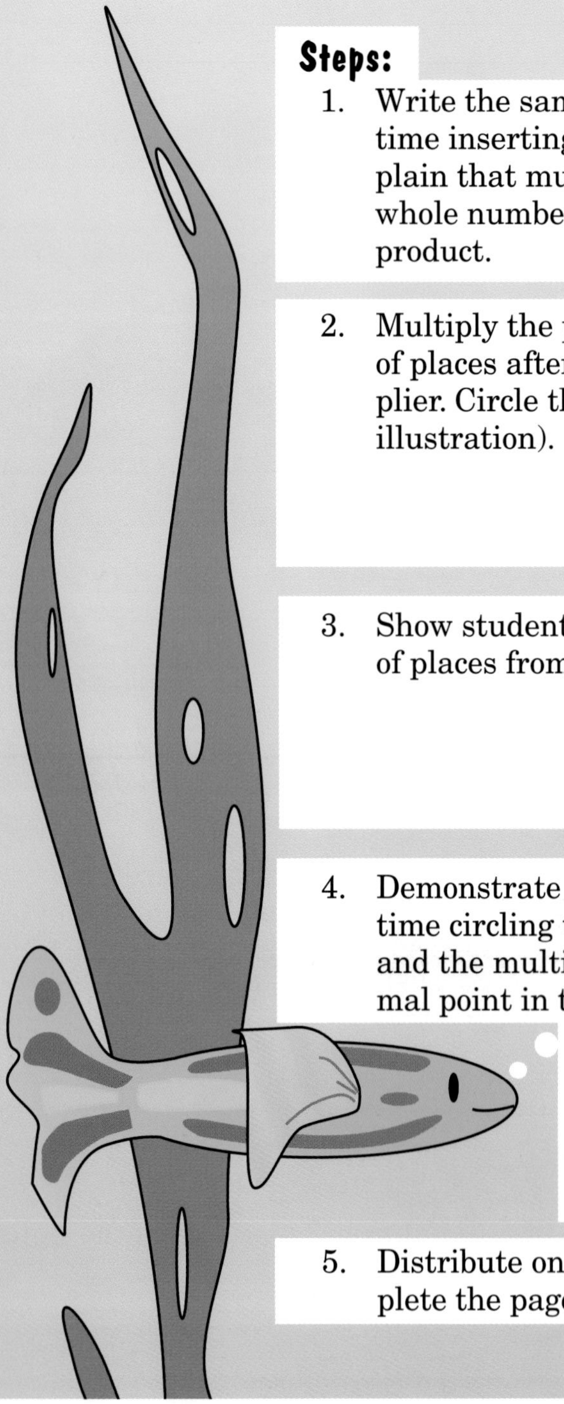

5. Distribute one copy of page 99 to each student. Instruct her to complete the page as directed.

Name_____

Diving Into Decimals

Get ready to dive into multiplying decimals! Solve each multiplication problem below; then look for the matching product in one of the fish. Use a crayon to color each matching fish.

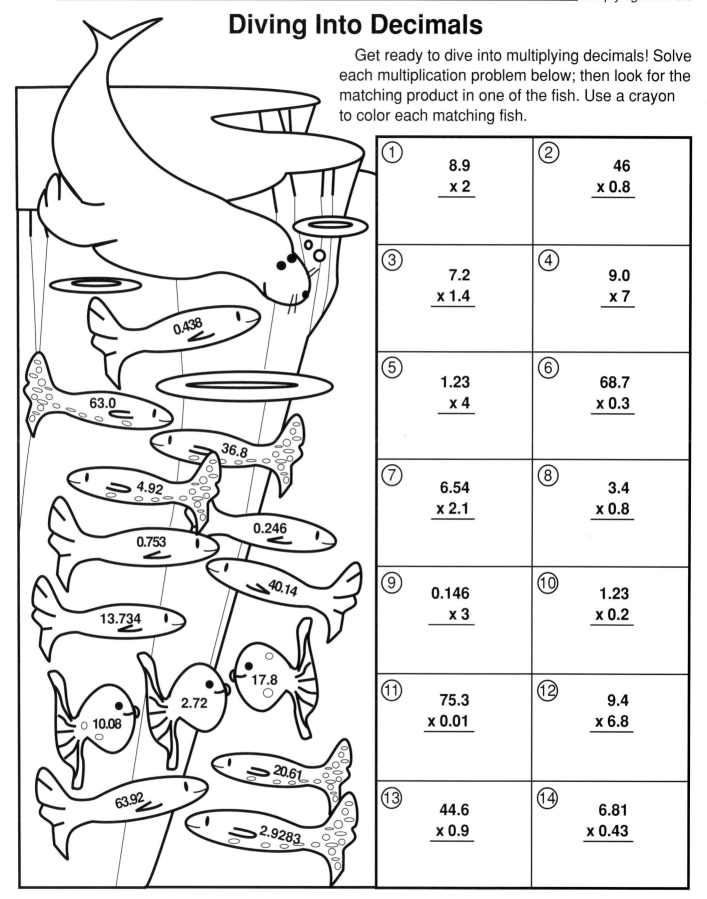

①	8.9 x 2	②	46 x 0.8
③	7.2 x 1.4	④	9.0 x 7
⑤	1.23 x 4	⑥	68.7 x 0.3
⑦	6.54 x 2.1	⑧	3.4 x 0.8
⑨	0.146 x 3	⑩	1.23 x 0.2
⑪	75.3 x 0.01	⑫	9.4 x 6.8
⑬	44.6 x 0.9	⑭	6.81 x 0.43

Fish values: 0.438, 63.0, 36.8, 4.92, 0.753, 0.246, 40.14, 13.734, 2.72, 17.8, 10.08, 20.61, 63.92, 2.9283

Bonus Box: On the back of this page, list the answers on the fish in numerical order from least to greatest.

How To Extend The Lesson:

- Divide your class into groups of five to eight students, and have each group sit in a circle. Give each student an index card on which to write a decimal multiplication problem. Instruct each group member to number a sheet of notebook paper with the same number as there are members in her group. On your signal have each member write and solve the problem that she created as problem number one on her paper. After about two minutes, call, "Pass," and have each student pass her card to the person sitting to her left. Then instruct each member to solve the problem on the card that she received as problem number two. Continue play until each member has solved each group member's problem. Instruct the group members to use a calculator to check the accuracy of each problem's answer.

- Distribute one calculator and one die to each student. Have her roll the die three times to create a three-digit number. Instruct her to write the number on a sheet of notebook paper, inserting a decimal point wherever she chooses. This number is the *multiplicand*. Next call out a one- or two-digit decimal number. Instruct her to write that number for the *multiplier* and solve the problem. Have her use the calculator to check her work.

- Review multiplying decimals with this variation of tic-tac-toe. Write the answers to the 15 decimal multiplication problems listed below on the chalkboard. Instruct each student to draw a tic-tac-toe board and write one of the chalkboard answers in each square. To play, call out one of the decimal multiplication problems at a time and have each student find the product. If the product is one that the student wrote on his board, direct him to draw an *X* in that square. Declare the first student to get three in a row as the winner. To play another round, replace the problems that you have already called with new ones.

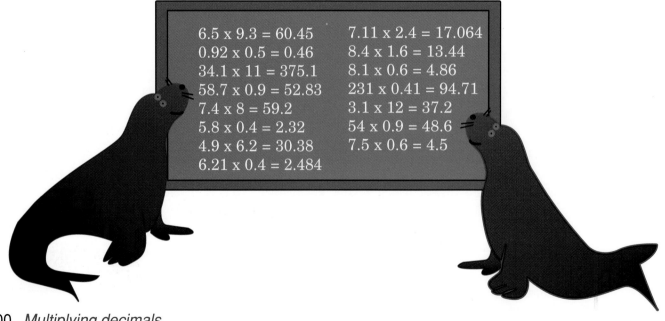

6.5 x 9.3 = 60.45
0.92 x 0.5 = 0.46
34.1 x 11 = 375.1
58.7 x 0.9 = 52.83
7.4 x 8 = 59.2
5.8 x 0.4 = 2.32
4.9 x 6.2 = 30.38
6.21 x 0.4 = 2.484

7.11 x 2.4 = 17.064
8.4 x 1.6 = 13.44
8.1 x 0.6 = 4.86
231 x 0.41 = 94.71
3.1 x 12 = 37.2
54 x 0.9 = 48.6
7.5 x 0.6 = 4.5

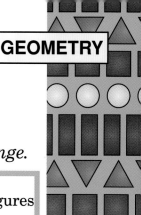

We're Talking Tangrams!

Give your students something to talk about with this tangram challenge.

Skill: Identifying, describing, comparing, and classifying geometric figures

Estimated Lesson Time: 1 hour

Teacher Preparation:
1. Duplicate one copy of the top portion of page 103 for each student on the thickest paper possible.
2. Make an overhead transparency of the bottom portion of page 103.

Materials:
1 copy of the tangrams pattern at the top of page 103 for each student
2 sheets of drawing paper for each student
1 sheet of loose-leaf paper for each student
1 blank transparency for creating a transparency of the bottom portion of page 103
scissors

- *Triangles* are polygons that have three sides and three angles.
- *Quadrilaterals* are polygons that have four sides and four angles.
- *Parallelograms* are quadrilaterals that have parallel line segments in both pairs of opposite sides.
- *Trapezoids* are quadrilaterals that have a pair of parallel sides.
- *Rectangles* are parallelograms with four right angles.
- *Squares* are rectangles that have sides of equal length.
- *Pentagons* are polygons that have five sides and five angles.
- *Hexagons* are polygons that have six sides and six angles.

Background Information:
A *polygon* is a two-dimensional shape, formed from three or more line segments that lie within one plane. A *regular* polygon has sides of equal length and angles of equal size. An *irregular* polygon has unequal sides and unequal angles. Polygons that are exactly the same size and shape are *congruent,* and those that are the same shape but not identical in size are *similar.*

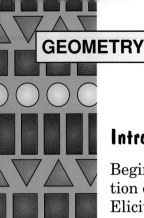

GEOMETRY

Introducing The Lesson:

Begin this lesson by displaying the transparency that you created of the bottom portion of page 103. Review the names of these six geometric shapes with your students. Elicit brief descriptions of these shapes—number of sides, types of angles, etc.—from your students (see page 101).

Steps:

1. Give each student two sheets of drawing paper, one sheet of loose-leaf paper, one copy of the tangrams pattern on the top of page 103, and scissors. Instruct her to cut out each of the seven tangram pieces.

2. Borrow a set of cutouts and paper from one of your students; then demonstrate how to trace the shape of a hexagon onto drawing paper as shown so that each tangram piece used in that shape is recognizable.

3. Explain that each student will have 15 minutes to use the tangram pieces to create and trace the six different shapes that are displayed on the overhead any way she can. Establish that the shape she creates can be regular or irregular and can be formed from any combination of two or all seven of her tangram pieces. Point out, too, that later in the lesson she will be challenging a partner to create the same shape, so she should try to use a complex combination of tangram pieces to create the shapes.

Create a rectangle using the two large triangles, the two small triangles, the square, and the parallelogram.

4. When time is up, have each student write on loose-leaf paper an instruction for each of the six shapes that she created. For example, if a student created the shape illustrated in Step 2, she should write "Create an irregular hexagon using the two small triangles and the square."

5. Divide your class into pairs and have the partners exchange the papers with the instructions. Challenge each student to create and trace her partner's shapes on a clean sheet of drawing paper. After the shapes have been created, allow each student to check her original tracings with those done by her partner. Give one point for each correct shape; then award each student who got all six correct with an inexpensive treat.

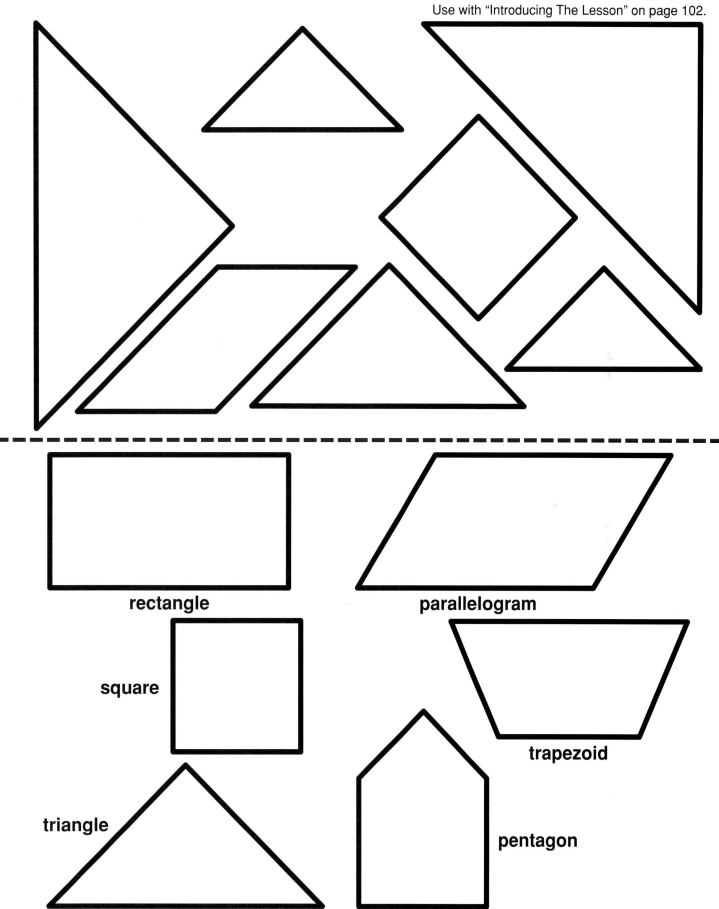

rectangle

parallelogram

square

trapezoid

triangle

pentagon

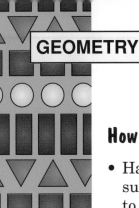
How To Extend The Lesson:

- Have your students explore further with tangram pieces to create other shapes—such as a hexagon, a rhombus, or even an irregular nonagon. Direct your students to use a marker to trace the shapes they create onto drawing paper; then cut out each shape. Label each shape with a number and post them on a bulletin board titled "What Am I?" Invite students to visit the board and identify each shape by writing its name next to a corresponding number on a sheet of loose-leaf paper. Reward each student who correctly identifies each shape with a small treat or homework pass.

- Help your students identify the characteristics of various shapes with this class game. Duplicate several copies of the tangram pieces at the top of page 103. Have a student volunteer cut out these pieces. Afterward place all of the tangram pieces inside a bag. Shake the bag; then have a student volunteer select one shape from the bag without revealing it to the class. Direct him to list three clues to the shape's identity on the board. Have the student call on a classmate to read the clues from the board and identify the shape. If he is correct, have him select the next shape from the bag and list three clues to its identity. If he is incorrect, have him call on another classmate to answer. Continue play until each student has had a chance to identify a shape.

- Have your students use the tangram shapes to create interesting works of art. Give each student a piece of cardboard with a sheet of white construction paper on top of it. Then have the student cut out one of the tangram shapes from a copy of page 103. Next instruct the student to thumbtack the shape to the center of the construction paper and cardboard (making sure the shape can rotate freely on the thumbtack). Have the student trace around the shape, turn it slightly, and trace it again. Direct the student to repeat this process until the shape is returned to its original position; then have him remove the thumbtack and the shape, and color his completed design. If desired, display each work of art on a bulletin board.

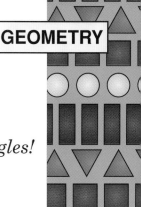

A Is For Angles!

Lead your class through this "mega-nificent" lesson on identifying angles!

Skill: Identifying acute, obtuse, and right angles

Estimated Lesson Time: 45 minutes

Teacher Preparation:
1. Duplicate one copy of page 107 for each student.
2. Make a transparency of the block letters displayed in Step 2 on page 106.
3. Duplicate one copy of the chart at the bottom of page 108 for each student.

Materials:
1 copy of page 107 for each
   student
1 copy of the chart on page
   108 for each student
1 ruler for each student
colored pencils or crayons
2 blank transparencies
1 transparency marker

Give me an *A!*
An *acute* angle
measures less
than 90 degrees.

Give me an *O!*
An *obtuse* angle
measures more than
90°, but less than
180 degrees.

Give me an *R!*
A *right* angle
measures exactly
90 degrees.

Background Information:
• An *angle* is a figure formed by two rays with a common endpoint.
• A *ray* is a part of a line that extends in one direction from an endpoint into infinity.
• A *vertex* is a common endpoint for two rays.

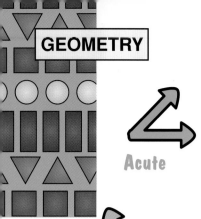

Acute

Obtuse

Right

Introducing The Lesson:

Draw a ray on the blank transparency and ask students to identify it. Explain the difference between a ray and a line. Then create an angle by drawing a second ray which shares the same endpoint as the first ray. Identify the figure as an angle and share the definition of an angle from the background information on page 105.

Steps:

1. Tell students that angles can be identified as acute, obtuse, or right. Draw examples of the three types of angles on the transparency; then use the background information to define each one.

2. Display the transparency you've prepared of the block letters displayed below. Explain that you have chosen letters of the alphabet that contain angles within their shapes.

Letter	# of Acute Angles	# of Obtuse Angles	# of Right Angles
A			
E			
F			
H			
I			
K			
L			
M			
N			
T			
V			
W			
X			
Y			
Z			

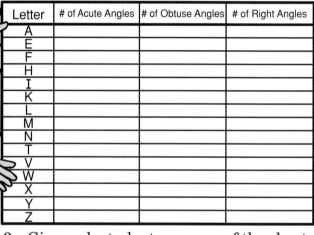

3. Give each student one copy of the chart on page 108. Instruct him to record the number of each type of angle in each letter on the transparency. For example, the letter A has zero right angles, two obtuse angles, and three acute angles. See the answer key on page 314.

4. As a class go over the correct answers. Then have each student write his first and last names in block letters on the back of his chart. Instruct him to create another chart beneath his name containing each letter in his name. Instruct him to identify the different types of angles in the letters of his name.

5. Decide which student's name has the most right, acute, and obtuse angles. Then determine which student's name has the least number of angles.

6. Follow up this activity by distributing one copy of page 107 and a ruler to each student. Have him complete the page as directed.

A Is For Angles!

Approach drawing from a new angle! Use a ruler to create a design in the space below. The trick? Your design must not include any curves. Make the entire design using straight lines and include at least four acute angles, four obtuse angles, and four right angles. Once your design is complete, circle the vertex of each acute angle in *red,* each obtuse angle in *blue,* and each right angle in *green.* Then, on the back of this page, create a table as you did earlier in this lesson to calculate the total number of different angles in your design.

Bonus Box: Use your ruler to measure the longest and shortest line segments (a part of a line defined by two endpoints) in your design. Compare your measurements with those of a classmate.

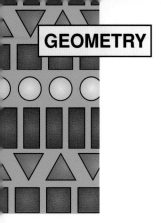

How To Extend The Lesson:

- Review identifying angles throughout the day by having students look at the class clock and identify the angle made by the two hands. Students will get practice identifying angles and telling time.

- Distribute one geoboard to each student or pair of students for extra practice in identifying angles. Call out the criteria for a specific shape as in the examples below. Then challenge the student to create the shape that you call out on her geoboard. Circulate throughout the room to assess students' understanding of acute, obtuse, and right angles.

Create a quadrilateral with at least one acute and one obtuse angle.
Create a triangle with one right angle.
Create a parallelogram. Identify the four angles as acute, obtuse, or right.
Create a quadrilateral with four right angles.
Create a figure that has no obtuse angles.
Create a figure that has no acute angles.

Letter	# of acute angles	# of obtuse angles	# of right angles
A			
E			
F			
H			
I			
K			
L			
M			
N			
T			
V			
W			
X			
Y			
Z			

©The Education Center, Inc. • *Ready-to-Go Lessons* • TEC1118

Note To The Teacher: Use with Step 3 on page 106. See the answer key on page 314.

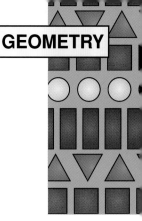

Mirror, Mirror!

Get your students to reflect on the geometric concept of symmetry with this challenging exercise!

Skills: Identifying symmetry; creating symmetric shapes

Estimated Lesson Time: 45 minutes

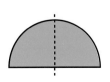

Teacher Preparation:

1. Duplicate one copy of page 111 for each student.
2. Enlarge and cut out each of the figures below from a sheet of paper.

Materials:

1 copy of page 111 for each child
1 handheld mirror

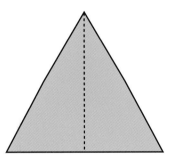
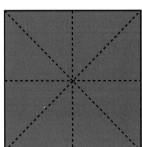
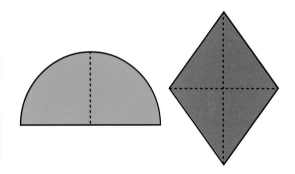

Background Information:

A figure is *symmetric* if a line divides it into two congruent or equal parts. The two parts are like mirror images of each other. Some figures have no lines of symmetry at all. Others may have anywhere from one to an infinite number of symmetry lines.

The dashed lines running through each shape below represent the figures' *lines of symmetry*.

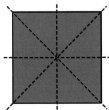
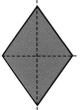

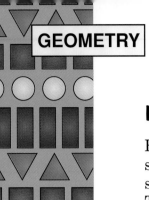

Introducing The Lesson:

Have a student volunteer come to the front of the classroom. Ask the remaining students what would happen if the volunteer were to look in a mirror. Guide students in responding that the mirror would reflect an exact copy of her image. Then have the volunteer look into a handheld mirror to illustrate the point. Point out that the mirror acts as the middle or line of symmetry between the two identical sides.

Steps:

1. Explain that the line of symmetry divides a figure directly down the middle. Then take the triangle shape and have a student point out the shape's line of symmetry. Direct the student to test the line of symmetry by folding the shape in half right along the dotted line. Have the student show the class the result, pointing out that the two folded halves are exactly the same or mirror images of each other.

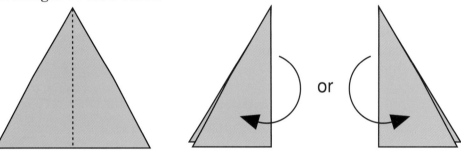

2. Point out that the isosceles triangle has only one line of symmetry, but the number of lines of symmetry varies among shapes.

3. Show your students the additional shapes and have them find the lines of symmetry in each one. Have students test the lines of symmetry by folding the shapes.

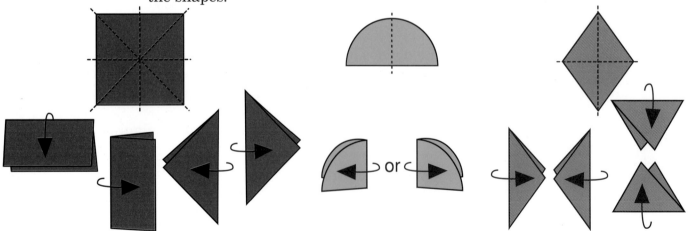

4. Provide each student with a copy of page 111. Direct the student to complete the reproducible as directed for more practice with symmetry.

The Most Symmetric Shapes Of All

Mirror, Mirror, on the wall, which shapes are symmetric?

Sorry, Prince, but it's up to you to make the call!

You have been summoned by His Royal Majesty Prince S. M. Atree. The magic mirror he usually consults for advice on important matters such as homework hasn't been very helpful lately. Now the prince is calling upon you to help him with his geometry homework. Remember, a figure is *symmetric* if a line divides it into two *congruent* or equal parts.

Look at each shape below. Draw a crown in the blank below each shape that is symmetric.

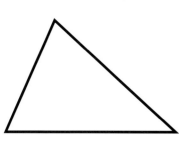 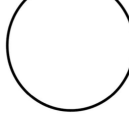 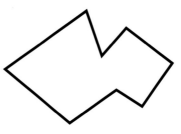 

1. _____   2. _____   3. _____   4. _____

Draw the lines of symmetry for each figure below. Then count and record the total number of lines of symmetry in the blank below each shape.

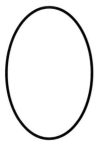 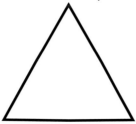 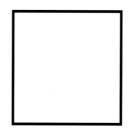 

5. _____   6. _____   7. _____   8. _____

Complete the design in each grid below to make a symmetric figure. Each bold line is a line of symmetry.

9. 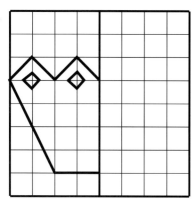   10. 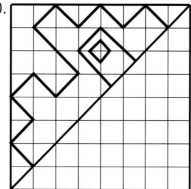   11.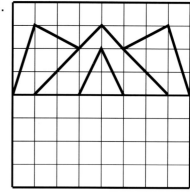

Bonus Box: On a sheet of graph paper draw one half of a symmetric design like those above. Then challenge a classmate to finish the design.

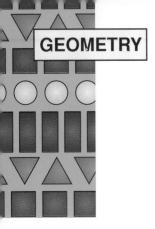
How To Extend The Lesson:

- Take your students on an expedition in search of symmetry. Divide your students into pairs; then direct each pair to find items located both in and around the school that are symmetric figures—figures that when divided in half by a line have two congruent or equal parts. Have each pair sketch each symmetric figure it observes and draw a dashed line down the middle of the figure to represent the figure's line(s) of symmetry. Invite each pair to share its findings with the rest of the class.

- Extend your study of symmetry to the arts by studying art forms in which symmetry plays an important role in design. Provide your students with architectural and art magazines and books. Direct students to find examples of symmetry and share them with the rest of the class, pointing out the line(s) of symmetry in each item.

- Create a "Gallery of Symmetry" by having each of your students fold a piece of construction paper in half. Direct each student to cut an interesting design from the paper, making sure not to cut completely across the fold. Then have the student unfold his paper design and use a thin marker to draw a dashed line or line of symmetry along the paper's crease. Display the student-created symmetric figures on a bulletin board.

Presto...It's A Palindrome!

*Have students work some math magic
by creating number palindromes!*

Skill: Recognizing palindromes

Estimated Lesson Time: 30 minutes

Teacher Preparation:
1. Duplicate one copy of page 115 for each student.
2. Enlarge and make a transparency of the hundreds board on page 116.

Materials:
1 copy of page 115 for each student
1 blank transparency

Background Information:
A palindrome is a word, verse, sentence, or number that reads the same both backward and forward. Sometimes palindromes can be made by adding a number and its reverse. For example, 431 + 134 = 565.

Introducing The Lesson:

Begin by writing five word palindromes—such as *mom, madam, dad, refer, wow, radar, noon,* and *eye*—on the chalkboard. Ask students what all five of the words have in common. Help students recognize that each word reads the same forward and backward.

Steps:

1. Explain to students that when a word, sentence, verse, or number reads the same both forward and backward, it is called a *palindrome.*

2. Display the hundreds board transparency on the overhead projector. Have students identify all the number palindromes between 1 and 100.
   (Answer: 11, 22, 33, 44, 55, 66, 77, 88, 99)

3. Demonstrate for students that some numbers that are not palindromes can be made into palindromes by adding the number and its reverse (see the examples below). Allow about five minutes for students to experiment with numbers to try to make a palindrome using this method.
   36 + 63 = 99 (palindrome) 143 + 341 = 484 (palindrome)

4. Explain that sometimes you need to keep reversing and adding to create a palindrome. (See the examples below.) Allow another five minutes for students to experiment with this new method of making palindromes.

$$\begin{array}{r} 64 \\ + 46 \\ \hline 110 \\ + 011 \\ \hline 121 \end{array} \text{(palindrome)}$$

$$\begin{array}{r} 84 \\ + 48 \\ \hline 132 \\ + 231 \\ \hline 363 \end{array} \text{(palindrome)}$$

5. Distribute one copy of page 115 to each student. Instruct the student to complete the reproducible as directed. Then have students explain why they think adding a number and its reverse will often result in a palindrome.

Name _____

Abracadabra!

Use your magic wand (a pencil will work nicely) to pull palindromes out of the hats below. Remember that a palindrome is a number that reads the same both forward and backward.

Each top hat contains a number that can be changed into a palindrome by reversing its digits and adding them to the original number. Sometimes the magic wand will need to be waved more than one time, so you may have to reverse and add the digits more than once. Show your work next to each hat; then write your answer on the line above each hat.

Here is an example to help you get started:

$$\begin{array}{r} 57 \\ + 75 \\ \hline 132 \\ + 231 \\ \hline 363 \end{array}$$ **Ta Da!**

1. _____

51

2. _____

82

3. _____

76

4. _____

162

5. _____

536

6. _____

785

7. _____

1,412

8. _____

2,651

9. _____

693

Bonus Box: On the back of this paper, create some number palindromes of your own.

How To Extend The Lesson:

- Give students additional practice in investigating number patterns with this activity. Create patterns to solve similar to those written below. Instruct each student to complete the next three items in the pattern series. Then challenge your students to create similar patterns of their own. Have each student write his pattern on the front of an index card, then write the answer on the back. Collect all of the cards and place them in your math center.

12, 9, 10, 7, 8, 5, 6, 3, _____, _____, _____ (4, 1, 2)

1, 2, 4, 8, 16, _____, _____, _____ (32, 64, 128)

16, 17, 19, 22, 26, 27, 29, _____, _____, _____ (32, 36, 37)

Dog, G, Ferret, T, Bird, D, Fish, _____, _____, _____ (H, any animal, last letter in animal word)

- Explain to each student that by using a pattern, he can make any year equal either 1 or 37. (See the examples below.)

1958: $(1 \times 1) + (9 \times 9) + (5 \times 5) + (8 \times 8) = 171$
171: $(1 \times 1) + (7 \times 7) + (1 \times 1) = 51$
51: $(5 \times 5) + (1 \times 1) = 26$
26: $(2 \times 2) + (6 \times 6) = 40$
40: $(4 \times 4) + (0 \times 0) = 16$
16: $(1 \times 1) + (6 \times 6) = \mathbf{37}$

1976: $(1 \times 1) + (9 \times 9) + (7 \times 7) + (6 \times 6) = 167$
167: $(1 \times 1) + (6 \times 6) + (7 \times 7) = 86$
86: $(8 \times 8) + (6 \times 6) = 100$
100: $(1 \times 1) + (0 \times 0) + (0 \times 0) = \mathbf{1}$

1	2	3	4	5	6	7	8	9	10
11	12	13	14	15	16	17	18	19	20
21	22	23	24	25	26	27	28	29	30
31	32	33	34	35	36	37	38	39	40
41	42	43	44	45	46	47	48	49	50
51	52	53	54	55	56	57	58	59	60
61	62	63	64	65	66	67	68	69	70
71	72	73	74	75	76	77	78	79	80
81	82	83	84	85	86	87	88	89	90
91	92	93	94	95	96	97	98	99	100

Note To The Teacher: Use the hundreds table above with Step 2, page 114.

Crafty Calculations

*Get your sleuths cracking on discovering
the mystery behind number patterns!*

Skill: Recognizing and continuing established patterns

Estimated Lesson Time: 45 minutes

Teacher Preparation:
1. Make a transparency of the sample input/output tables shown in Step 2 on page 118.
2. Label an index card with an answer for each problem on each input/output table shown in Step 2 on page 118.
3. Duplicate one copy of page 119 for each student.

Materials:
1 transparency of the input/output tables on page 118
1 transparency marker
an overhead projector
1 labeled index card for each student
1 copy of page 119 for each student

Background Information:
A pattern is an arrangement of things re-peated in an orderly, recognizable fashion. Numbers in a problem that are not given can be found by using the established pattern.

Example:
What is the pattern on the paw prints below and what is the next number in the pattern?
The pattern is that 2 is added to every number. So the next number is 13.

Introducing The Lesson:

Draw a large circle on the board. Place two prime numbers in the center of the circle. Then have each student name a number. If the number fits the pattern, write it in the circle. If it does not fit the pattern, write it outside the circle. Continue having students name numbers until they can identify the pattern.

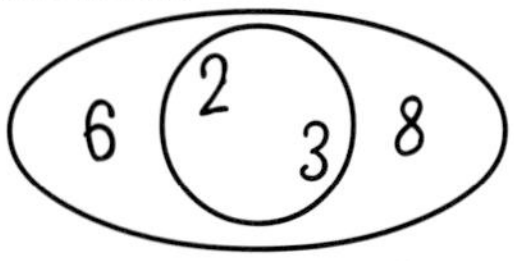

Steps:

1. Explain how to recognize and continue an established pattern using the background information and example on page 117.

2. Distribute a labeled index card to each student. Then place the previously programmed transparency on an overhead projector. Explain to students that in an *input-output table,* a number is entered on the *input* side of the table, a rule is established, and then the answer is placed in the *output* side of the table.

Input	Output
4	14
7	17
9	19
1	
6	
10	
2	
5	
8	
3	
0	
11	

Rule: Add 10.

Input	Output
4	16
7	28
9	36
1	
6	
10	
2	
5	
8	
3	
0	
11	

Rule: Multiply by 4.

Input	Output
3	1
8	6
5	3
10	
7	
4	
9	
6	
2	
17	
22	
13	

Rule: Subtract 2.

3. Point out the first three input and output numbers on the first table. Challenge students to identify the rule that is being used, and to find the next number in the established pattern. *(11)*

4. Have the student who has the index card labeled with the next number in the pattern write the number in the appropriate place on the chart. (If no one has the card with the next number in the pattern, check the pile of cards that was left after giving each student one card.)

5. Continue the process to complete the patterns on the other two charts.

6. Distribute a copy of page 119 to each student. Direct each student to complete the reproducible as directed. After each student completes the activity, discuss the answers as a class.

Crack The Code!

A pattern is an arrangement of things repeated in an orderly and recognizable fashion. Numbers in a problem that are not given can be found by using the established pattern.

Directions: Help ace detective I. M. Stumped and his dog, Sherlock, figure out the code to each of the patterns below. Write the letter that matches the rule for the pattern on the magnifying glass by each number; then continue the pattern by filling in the remaining blanks.

Example: 10 12 11 13 12 14 13 15 14   **Rule:** Add 2; then subtract 1.

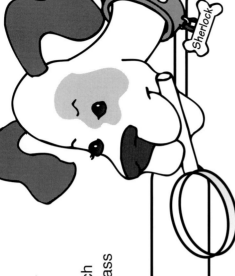

Rules:

A. Alternate an increasing multiple of 11 with its factor.
B. Subtract 1; then add 2.
C. Double the number.
D. Alternate dividing by 2 with multiplying by 4.
E. Alternate multiplying by 10 with adding 100 to the previous alternate number.
F. Add 9 to each multiple of 10.
G. Write the number 5; then subtract 5 from the number before the 5.
H. Subtract a multiple of 3.
I. Alternate multiples of 2 with a number that is 2 less than the number that is 2 places before it.
J. Add $.25.

1. 100 1,000 200 _____ 300 3,000 _____

2. 10 19 20 29 _____ 39 _____

3. $1.00 $1.25 _____ $1.75 $2.00 _____ $3.00

4. 100 99 101 _____ 102 _____ 102 _____

5. 75 5 70 _____ 65 5 _____

6. 5 10 _____ 40 80 _____ 640

7. 123 120 114 _____ 93 _____ 39 15

8. 400 200 800 400 _____ 800 _____ 1,600

9. 11 1 _____ 2 33 _____ 44 4

10. 99 2 97 4 _____ 6 93 _____

Bonus Box: Choose three of the patterns above. Then, on the back of this sheet, extend each of the patterns four more places.

Note To The Teacher: If desired, have each student complete the pattern for each problem; then write each rule together as a class.

How To Extend The Lesson:

• Have students construct their own input/output tables. Direct each student to fill in the first three numbers on each side of his table to establish a pattern. Then have the student exchange his paper with a classmate to continue the pattern.

• Once students are comfortable with one-step patterns (such as adding 1 to a number), set up an input/output table that involves a multistep rule (such as multiply by 2, then add 1). Then challenge them to create their own multistep tables.

• Introduce students to patterns that are other than numeric. (See the example below.) Then have students create their own patterns with items such as shapes, colors, letters, and numbers that repeat.

• Give students practice identifying multiples of a number while using patterns. Duplicate a copy of a hundred chart for each student. Direct the student to fill in each multiple of the numbers 1–10 with a different-colored crayon or colored pencil. Students will readily see the multiples using the color patterns they created.

• Write several palindromes (see page 113), such as 33, 212, and 1001 on the chalkboard. Have your students identify the pattern. *(The numbers are the same forward and backward.)* Then have each student create his own palindromes using not only numbers, but words like *dad, mom,* and *Hannah.*

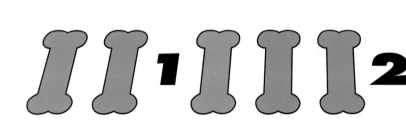

Mousing Around With Measurement

Challenge your students to use their knowledge about the area of a rectangle to complete this thought-provoking activity!

Skill: Finding the area of irregularly shaped figures by using the formula for the area of squares and rectangles

Estimated Lesson Time: 1 hour

Teacher Preparation:
Make one copy of page 123 for each student.

Materials:
1 copy of page 123 for each student
colored pencils or crayons
1 centimeter ruler for each student
1 blank transparency

Background Information:
- To find the area of a rectangle, multiply length times width.
- To find the area of an irregular figure, divide the figure into rectangles, find the area of each rectangle, and then add the areas of the rectangles together.

3 cm

3 cm

The area of this rectangle is 3 cm x 3 cm = 9 cm²

Divide into separate rectangles

2 cm

1 cm

The area of this rectangle is 2 cm x 1 cm = 2 cm²

The area of this irregularly shaped figure is 9 cm² + 2 cm² = 11 cm²

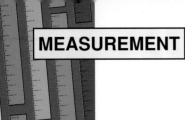

Introducing The Lesson:

Introduce this lesson by drawing a rectangle on the blank transparency. Place the transparency on an overhead projector and ask students how to find the area of the figure *(length times width)*. Use a centimeter ruler to find the measurement of both the length and width of the rectangle. Have students compute the area of the figure.

Steps:

1. Draw the figure below on an overhead transparency. Ask students how they can determine the area of the figure. Guide them into recognizing that the figure can be divided into two rectangles.

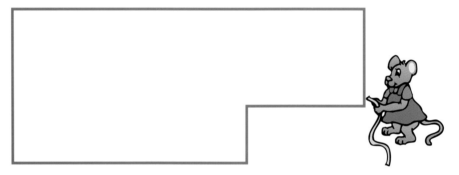

2. Divide the figure into two rectangles. Demonstrate how to compute the total area by first finding the area of each rectangle; then adding the two areas together.

3. Draw the three figures below on a transparency. For extra practice, have students explain how they would divide each figure to find the area.

4. Give each student a centimeter ruler, a copy of page 123, and colored pencils or crayons.

5. Have students complete page 123 as directed.

Mousing Around With Measurement

Mrs. Mouse brought home a large piece of cheese for her nine children. After she divided the cheese into nine pieces, some of the children began to complain about the size of their pieces. Use your centimeter ruler to find the area of each piece of cheese to see if Mrs. Mouse was fair to all nine children. Write the area of each mouse's piece of cheese next to his or her name. The first one has been done for you. Then follow the directions at the bottom of the page to color the cheese pieces.

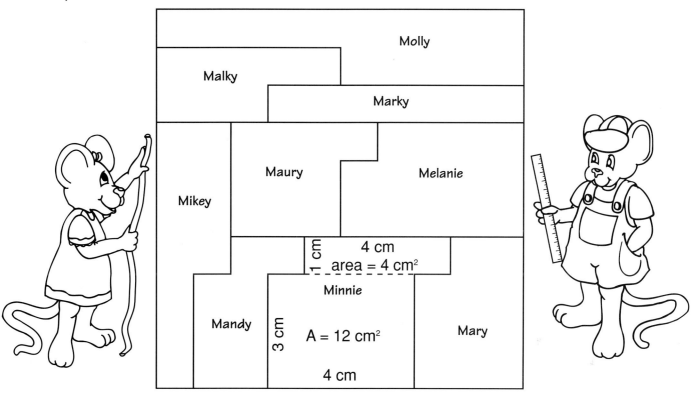

1. Minnie's __16__ cm²

2. Marky's _____ cm²

3. Mary's _____ cm²

4. Mikey's _____ cm²

5. Melanie's _____ cm²

6. Molly's _____ cm²

7. Mandy's _____ cm²

8. Maury's _____ cm²

9. Malky's _____ cm²

10. Color the piece with the largest area red.

11. Color the two pieces that have the same area and have a combined area of 22 cm² blue.

12. Color the piece that can be divided into two different sized squares orange.

13. Color the piece with the smallest area yellow.

14. Color the two pieces with the second-smallest area purple.

15. Color the remaining two pieces green.

Bonus Box: Is there a way that Mrs. Mouse could have divided the piece of cheese so that each mouse would get an equal share? Explain your answer on the back of this paper.

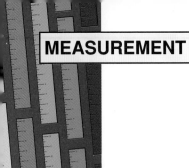

How To Extend The Lesson:

- Have students create their own puzzles similar to the one on page 123. Instruct each student to divide a square into five irregularly shaped figures. Tell students that each piece must have a length and a width that are whole numbers and can be divided into rectangles. Have students label the squares and switch papers with a partner. Have each student find the area of his partner's five figures.

- Have students find irregular shapes in the school environment to calculate the area of, such as the classroom, the playground, or the office. As a class devise a plan to determine the area of each location. Have students decide which measuring tool (tape measure or yardstick) best suits the job. Post the results of each calculation in the hallway for other classes to see.

- Use manipulatives to practice finding the area of irregular figures. Have students use pentominoes, pattern blocks, or Cuisenaire® Rods to create designs. Instruct each student to trace his design on drawing paper, then calculate the total area of his creation.

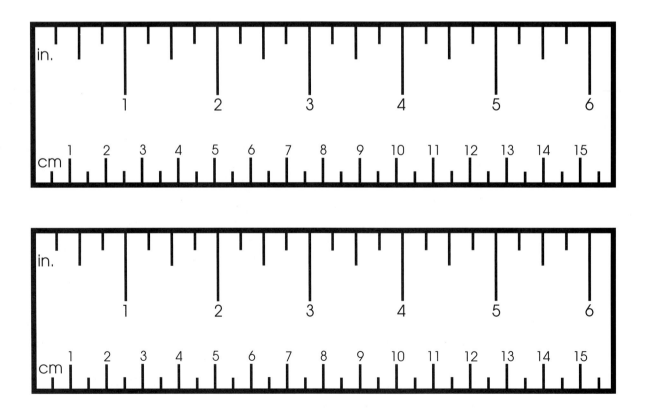

Perimeter Party!

Your students will want to dive right into this exciting lesson on perimeter!

Skill: Calculating perimeter

Estimated Lesson Time: 1 hour

Teacher Preparation:
Duplicate one copy of page 127 for each student.

Materials:
1 copy of page 127 for each student
scissors for sharing

6cm

6cm   6cm

6cm

Background Information:
Perimeter is the distance around the outside edge of a polygon. A *polygon* is a closed plane figure with three or more straight sides. In a polygon two sides meet to form a vertex. The perimeter of a polygon is found by adding together the lengths of all its sides. For example, in the polygon above, the perimeter is 24 centimeters.

Introducing The Lesson:

Draw the polygons below on the chalkboard, but do not label their perimeters. Tell students that each of the six squares in the polygons represents one square yard. Then point out that the shapes shown represent different styles of swimming pools from which each child must select one. Explain that each pool's owner must also compute the cost of installing safety railing around his pool. Tell each student that in order to do this, he must compute the distance around the outside edge of the pool, or its perimeter. Next have students tell you how they would determine the perimeter of each pool. Guide students to conclude that the perimeter can be determined by adding the sum of the number of exposed square sides around the outside edge of each polygon.

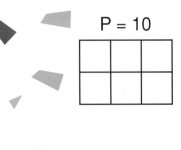

P = 10   P = 12   P = 12

P = 14

P = 14

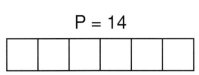

P = 14

Steps:

1. Review the definition of perimeter found on page 125.

2. Show students how to calculate the perimeter of one of the pools by counting aloud the number of exposed square sides. Remind the students that each square side is equal to one yard. Record the number of exposed square sides, or the perimeter, on the board beneath the pool.

3. For each of the five remaining pools, select a different student volunteer to point out and count aloud each of the exposed square sides of her assigned pool.

4. Once each student computes each pool's perimeter, tell students that the price of pool railing is $10 per yard. Have each student work independently to compute the cost of installing railing around each pool. Then have each child indicate the pool requiring the least amount of money for railing. Once each student has made her selection, ask a volunteer to explain the most economical arrangement—the pool with a perimeter of 10. Point out that its railing cost would be $100, while railing for the other pools would be more expensive given their larger perimeters.

5. Give each student a copy of page 127 for additional practice in computing perimeter.

Perimeter Pizza

For your upcoming pool party, you have decided to order a jumbo pepperoni pizza from Paul's Perimeter Pizza Shop. At Paul's each pizza's price is based on its perimeter and you choose the shape of the pizza. To get the best deal, you will want to be sure to choose the pizza with the smallest perimeter.

Cut out the four squares at the bottom of this sheet. **Each square side is 1 foot in length.** Then use the squares to design as many different-shaped pizzas as possible without repeating a design. Shade the pizzas you create in the grids numbered 1–5. Then calculate their perimeters. Remember that each pizza must be made up of four squares and one side of each square must completely touch the side of another square.

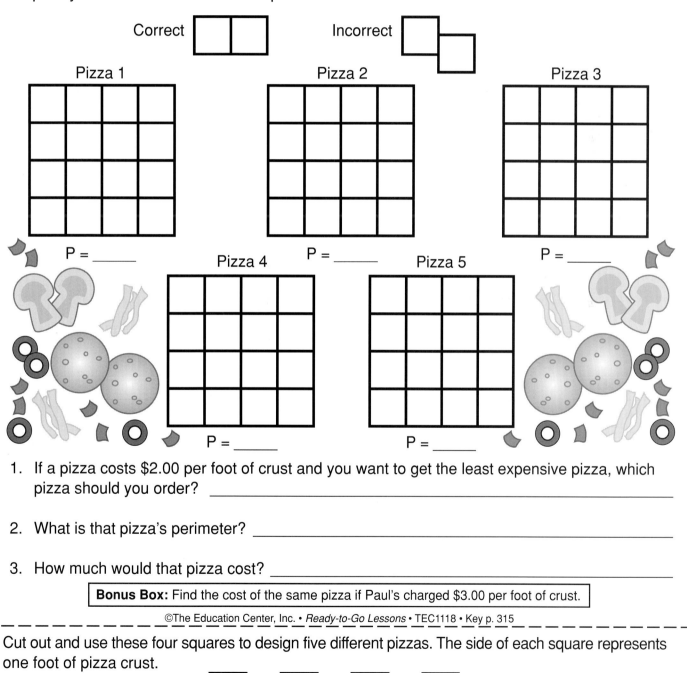

Correct   Incorrect

Pizza 1   Pizza 2   Pizza 3

P = _____   P = _____   P = _____

Pizza 4   Pizza 5

P = _____   P = _____

1. If a pizza costs $2.00 per foot of crust and you want to get the least expensive pizza, which pizza should you order? _____

2. What is that pizza's perimeter? _____

3. How much would that pizza cost? _____

> **Bonus Box:** Find the cost of the same pizza if Paul's charged $3.00 per foot of crust.

Cut out and use these four squares to design five different pizzas. The side of each square represents one foot of pizza crust.

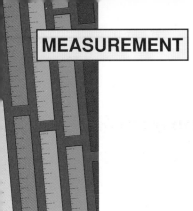

How To Extend The Lesson:

- Create a chart like the one below on your board. Then select ten polygons in your classroom and record their names in the column labeled "Object." Have each student copy the chart onto a sheet of paper. Select one object at a time and direct the student to record an estimate of the perimeter of the item using inches or centimeters. Then measure the item to determine its exact perimeter and direct each student to record that information in her chart. Continue this process until all items have been measured. Ask each student if her estimates became more accurate with more practice.

OBJECT	ESTIMATED PERIMETER	ACTUAL PERIMETER
Desk	80 inches	85 inches
Book	33 inches	39 inches
Classroom	80 feet	70 feet

- Explain to students that they have been building shapes that have the same area but different perimeters. Then have them use centimeter cubes or tiles to create five different shapes whose perimeters are exactly the same. Have them trace the shapes they come up with, then determine which of the five same-perimeter shapes has the biggest area. Explain that the answer is a square or a rectangle whose sides are the same length.

- Provide each student with the following three shapes—a square, a rectangle, and an equilateral triangle. Challenge students to use what they know about perimeter to determine alternate methods of calculating perimeter besides adding together the length of all the shape's sides. Have students think about how multiplication can be intergrated into a formula.

Finding perimeter

How Sweet It Is!

Sweeten your students' day with this hands-on volume lesson!

Skill: Finding the volume of rectangular prisms

Estimated Lesson Time: 1 hour

Teacher Preparation:
Duplicate one copy of page 131 for each student.

Materials:
1 or 2 boxes of sugar cubes (enough for each student to have 4 cubes)
1 copy of page 131 for each pair of students

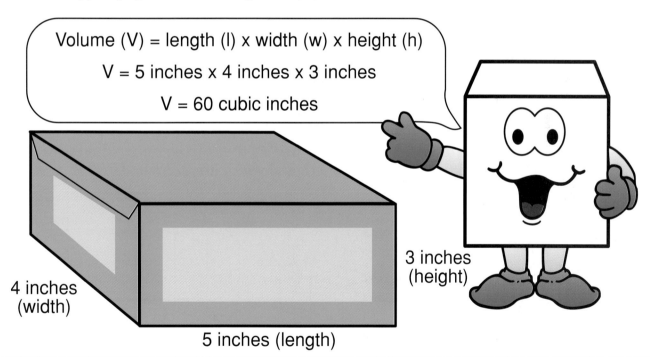

Volume (V) = length (l) x width (w) x height (h)

V = 5 inches x 4 inches x 3 inches

V = 60 cubic inches

4 inches (width)

3 inches (height)

5 inches (length)

Background Information:
• *Volume* is the amount of space inside a container.
• A *rectangular prism* is a three-dimensional figure with six faces, each of which is a rectangle.
• To find the volume of a rectangular prism, multiply *length* by *width* by *height*.
• Volume is measured in *cubic* units.

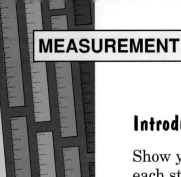
Introducing The Lesson:

Show your students the box of sugar cubes. Remove one cube from the box so that each student can see its size; then ask students to estimate how many cubes it takes to fill one sugar-cube box. Record each student's response on the board. Tell students that *volume* is the term used to explain how much space is contained in a three-dimensional shape. Explain that the volume of a container remains the same, regardless of whether it is filled with sugar cubes, noodles, or air.

Steps:

1. Tell students that the sugar-cube box is a rectangular prism. Read to your students the definition of a rectangular prism on page 129. Then ask them how the actual volume of this box can be determined. Guide your students into concluding that the volume can be found by counting each cube in the box.

2. Demonstrate how to calculate the volume of the box by using the formula for volume—*Volume = length x width x height*. Multiply the number of cubes long by the number of cubes wide by the number of cubes high.

3. Compare the volume calculated using the formula to that of the volume determined by counting the sugar cubes. Explain that volume is always measured in cubic units; then write the volume of the sugar-cube box using cubic centimeters.

4. Give each student four sugar cubes. Challenge her to use the cubes to build the four different rectangular prisms that can be constructed using just four cubes. Explain that the length and width are interchangeable.

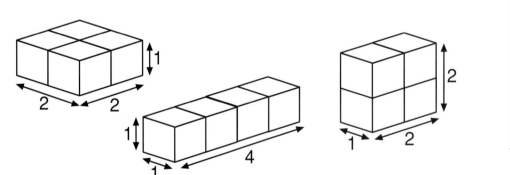

5. Counting one side of a cube as a unit, calculate the volume of each of the four rectangular prisms. Point out that the volume is the same for each prism, because each is constructed of four sugar cubes.

6. Pair your students; then instruct the members of the pair to combine their sugar cubes for a total of eight cubes. Give each pair one copy of page 131. Instruct each pair to complete the page as directed.

Operation: Rescue Sugartown

Oh no! Heavy rain is predicted in Sugartown and the neighborhood is in desperate need of your help. Each homeowner has been given eight blocks with which to build a portion of a wall to keep the river from flooding Sugartown.

Working with a partner, use all eight sugar cubes to make six different possible rectangular prisms (walls). Keep in mind that the length and width can be switched and still create the same figure. Record the dimensions of each wall on the chart below. Then answer the questions that follow.

Design	Length	Width	Height
A			
B			
C			
D			
E			
F			

1. Which wall would you recommend that each homeowner in Sugartown build? Explain your reason.

   _____

   _____

   _____

   _____

2. Find the volume of each wall design. Explain the method that you used to calculate each volume.

   _____

   _____

   _____

   _____

Bonus Box: On the back of this page, explain a method that you might use to determine the number of sugar cubes it would take to fill your classroom.

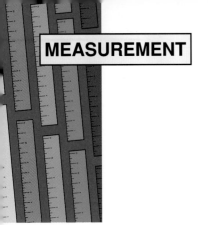

How To Extend The Lesson:

- Have each student bring from home four different rectangular boxes. During the next math class, have the student predict which of his boxes has the largest volume. Next instruct him to use a ruler to measure the dimensions of each box, then sketch a model of it on a sheet of drawing paper. Finally, have him calculate the actual volume to test his prediction.

- Bring in several boxes of different sizes and display them in your learning center. Have each student who visits the center estimate the volume of each box, then use a ruler to measure the length, width, and height of each box. Finally, have the student use the formula for volume to calculate the volume of each box and compare it against his estimates.

- Place a box of sugar cubes in your math learning center. Challenge any student who visits the center to determine how many different rectangular prisms can be made with a volume of 12, 14, and 24 cubic centimeters. Provide copies of the blank table below on which a student can record his findings.

Design	Length	Width	Height
A			
B			
C			
D			
E			
F			
G			
H			
I			
J			
K			
L			

Opening Night

It's curtain call for a new problem-solving method—making a table.

Skill: Making a table

Estimated Lesson Time: 45 minutes

Teacher Preparation:
1. Duplicate one copy of page 135 for each student.
2. Make a transparency of page 135.
3. Write the problem from step one on page 134 on a blank transparency.

Materials:
1 copy of page 135 for each student
1 transparency of page 135
1 blank transparency
overhead projector pen
6 pencils
2 index cards: any size

Background Information:
Problem solvers who use the strategy of making tables can easily organize data, spot patterns, and identify missing information.

Introducing The Lesson:

Problem solving is sure to get positive reviews in your room after this lesson. Begin by asking each student to name a method or strategy he currently uses when problem solving. List each response on the board.

Steps:

1. Tell students that they will be learning a new problem-solving strategy—*making a table;* then show the transparency of the problem below.

   Sharon's school is putting on its first musical. In order to encourage attendance, the principal offered to give door prizes. Every second person who walks in the door will receive a school pencil. Every fifth person to come in will receive a school T-shirt. Of the first 12 people to walk through the door, will anyone receive both a pencil and a T-shirt?

2. Read the problem to your students. Be sure each child understands what the problem is asking. Tell students that first they will try to solve the problem by acting it out.

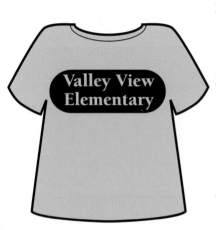

3. Select 12 students to form a straight line to simulate the people entering the door. Select one child to hand out a pencil to every second student and one child to hand out a T-shirt (index card) to every fifth student. Once the items have been distributed, point out that only one student received both items.

4. Draw the table below (leaving out the Xs) on a transparency to display the problem. Demonstrate for your students how they can solve the same problem by filling out the table as shown.

Student	1	2	3	4	5	6	7	8	9	10	11	12
pencil		X		X		X		X		X		X
T-shirt					X					X		

5. Distribute one copy of page 135 to each student. Have him solve each problem by making a table.

6. Have selected students use the transparency of page 135 to show how they obtained their answers for each problem.

Behind The Scenes

The production of a musical involves a great deal of planning. Help the actors out by solving the problems below. Each one can be solved by making a table. Be sure to write each solution in a complete sentence.

1. Before the musical, the dancers will need to rehearse by themselves and with the singers. The singers will also need time to rehearse by themselves. They decided on the following schedule: Every third day the dancers will rehearse, and every second day the singers will rehearse. In the first three weeks of rehearsal, how often will the dancers and singers rehearse together as a group?

Day	1	2	3	4	5	6	7	8	9	10	11	12	13	14	15	16	17	18	19	20	21
Dancers																					
Singers																					

Solution: _____

2. The dancers were given the opportunity to design their butterfly costumes that Stacey's mother made. As a group, they decided the costumes should look similar but not identical. They asked Stacey's mother to put purple polka dots on every second costume she made and pink polka dots on every third costume she made. If Stacey's mother made 15 costumes, how many had both pink and purple polka dots?

Costume	1	2	3	4	5	6	7	8	9	10	11	12	13	14	15
Pink															
Purple															

Solution: _____

3. After the musical, the director wanted to treat the performers to ice-cream sundaes. Jesse's dad planned to dish the ice cream ahead of time so the students wouldn't have to wait long. He knows how picky people are about their ice cream, so after putting ice cream in every dish, he decided on the following plan: In every third dish he put chocolate syrup, in every fourth dish he put whipped cream, and on top of every sixth dish he sprinkled peanuts. If he prepared 30 dishes, how many had peanuts and chocolate syrup? How many dishes had all three toppings?

Sundae	1				5					10					15
Chocolate Syrup															
Whipped Cream															
Peanuts															

Sundae					20					25					30
Chocolate Syrup															
Whipped Cream															
Peanuts															

Solution: _____

_____

_____

Bonus Box: What would the answer to the last problem be if he prepared 60 dishes of ice cream?

How To Extend The Lesson:

- Give students problems that can be solved using the make-a-table strategy, but ask them to solve these problems using least common multiples. This will not only provide practice with LCMs, but will also show that there is more than one way to solve a problem.

Example: If every third day (3) the dancers practiced and every sixth day (6) the singers practiced, then you can figure that on every day that is a multiple of six, they will both practice *(the LCM of 3 and 6 is 6)*. Therefore, in 21 days the dancers and singers will practice together three times: on the sixth day *(6 x 1 = 6)*, on the twelfth day *(6 x 2 = 12)*, and on the eighteenth day *(6 x 3 = 18)*.

- For additional practice on this problem-solving strategy, have students solve the following problems:

1. Every morning Gina looks out her bedroom window. She has noticed that every three days she sees a rabbit in her yard and every seventh day she spots a squirrel. How many times in six weeks will Gina see the rabbit and squirrel on the same day? *(Gina will see the rabbit and squirrel on the same day once in three weeks; therefore she will see them twice in six weeks.)*

2. Jeremiah worked during the summer as a peach inspector at an orchard. He noticed that 2 out of every 7 peaches had wormholes. How many good peaches did he find in a basket containing 70 peaches? *(Jeremiah found 50 out of 70 good peaches in the basket.)*

3. Tia spends twice as much time practicing basketball as practicing the piano. One week her total practice time was 24 hours. How many hours did she practice the piano? *(Tia practiced the piano for eight hours.)*

Put It In Reverse!

Reverse your students' thinking by having them work backward to solve problems.

Skill: Working backward to solve a problem

Estimated Lesson Time: 45 minutes

Teacher Preparation:
1. Duplicate one copy of page 139 for each student.
2. Write the word problems from Step 1 and Step 4 on page 138 on a blank transparency.

Materials:
1 copy of page 139 for
   each student
blank transparency
overhead projector
   pen

Background Information:
Working backward to solve a problem involves making a series of computations, starting with the data mentioned at the end of the problem and ending with the data mentioned at the beginning of the problem.

Introducing The Lesson:

Begin this lesson by asking students which problem-solving strategies they have learned this year. Possible answers include: *using logical reasoning, drawing a picture, acting it out, making a table or organized list, guessing and checking, looking for a pattern,* and *simplifying.* Inform students that they will be learning a new problem-solving strategy in this lesson called *working backward*.

Steps:

1. Read the problem below to your class as you display the transparency that you created.

   Katlyn went to the store and bought a pen for $0.50 and a postcard for $0.75. If Katlyn has $3.75 left, how much money did she have when she arrived at the store?

2. Explain to students that some problems can be solved using the *working-backward* strategy. Share the definition from the background information on page 137; then show students how to create a flowchart—like the one below—to help with this strategy.

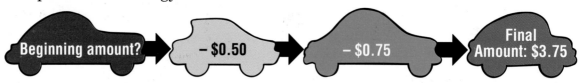

3. Show students how to reverse the flowchart using inverse operations to come up with a solution to the problem. Point out that Katlyn had $5.00 when she arrived at the store.

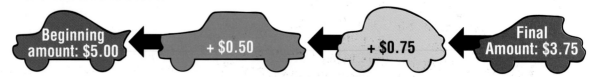

4. Read the next two problems below, one at a time, as you display the transparency that you created. *(Be sure to cover the answer when displaying each problem.)* Instruct each student to use flowcharts to solve each problem; then go over the correct answers.

   Bill has the same number of pens and pencils. His pens are red and blue and he has the same number of each color. If Bill has five red pens, how many total writing instruments does he have? (Answer: 20 writing instruments)

   Wendy received her allowance on Monday. On Tuesday she spent $1.75 at the store and on Wednesday she gave her brother $1.00. Wendy has $2.00 left. How much is her allowance? (Answer: $4.75)

5. Give each student one copy of page 139 and instruct him to complete the page as directed.

Put It In Reverse!

Sometimes going backward will actually put you ahead! Prove it by using the *working-backward* strategy to solve each of the problems below. Create a flowchart from the information in the problem; then reverse its operations to arrive at the problem's solution.

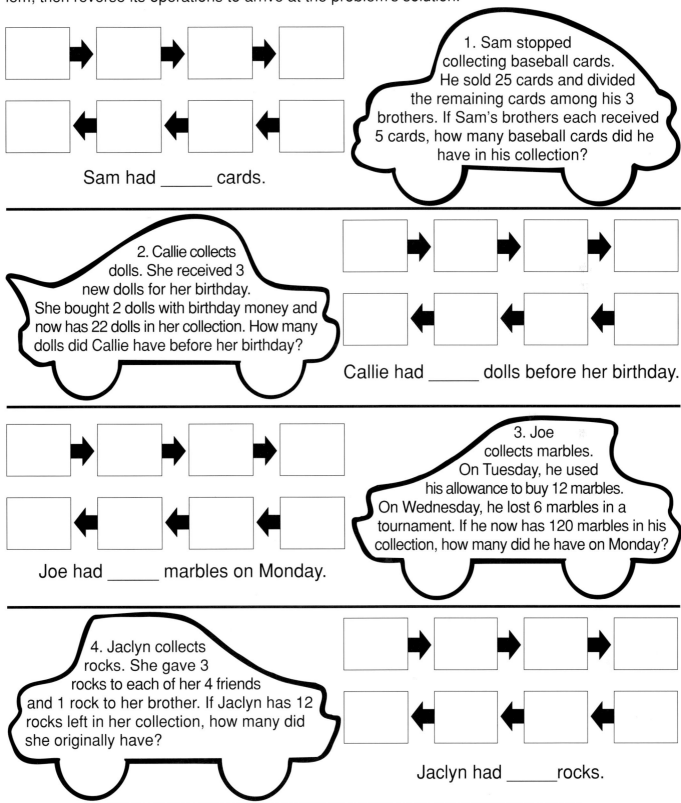

Sam had _____ cards.

1. Sam stopped collecting baseball cards. He sold 25 cards and divided the remaining cards among his 3 brothers. If Sam's brothers each received 5 cards, how many baseball cards did he have in his collection?

2. Callie collects dolls. She received 3 new dolls for her birthday. She bought 2 dolls with birthday money and now has 22 dolls in her collection. How many dolls did Callie have before her birthday?

Callie had _____ dolls before her birthday.

Joe had _____ marbles on Monday.

3. Joe collects marbles. On Tuesday, he used his allowance to buy 12 marbles. On Wednesday, he lost 6 marbles in a tournament. If he now has 120 marbles in his collection, how many did he have on Monday?

4. Jaclyn collects rocks. She gave 3 rocks to each of her 4 friends and 1 rock to her brother. If Jaclyn has 12 rocks left in her collection, how many did she originally have?

Jaclyn had _____ rocks.

Bonus Box: On the back of this page, compute the average number of items in all four of the collections above.

How To Extend The Lesson:

- Create a work-backward game for your math learning center. Program a set of index cards with different operations using even whole numbers. For example, "add 4," "subtract 6," "divide 2," "multiply 8." Include a set of directions that tells the student to draw two cards from the top of the deck and select an *even* number as the end number. Have him create a flowchart, then a reverse flowchart to come up with a starting number. For example, if the cards *add 4* and *divide 2* were drawn and the student chose *48* as an end number, then the solution would be *92* (see the illustration). Assign each child who visits the learning center to play a total of five rounds.

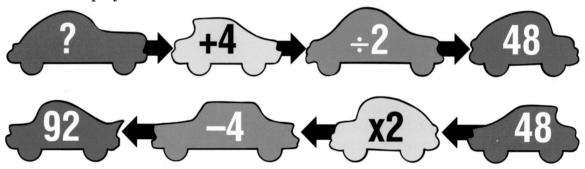

- Play the mind-reading game with your students to practice the work-backward problem-solving strategy! Create a variety of problems similar to the one shown below. Write each problem on the board and then read the problem aloud to your students. Have them work backward through the information presented in the problem to determine the mystery number. After a few rounds of the game, challenge each student to come up with a problem for his classmates to solve.

  I am thinking of a number. If you multiply that number by 2, add 9, subtract 7, and divide by 2, the result is 14. What number am I thinking of?

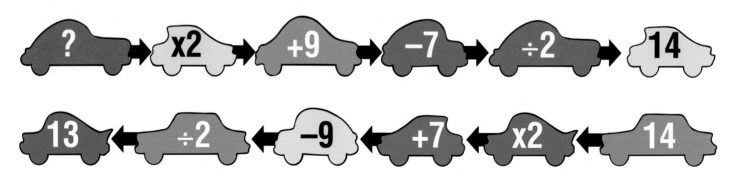

Solution: You are thinking of the number 13.

A Picture Is Worth A Thousand Words

With a little practice, your students will master the art of solving word problems using pictures or diagrams!

Skill: Solving word problems using pictures or diagrams

Estimated Lesson Time: 45 minutes

Teacher Preparation:
1. Duplicate one copy of page 143 for each student.
2. Make one transparency of the word problem and illustrations found in Step 1 (page 142).
3. Write each word problem listed on page 144 on a separate transparency.

Materials:
1 copy of page 143 for each student
1 transparency of Step 1 (Page 142)
5 blank transparencies
1 transparency marker for each group of students
overhead projector

Background Information:
Drawing a picture or a diagram when solving some word problems is a very helpful strategy for students to use. Stress to students that while the drawing should be an accurate picture and match the information given in the word problem, they do not need to worry about its being well drawn.

Introducing The Lesson:

Tell students to imagine that they are traveling east from St. Louis, Missouri to Norfolk, Virginia; then north to Washington, D.C. Ask students how many states they have to pass through to do this. Accept reasonable responses. Then ask students what would help them answer the question more accurately *(a map of the United States)*. Display a U.S. map; then have a student volunteer come up to the map and count the number of states *(5)*. Explain to students that using a picture or diagram is often a very helpful strategy when solving word problems in math.

Steps:

1. Display the transparency of the word problem below on an overhead projector. Tell students to choose one of the pictures to help solve the word problem.

   Two treasure hunters are hiking through a forest in search of a lost treasure. The hunters walk 5 miles south, 1 mile west, 4 miles north, and 1 mile east. How far are they from their starting point?

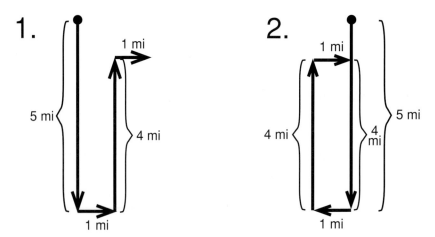

2. Show students step-by-step how picture 2 was drawn using the details given in the word problem to find the correct answer. *(1 mile)*

3. Next divide students into five groups. Give each group one transparency containing one of the word problems from page 144 and a transparency marker. Instruct each group to read its word problem, then draw a picture or diagram on the transparency to help solve its problem.

4. Have each group display its transparency on the overhead projector and share how it used the picture to determine an answer.

5. Give each student a copy of page 143. Direct each student to follow the directions on the reproducible to complete the activity. After each student has completed the activity, have a different volunteer share her picture and discuss her answer for each word problem.

A Happy Hunting Party!

The Thompson twins, Tracey and Thomas, are planning a party to celebrate their 11th birthday. Tracey suggested having a treasure-hunt theme. She and Thomas needed some help with the planning and decorating, so they called on a few of their close friends.

Help the friends plan for the party by solving each of the problems below. Draw a picture or diagram on the back of this sheet to help you solve each problem; then write your final answer on the line provided.

1. Tracey asked T. J. to pick up some special party supplies. T. J. plans to leave his home and ride his bike 10 blocks west to Andy's Art Supply Store, 5 blocks north to The Party Place, and then 3 blocks east to Sam's Supermarket. Before heading home he'll travel 2 blocks south to Terrific Toys. How far and in what direction will he have to travel to get back to his house? _____

2. Thomas is setting up four tall posts at each corner of the patio. He wants to tie each post to each of the other three posts. How many pieces of string will he need? _____

3. Tracey is hanging decorations on the outer posts and outer strings that Tom set up. The posts are 12 feet apart and Tracey will hang each decoration 3 feet apart. How many decorations will she hang in all? _____

4. Terry and Terrel are constructing a trail in the backyard on which to hide treasures. The trail extends 10 feet north, 5 feet west, 5 feet north, 10 feet east, and then 7 feet south. If the trail then continues 2 feet west, how far and in what direction will Terry and Terrel have to go to reach the starting point again? _____

5. Thomas and his four friends walk in a single file line as they hide the treasures for the hunt. Thomas is walking between Terrence and Tammy. Thomas is walking in front of Tammy. Tara is walking in front of Terrence but behind Travis. Where is Thomas in the line? _____

6. If the treasures are hidden 1 foot apart, how many will be hidden in all? _____

7. Tara and Tammy are helping to set up the food tables. There are seven tables. If they set the tables end-to-end and in a *U* shape, at how many sides will they not be able to set chairs? _____

8. Tracey wants to deliver the party invitations personally. She and her mother have to travel by car north for 3 miles, west for 3 miles, and then north again for 2 miles. If they then have to travel east 2 times farther than they did west, and then travel south the same distance that they traveled north, how much farther will they have to travel to get back home?

_____

Bonus Box: Create a new party problem for Tracey and Thomas on another sheet of paper. Give the problem to a friend to solve; then check to see if your friend's picture and answer are correct.

How To Extend The Lesson:

Have each student bring in a photograph that shows him involved in a favorite activity. Direct each student to fold a light-colored, 9" x 12" sheet of construction paper in half, greeting-card fashion. Instruct the student to glue or tape his photograph to the left-front side of the card, then write a word problem based on the picture on the right side with a black marker. On the inside of the card, have the student draw a picture or diagram that solves the word problem. Next have the student use a hole puncher to put a hole through the bottom of the card, then tie the card closed with a 12-inch piece of string as shown. Post each student's card on a wall or bulletin board titled "Picturesque Word Problems!" Finally challenge each student to choose five of the word problems to solve. After the student solves the word problems, have him untie the cards to check his answers.

During basketball practice, our coach threw the ball back and forth between me and five other players. I was next to Margaret. Jerry was between Audrey and Donald. Margaret was to the left of Donald, and Beth was to the right of Audrey. Who was at the left end of the line? Who was second from the right end of the line? Written by: Sallie Marshall

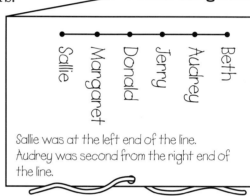

Sallie was at the left end of the line. Audrey was second from the right end of the line.

Word Problems

- Draw a three-row, three-column grid. Place an *X* on three different places so that no one row, column, or diagonal has more than one *X* in it.

- Four friends are riding single file on a bike trail. Alan is ahead of Ian. Jeff is behind Ian. Alan is behind Katie. Who is the front rider? Who is the last rider? *(Katie is the front rider, Jeff is the last rider.)*

- The basketball team from the local YWCA is having its picture taken. Amy wants to frame her 11" x 14" picture so that there is a three-inch boarder around it. How large will the framed picture be? *(17" x 20")*

- Don's mother, father, brother, and sister are sitting on the bleachers watching his football game. His neighbors, Mr. and Mrs. Johnson and their daughter, Ashley, are also there. Each female has a bag of popcorn and each male has a hot dog. For each hot dog, there are 2 sodas. How many bags of popcorn, hot dogs, and sodas are there altogether? *(4 bags of popcorn, 3 hot dogs, and 6 sodas)*

- Mary and her mom were driving to the public library. After driving 4 blocks, Mary realized she had forgotten her book. She and her mother drove back, got the book, and then drove another 6 blocks to the library. How many blocks did they drive in all? *(14 blocks)*

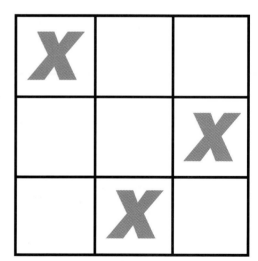

Note To The Teacher: Write each word problem in the box above on a separate transparency and use with Step 3 on page 142.

Supplying The Solution

When faced with a problem where data isn't in short supply, guess and check is a problem-solving method your students will definitely want to try!

Skill: Using the guess-and-check technique to solve math problems

Estimated Lesson Time: 45 minutes

Teacher Preparation:
Duplicate one copy of page 147 for each student.

Materials:
overhead projector
transparency
transparency marker
1 copy of page 147 for each student
1 sheet of paper and a pencil for each student

Background Information:
One method of problem solving is called *guess and check*. Guess and check involves guessing the answer to a problem and then checking to see if it is correct. This process of guessing and checking continues until a solution is reached. Guessing and checking is especially desirable when a problem contains many pieces of data.

Introducing The Lesson:

Explain to students that they will be playing Guess The Magic Number. Write a number between 1 and 100 on a sheet of paper, making sure to keep the number hidden from your students. Explain to students that they will each be attempting to guess the number you recorded by asking you any question that can be answered with a yes or no response. Guide students in determining that certain questions help narrow the field of possible answers. These questions might include "Is the number even?", "Is the number between 10 and 20?", and "Is the number greater than 50?" Continue this process until the answer has been guessed. As the students get more skilled at the game, increase the range of numbers from which you select the mystery number.

Steps:

1. Explain to students that they were able to identify the answer by the guess-and-check method of problem solving.

2. Write the following problem on a transparency on the overhead projector:

   Jane has ten books. She stores the books on two shelves. One shelf has two more books on it than the other. How many books are on each shelf?

3. Read the problem on the overhead aloud to the class. Explain that the guess-and-check strategy can be used to help solve this problem. Model the process for your students by guessing that there are three books on one shelf. Explain to students that that would mean there were five books on the other shelf because three plus two is five. Then check your guess by adding three and five together. Point out that with your guess, eight is the total number of books, so that answer is incorrect since Jane has a total of ten books on her shelves.

4. Have a student volunteer make another guess; then check the guess. Continue allowing students to guess and check until the solution—four books on one shelf and six books on the other—is reached.

5. As a class, work each of the following problems on the overhead using the guess-and-check method:
   - *Bill bought 24 pieces of fruit. He had 12 more oranges than apples. How many apples did he buy? How many oranges? (answer: 6 apples, 18 oranges)*
   - Mr. Reitz has 24 students in his class. There are 2 more boys than girls. How many boys are in the class? How many girls? (answer: 13 boys, 11 girls)
   - Jake has $4 more than Jennifer. The combined sum of their money is $20. How much money does Jennifer have? How much does Jake have? (answer: Jennifer has $8, Jake has $12)

6. Give each student a copy of page 147 for additional practice using the guess-and-check method.

Silly Sam's Inventory Jam

Silly Sam owns a school supply store, but he is not very good at keeping inventory records. Sam has written some notes about his store's inventory on several scraps of paper. Read each note carefully. Then use the information on each note to figure out how many of each item Sam has in his store. Then record your answers in the chart.

I have 11 three-ring binders in stock. There are three more red binders than blue binders.

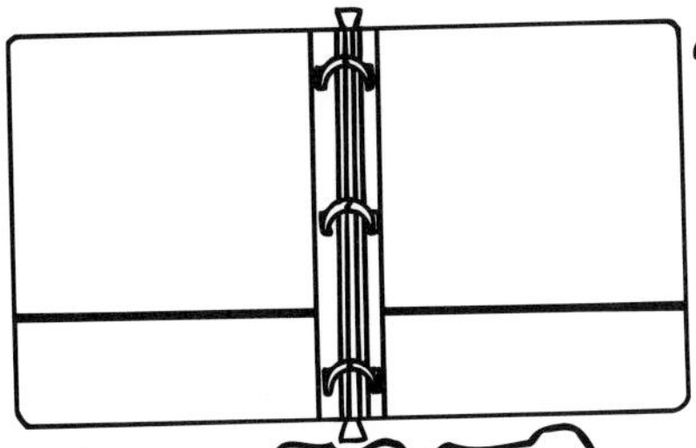

I have 55 pens. There are 15 fewer red pens than blue pens.

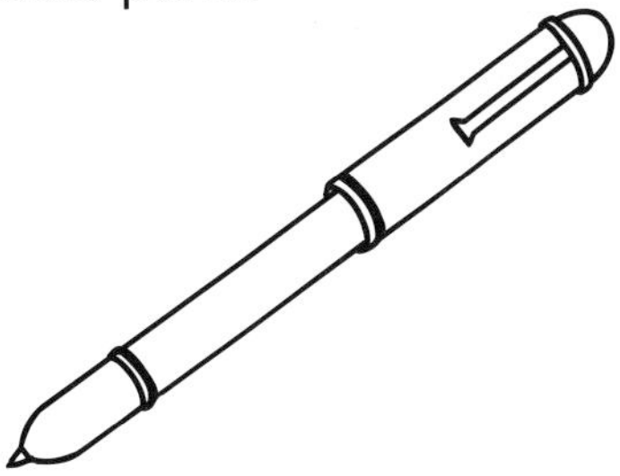

I counted 15 notebooks. There are seven more blue notebooks than red notebooks.

There are 44 pencils in stock. I have 12 more red pencils than blue pencils.

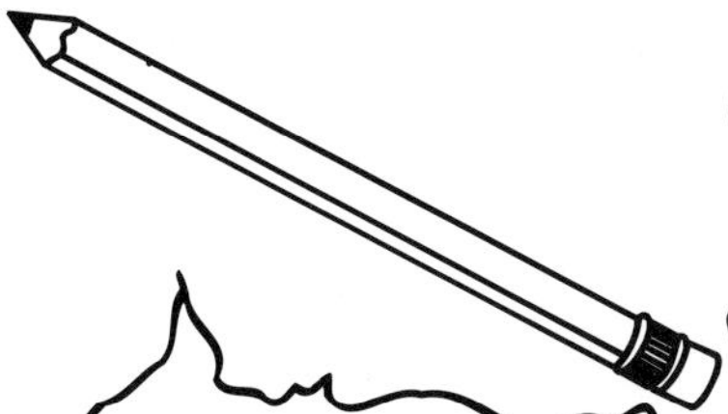

The store has 36 folders. There are eight more red folders than blue ones.

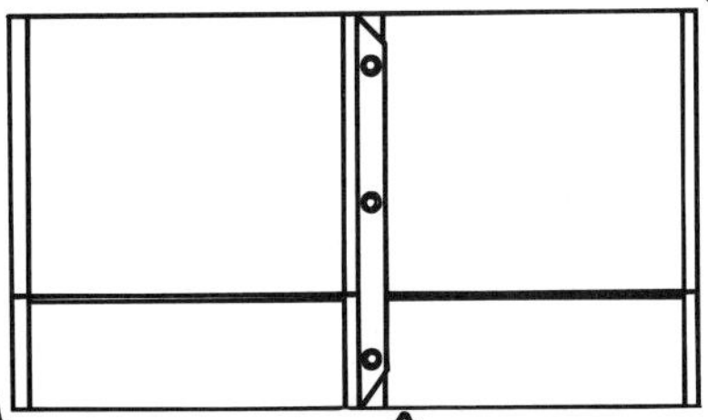

We have 14 bookbags in the store. There are two more red bookbags than blue bookbags.

	pens	notebooks	pencils	bookbags	folders	3-ring binders	erasers
red							
blue							
total number							36

Bonus Box: On the back of this sheet, record an additional clue for determining the number of red erasers and the number of blue erasers. Then record the answers in the chart.

How To Extend The Lesson:

- Ask a student volunteer to step outside the classroom for a minute. Select a number and play Guess The Magic Number (as described in the introduction on page 146) with the remaining students. Record the number of guesses the class required to guess the recorded number. Then invite the student volunteer to return to the class and attempt to guess that same number without the help of any clues. Count the number of times it takes the volunteer to guess the recorded number. Compare the number of guesses it took the volunteer with the number of guesses it took the class to determine the magic number. Then discuss how important it is to use all the given information when solving problems.

- Read the following riddle aloud and have each student solve it.
  I am an even number. My ones digit is less than my tens digit. I am less than 50 but greater than 10. What number am I? (answers: 20, 30, 32, 40, 42)

  After each student has arrived at a solution, discuss the answer. Then have each student write a similar riddle. Instruct each student to exchange his problem with another student and solve each other's riddle.

- Challenge your students to find at least five different answers to the following riddle:

  I am an even number. My ones digit is less than my tens digit. I am less than 100 but greater than 1. List the numbers. (one possible answer: 10, 32, 54, 76, 98)

- Have each student make a back-to-school shopping list of school supplies from Silly Sam's School Supply Store. Then display the list of prices shown below. Have each student use the price information to calculate the cost of the supplies on her list.

New Lower Prices!!!

3-ring binder	$2.49
folder	$.99
notebook	$1.29
pencil	$.10
pen	$.30
bookbag	$19.99
eraser	$.05

Act It Out!

*Actions definitely speak louder than words
when students use this helpful problem-solving strategy!*

Skill: Solving word problems by acting them out

Estimated Lesson Time: 1 hour

Teacher Preparation:

1. Obtain nine small index cards for each group of four students.
2. Duplicate page 151 for each group of four students.

Materials (for each group of four students):

9 small index cards
scissors
markers
1 copy of page 151

Background Information:

There are many situations in which students may have difficulty visualizing a problem or the steps necessary to solve it. Acting out the problem is an effective problem-solving strategy. People or objects can be used exactly as they're described in a problem, or things can be used to represent people and objects. Acting out a problem often leads to its answer, or it may lead to another strategy that can help solve it.

Introducing The Lesson:

Invite four students to come to the front of the class. Ask the class, "If these four students shake hands with each other—one time each—how many total handshakes would that be?" Share with the class that since visualizing this problem is difficult, the four students are going to act it out to reach a solution. Next direct Student A to shake hands with students B, C, and D. Write each combination on a chalkboard or a transparency, replacing the letters with students' names. Then have Student B shake hands with students C and D, and write these two combinations on the board. Ask the class, "Should Student B also shake hands with Student A?" *(No, this combination has already been made.)* Next direct Student C to shake hands with Student D. Write this combination on the board. Ask the class, "Should Student D shake hands with students A, B, or C?" *(No, those students have already shaken hands with Student D.)* Point out to the class that acting out this problem—then writing each possible answer in an organized list—is a helpful strategy to use.

Steps:

1. Divide students into groups of four.

2. Provide each group with a copy of page 151, nine small index cards, scissors, and markers.

3. Direct each group to:
    a. Fold eight of the index cards in half.
    b. Unfold each card and cut it in half along the crease line.
    c. Label each of eight halves with "$10."
    d. Label each of the other eight halves with "$5."
    e. Decorate the ninth index card to resemble a baseball card.

4. Read problem 1 on the reproducible to the class. Instruct two students within each group to act out the problem: both students should begin with $60 (four $10s and four $5s) each; one student "owns" the baseball card. Then have the other two students act out the problem.

5. Direct each group of students to record its solution in the answer blank for number 1, and then continue working together to solve the remaining problems.

Lights, Camera, ACTION!

Sometimes it's hard to decide how to solve a problem. In some cases, you may find it helpful to "act it out." You can use people or objects, just like they're described. Or you can use items to represent people or objects. Solve each problem below by acting it out with your group members. Remember: You can also use other strategies with acting it out.

1. Suppose you have $60 and you buy a valuable baseball card for $30. Then you sell it for $40. Next you buy the card back for $50. Then finally, you sell it for $60. How much money did you make or lose in buying and selling the baseball card?

2. Joe is younger than Flo, but older than Moe. Bo is older than Joe, but younger than Flo. Who is the youngest?

_____

3. Fred, Jed, Ted, and Ned ran in a 1,000-meter race. Jed finished third. Ned finished after Ted, but ahead of Jed. In what place did Fred finish the race? _____

4. Tam sits to the right of Sam. Sam sits to the right of Cam. Tam sits between Sam and Pam. In what order are the four students sitting?

_____

5. Three soccer players wear green, gold, and teal jerseys. None wears the same color. Susan's jersey is not gold or teal. Suzanne's jersey is teal. What color is Sue's jersey? _____

6. A football league has four teams: the Panthers, Bobcats, Tigers, and Cougars. If the teams play each other twice, how many games will each team play? _____ How many total games will the teams in the league play? _____

7. Marie is standing in the middle of a line of moviegoers. There are six people behind Marie. How many total people are in the movie line? _____

Hint: Use the small index cards from problem 1 to help you solve problems 7 and 8.

8. A parking lot with spaces numbered 1–16 is full. All of the cars in the even-numbered spaces leave. Then every third car of those remaining leaves. And finally, half of the remaining cars leave. How many cars remain in the parking lot?

_____

Bonus Box: Dan has an 8-page photo album. Each side of a page has 6 pockets for photos—except pages 1 and 8. The front of page 1 and the back of page 8 do not have pockets. If Dan's album is half full of photos, how many photos does it contain? _____

How To Extend The Lesson:

- When checking and discussing problems 1–6 on page 151, have groups of students take turns acting out each one in the front of the classroom. For problem 7, have a student come to the front of the class to represent Marie; then have six students line up behind her. Ask a volunteer to explain the solution to this particular problem. To solve problem 8, have 16 students line up across the front of the classroom to represent 16 cars. Then read each step of the problem as the students act it out. For the Bonus Box, invite a student volunteer to draw its solution on the chalkboard.

	green	gold	teal
Susan	✔	X	X
Suzanne	X	X	✔
Sue	X	✔	X

- Review with students that the act-it-out strategy is often used with other strategies, such as making organized lists, recognizing patterns, and using models and diagrams. Extend problem 5 on the reproducible by showing students how to construct and use a logic box. Since the problem consists of three attributes (colors) and three people, draw a box on a chalkboard or transparency that has three columns and three rows. Label the rows and columns as shown. Then fill in each individual section of the box with either a √ for information that is true or an *x* for information that is not true. Remind students that the different parts of the problem can be read in any order; thus a check can be made in the box that matches *Suzanne* and *teal*. Complete the logic box with students' responses. Point out to students that a logic box provides a visual display for some problems.

- Working in groups of four, have students make up additional problems that can be solved by acting them out. Have students use the problems on the reproducible as models, or come up with situations of their own. Have each group share its problem with the rest of the class.

"Un-bee-lievably" Organized!

*Get your students buzzing about this "un-bee-lievably"
organized approach to problem solving!*

Skill: Solving word problems using an organized list

Estimated Lesson Time: 1 hour

Teacher Preparation:

1. Fill one resealable plastic bag with four different-colored
   candies—such as jelly beans, M&M's®, or Starbursts®—for each
   student. If desired, substitute four different-colored pieces of
   construction paper for the candies.
2. Duplicate one copy of page 155 for each student.

Materials:

1 copy of page 155 for each student
1 small resealable plastic bag for each
   student
a supply of candies of various color combinations, such as jelly beans,
   M&M's®, or Starbursts®

Background Information:

Making an organized list when solving some word problems is a very helpful strategy
for students to use. An organized list can be used when items need to be put in a
given order or all of the possible combinations of a group of items need to be known.
Encourage systematic listing to ensure that choices are not left out or repeated.

Introducing The Lesson:

Direct three student volunteers to stand at the front of the classroom. Explain to the class that the volunteers are going to have an imaginary group photo taken. Ask the class how many different ways the three can be arranged in line from left to right for the photo. *(Six combinations are possible: 1, 2, 3; 1, 3, 2; 2, 1, 3; 2, 3, 1; 3, 1, 2; 3, 2, 1.)* Suggest that the class list all the possible choices beginning with the volunteer on the left. For each choice given, have the volunteers move to show the arrangement; then list the arrangement on the board. Continue until each possible arrangement has been given. Explain to students that making an organized list can be used to show all possible choices and ensure that choices are not left out or repeated when solving word problems in math.

Steps:

1. Place a small plastic bag filled with four different-colored candies on each student's desk. Direct each student to list all the possible ways the candies can be arranged in line from left to right. Instruct the student to use a systematic approach and list each possible arrangement on a sheet of paper. *(There are 24 different possible arrangements, six for each color of candy. See the example below.)*

2. Pair each student, and have partners check one another's lists. After students have checked one another's lists, invite each student to eat her candies.

3. Give each student a copy of page 155. Instruct the student to follow the directions on the reproducible to complete the activity. After each student has completed the activity, discuss the answers as a class.

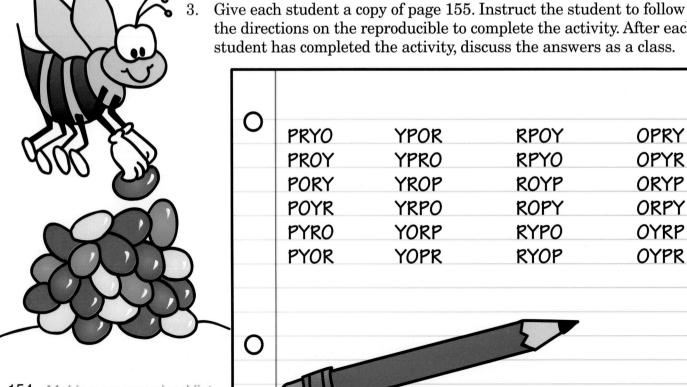

PRYO	YPOR	RPOY	OPRY
PROY	YPRO	RPYO	OPYR
PORY	YROP	ROYP	ORYP
POYR	YRPO	ROPY	ORPY
PYRO	YORP	RYPO	OYRP
PYOR	YOPR	RYOP	OYPR

Name_____ *Making an organized list*

Bumble Bee's Booming Business

Beatrice Bee and her young swarm—Bernard, Bonnie, Brittany, Borris, and Brenda Bee— buzzed downtown for a shopping spree! Bumble Bee's business was booming that day with bees and buzzes going every which way. So Beatrice said, "Kids, there's no time to play; get what you need and let's be on our way!"

Directions: Make an organized list of all possible answers to each of the following Bee family problems. Record your lists on the spaces provided; then check each list to make sure that you have not repeated or left out any items.

1. Bernard Bee, the oldest brother bee, is incredibly hooked on all kinds of books! Bernard buzzes over to the literature section and buys four of his favorite kinds of books: mystery, historical, adventure, and science fiction. List all the different ways the books can be arranged on his shelf if the mystery book is always placed on the left.

2. Bonnie Bee, the fashion bee, buys socks and sneakers in colorful threes. Bonnie has banana-, cherry-, and peach-colored sneakers. She wants to purchase strawberry-, lemon-, and lime-colored socks. List all the possible color combinations of sneakers and socks she can wear.

3. Brittany Bee (who is only three) said, "I'm buying flowers just for me!" Brittany found five flowers: white, pink, purple, yellow, and blue. List all the possible ways she can make a bouquet with two flowers.

4. Borris Bee, who just eats and eats, loves nothing more than nutritious treats! Borris sees peanut butter, carrots, bagels, juice, spring water, and milk. If he consumes two foods and one drink at a time, list all the possible combinations he can have.

5. Brenda Bee, whose nickname is Flea, loves to drink mint-flavored tea! She has 1 quarter, 3 dimes, 6 nickels, and 10 pennies. If the tea she wants costs 55 cents a box, how many different coin combinations can she use? List all the possible combinations.

Bonus Box: Create a rhyming word problem for Beatrice Bee on the back of this sheet; then make an organized list of all possible answers to the problem on a separate sheet of paper. Give the problem to a friend to solve; then check to see that your friend does not repeat or leave out any items.

How To Extend The Lesson:

- Make a 4' x 1' rectangle with masking tape on a section of your classroom floor. Divide the rectangle into four 1-foot sections. Then label four index cards with *A, B, 1,* and *2*. Place each card in a square on the rectangle in the order listed below. Next pair students; then instruct each pair to systematically list all of the possible letter/number combinations on a sheet of paper. After each pair has completed the activity, discuss students' findings (see the list below).

| A | B | 1 | 2 |

AB12	BA12	1AB2	2AB1
AB21	BA21	1A2B	2A1B
A12B	B12A	1BA2	2BA1
A1B2	B1A2	1B2A	2B1A
A21B	B21A	12AB	21AB
A2B1	B2A1	12BA	21BA

- Gather three shoeboxes. Fill each box with a group of five items such as coins, shells, and buttons; then place the boxes at a center. Create an answer key (an organized list) for each group of items; then attach each key to the bottom of its box. Next invite three students to the center and have each student choose one of the boxes. Instruct each student to systematically list all of the possible arrangements of the items found in his box on a sheet of paper. When each student is finished, have him exchange his list with another student in the group. Direct the group to check one another's lists using the provided keys. Finally, have the students return the items to the appropriate boxes for the next group of students to use.

- Instruct each student to gather four household items, such as cans of soup, keys, cups, or CD cases. Direct the student to challenge a family member to list all the possible ways the four items can be arranged in line from left to right. Instruct the student to make a list of the family member's arrangements, then check the completed list. If the student finds the family member has repeated or left off an arrangement, direct him to show the family member how to use an organized approach. Finally, have each student write a paragraph about his experience and share it with the class.

Loading Up On Logic

Top off your study of problem-solving strategies with this logical-reasoning lesson!

Skill: Using logical reasoning

Estimated Lesson Time: 1 hour

Teacher Preparation:

1. Duplicate one copy of page 159 for each student.
2. Make a transparency of page 159.

Materials:

1 transparency of page 159
1 copy of page 159 for each student
transparency pen

Background Information:

Logical reasoning is a general problem-solving strategy that enables a person to see how several facts work together to make a solution. Displaying the data for this type of problem in a chart or matrix is very helpful.

PROBLEM SOLVING

Introducing The Lesson:

Begin by asking students which problem-solving strategies they have learned this year. Possible answers include *draw a picture, act it out, make a table, make an organized list, guess and check, use or look for a pattern, working backwards,* and *make it simpler*. Inform students that they will be learning a new problem-solving strategy called *logical reasoning* in this lesson.

Steps:

1. Display the transparency that you created of page 159. Use a sheet of paper to cover the bottom half of the transparency so that only problem number one is displayed.

2. Read problem number one all the way through; then tell students that they can use the clues listed and the matrix to solve the problem.

3. Reread the problem until you come to the first clue; then underline the clue. Place an *X* on the matrix to indicate the topping each person didn't order. For example, in clue number one, since no person ordered a topping that starts with the same letter as his or her name, place an X in the matrix boxes shown below.

	Tramal	Leeza	Karl	Colleen	Brad
lettuce		X			
tomato	X				
ketchup			X		
cheddar				X	
bacon					X

4. Read the remaining clues one at a time, underlining each. Place an *O* on the matrix to match each person with the topping that he or she ordered. Place an *X* to indicate each topping that the person didn't order.

5. Show students how to read the matrix to write the solution to the problem. *(See the completed matrix and solution in the answer key for page 159 at the back of this book.)*

6. Distribute one copy of page 159 to each student. Have the student redo the first problem, using your transparency as a reference. Then instruct him to complete the second problem using the same strategy.

Hamburger Helpers

Use what you know about logical reasoning to help you solve the two problems below.

1. Tramal, Leeza, Karl, Colleen, and Brad each had a hamburger for lunch. They each ordered a different extra topping for their burgers. No one ordered a topping that begins with the same letter as his or her name. Colleen and Tramal don't like condiments because they make bread soggy. Brad says that green vegetables are meant for rabbits. Leeza loves cheese and Karl ordered the bacon. The topping choices are lettuce, tomato, ketchup, cheddar, and bacon. Which extra topping did Tramal order on his hamburger?

Solution:_____

	Tramal	Leeza	Karl	Colleen	Brad
lettuce					
tomato					
ketchup					
cheddar					
bacon					

2. Tramal, Leeza, Karl, Colleen, and Brad decided to eat dessert after they finished their hamburgers. Neither Leeza nor Brad likes pie. Brad's dessert melted all over his hands. Tramal is allergic to citrus fruits and carrots. Colleen only eats dessert if there is chocolate in it. The waitress placed an order for one slice of lemon pie, one piece of carrot cake, one chocolate surprise, one ice-cream cone, and one slice of peanut-butter pie. What did Karl have for dessert?

Solution:_____

	Tramal	Leeza	Karl	Colleen	Brad
lemon pie					
carrot cake					
chocolate surprise					
ice-cream cone					
peanut-butter pie					

Bonus Box: If a hamburger with one extra topping costs $3.50 and each dessert costs $2.25, how much was the total bill at lunch for all five people?

How To Extend The Lesson:

- Challenge your students to solve the following problems using logical reasoning:

1. Sandra, Sally, Sara, Samantha, and Sabrina are visiting West Lake Elementary for its Career Day celebration. Sally and Sabrina don't like animals. Sara faints at the sight of blood. Either Sara or Samantha is a decorator. Sally carries a toothbrush and dental floss wherever she goes. Samantha works with food. The five women have five different jobs: doctor, dietitian, dentist, dog groomer, and decorator. Which woman is the decorator?
(Sara is the decorator.)

2. Russell, Tyler, Keaton, Neil, Erik, and David each brought a different pet to school for show-and-tell. Neither Neil's nor Tyler's pet is a mammal. Keaton takes his pet to the groomer. Russell's pet has four legs and David's has fins. Neither Erik nor Russell has a cat. Neil's pet can say, "Hello." Russell's name starts with the same letter as the pet that he brought. Together the boys brought a dog, snake, parrot, fish, rabbit, and cat to school. Who brought the snake to show-and-tell?
(Tyler brought the snake to show-and-tell.)

3. While at the movies, Tim, Bill, Andrea, Ryan, and Maria each ordered a different drink. Neither Tim nor Andrea ordered a carbonated drink. Both Ryan and Andrea ordered drinks that were crystal clear. Maria always drinks Coca-Cola®. The movie theater sells water, Coca-Cola®, Sprite®, iced tea, and diet Coke®. What did Tim order to drink?
(Tim ordered the iced tea.)

	Tim	Bill	Andrea	Ryan	Maria
water	X	X		X	X
Coca-Cola®	X	X	X	X	
Sprite®	X	X			X
iced tea		X	X		X
diet Coke®	X		X	X	X

Double Your Fun!

Your students will experience double the fun with this double bar graphing activity.

GRAPHING, PROBABILITY & STATISTICS

Skill: Making and interpreting a double bar graph

Estimated Lesson Time: 45 minutes

Teacher Preparation:
1. Duplicate one copy of page 163 for each student.
2. Obtain two 2" x 1 1/2" sticky-note pads, each a different color.
3. Draw the graph illustrated in Step 1 on page 162.

Materials:
1 copy of page 163 for each student
two 2" x 1 1/2" sticky-note pads, each a different color
crayons
scissors

Background Information:
Graphs are a visual method of displaying data. There are many types of graphs. Double bar graphs compare two related sets of data on one graph. Every bar graph has a title, two axes (vertical and horizontal), labels for each axis, and a scale of measurement for the data.

Making and interpreting double bar graphs   161

Introducing The Lesson:

Ask your students what a graph is used for. Record students' responses on the board. Show several examples of graphs from textbooks and periodicals, discussing the information shown in each graph.

Steps:

1. Tell your students they will be helping you create a double bar graph; then draw the graph below on the board for your students.

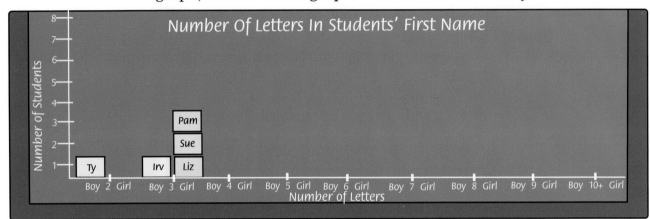

2. Point out the importance of the title at the top of the graph. Inform students that the title quickly tells what kind of information the graph displays. Next point out the titles of the vertical axis (y-axis) and the horizontal axis (x-axis).

3. Provide each female student with a blue sticky note and each male student with a yellow sticky note. Have him record his first name on it. Call each male student with a two-letter first name to the board and have him place his sticky note above the number two on the graph. Then call each female student with a two-letter first name to the board and have her place her sticky note in a column above the number two on the graph, making a separate girls' column next to the boys' column. Repeat this process, calling in turn the male and then female students with three-letter first names, four-letter first names, and so on until each child has affixed his or her sticky note to the board.

4. Ask your students questions related to the data presented on the completed graph. Then write the name of each month across the chalkboard. Provide each student with a copy of page 163. Direct each student to follow the directions for completing the candle pattern. Then instruct each student to tape his candle pattern under the appropriate month labeled on the board. Have each student use this birth-month data to complete the graph on his reproducible.

Name _____

☆ Birthday Fun ☆

Directions: Record your name and the month of your birth on the candle pattern to the left. Color your candle green if you are a boy and red if you are a girl. Cut out your candle and then tape it under the appropriate month labeled on the board. Organize the birth-month information presented on the board into a double bar graph. Be sure to label each axis and give the graph a title. Create a key indicating which color on the graph represents boys and which color represents girls.

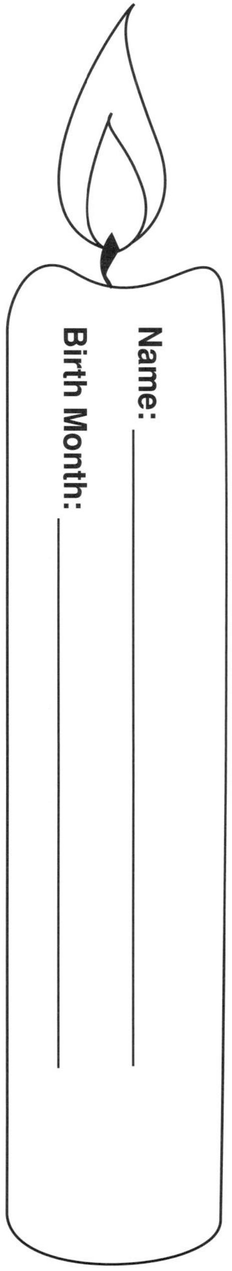

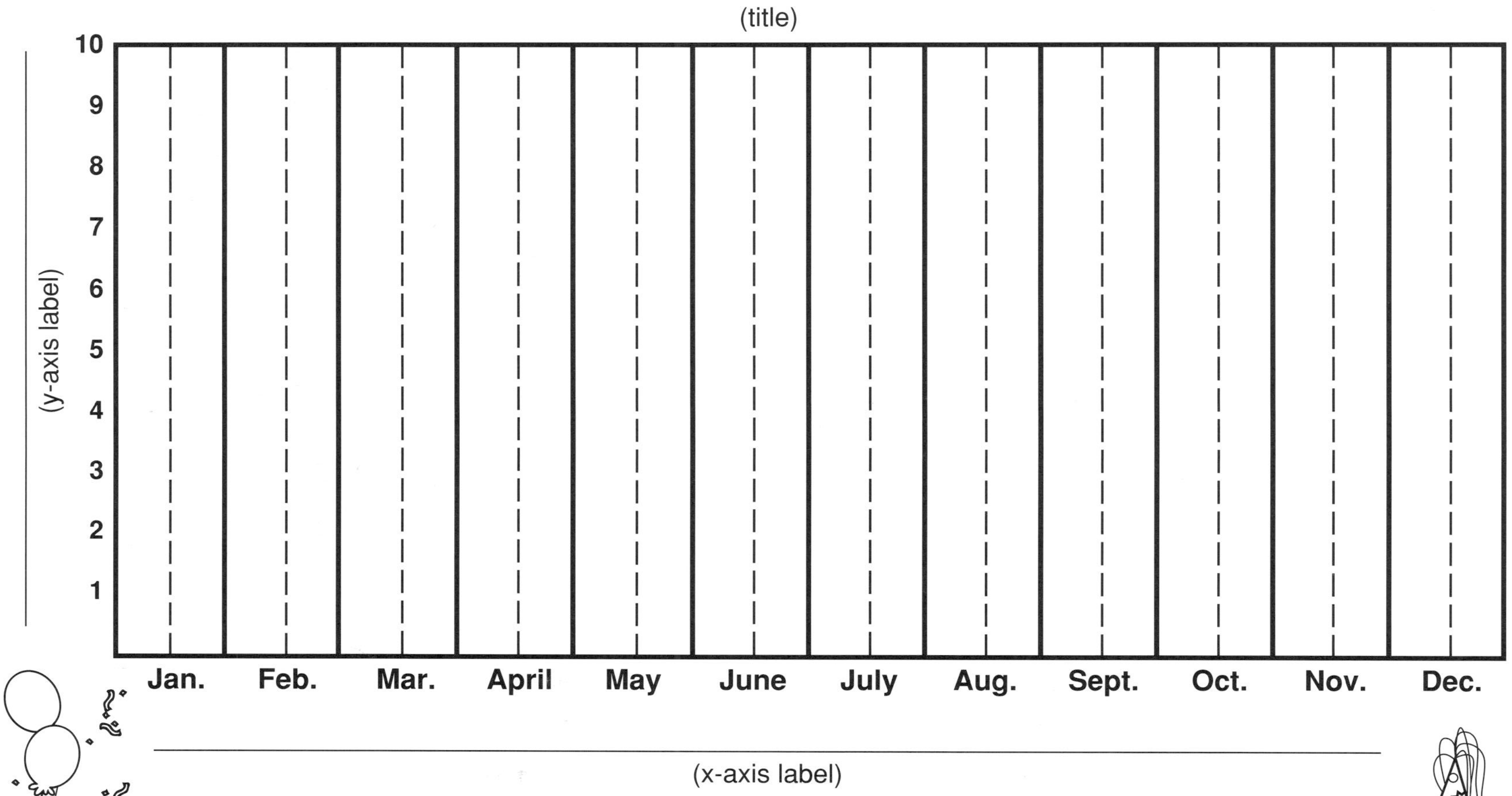

(title)

Jan.	Feb.	Mar.	April	May	June	July	Aug.	Sept.	Oct.	Nov.	Dec.

10
9
8
7
6
5
4
3
2
1

(y-axis label)

(x-axis label)

Key ☐ = boys   ☐ = girls

Bonus Box: On the back of this sheet, record three other topics that would make interesting double bar graphs.

©The Education Center, Inc. • *Ready-to-Go Lessons* • TEC1118

Name: _____

Birth Month: _____

163

How To Extend The Lesson:

- Challenge each student to find examples of different types of graphs in newspapers and magazines. Have each student cut out and attach his graphs to a piece of construction paper. Then direct the student to write a short summary of what each of his selected graphs conveys.

- Have each student use the temperature to create a double bar graph comparing the highs and lows of daily temperatures for a week.

- Provide your students with practice in creating different types of graphs by having them present the same data using a bar graph, line graph, pictograph, and circle graph. Hair color, eye color, and favorite food are quick and easy topics for students to survey and graph for this activity.

- Divide your class into cooperative groups of three to four students. Direct each group to come up with a survey question to ask students in the school; then have each group interview other students to collect data. After each group has collected its data, have it create a bar graph detailing its findings.

Picture This!

Your students will be sure to get the picture about pictographs with this exciting graphing activity!

Skills: Making and interpreting pictographs; classifying information

Estimated Lesson Time: 45 minutes

Teacher Preparation:

1. Duplicate one copy of page 167 for each student.
2. Duplicate one copy of the suitcase pattern on page 168 for each student.
3. Duplicate one copy of the suitcase pattern on page 168 for use in the pictograph key.

Materials:

1 copy of page 167 for each child
1 copy of the suitcase pattern on page 168 for each student and 1 copy for use in the pictograph key
masking tape
several examples of graphs—such as bar graphs, line graphs, and pictographs—from textbooks or periodicals
chart paper

Background Information:

Graphs are a visual method of displaying data. There are many types of graphs. Pictographs use pictures or symbols to communicate information. Pictographs have:

- a title
- two columns
- a symbol to represent data
- a key that gives the value of the symbol

Introducing The Lesson:

Begin by asking your students to name all the different types of graphs they've seen. List their responses on the board. Ask students to describe the different types of information they have seen represented in graphs. Guide students in determining that graphs are used to arrange and communicate important data.

Steps:

1. Tell students that a pictograph is a graph that uses pictures or symbols to convey information. Explain that each symbol represents a specific value. Next share with students the elements of a pictograph outlined on page 165.

2. Tell students that they will be creating a graph using suitcase cutouts to represent data. Draw a two-column by seven-row chart on a sheet of chart paper, making the second column of the chart three times as large as the first. Title the graph "Dream Vacation Destination." Explain to students that the graph's title identifies its subject.

3. In each of the seven rows of the first column, record the name of one of the seven continents.

Dream Vacation Destination

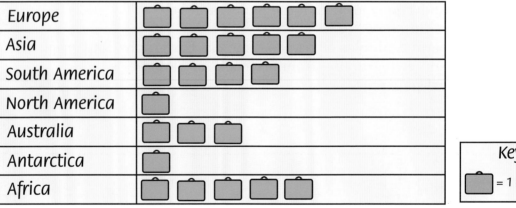

Europe	🧳 🧳 🧳 🧳 🧳 🧳
South America	🧳 🧳 🧳 🧳
North America	🧳
Australia	🧳 🧳 🧳
Antarctica	🧳
Africa	🧳 🧳 🧳 🧳 🧳

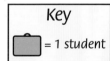

Key

🧳 = 1 student

4. Give each student a cut-out suitcase pattern (page 168) with a rolled piece of masking tape on the back. Explain to each student that her suitcase will be used to represent her vacation preference in the pictograph. Affix an additional suitcase cutout in a key below the graph and record the value of the symbol beside it—in this case, the symbol's value is one student.

5. Have each student place her cutout on the graph beside the name of the continent she would most like to visit.

A Picture-Perfect Vacation

As a travel agent at the Picture-Perfect Travel Agency, you are always looking for the best value to pass along to your customers. Sharon and James Newton explained to you that their only requirement for their upcoming vacation to Hawaii is that the airline on which they fly be the most economical. To make their airline choice clearer, they have asked you to create a pictograph showing the current cost of the round-trip airfare on each of the major airlines from their home in Louisville, Kentucky, to Honolulu, Hawaii.

Directions: Use the airline advertisements from the local newspaper below to create a pictograph for the Newtons. Be sure your pictograph includes these important details:
- a title
- a symbol to represent data
- two columns
- a key that gives the value of the symbol

TRAVEL

Don't Miss Out On Air Across America's Summer Sizzlers!
Newark $80
Miami $185
San Diego $260
Honolulu $620

Friendly Air—We Get You There!
Dallas/Ft. Worth $200
Detroit $175
Honolulu $590
Seattle $435
Washington, DC $155

Fly By Night Airlines Our Name Says It All!
Honolulu $550
New York $175
Salt Lake City $250
Tampa $160

Golden Wing Airlines
Atlanta $145
Baltimore $190
Honolulu $625
Orlando $180
San Antonio $235

Graph Title: _____

Air Across America	
Friendly Air	
Fly By Night Airlines	
Golden Wing Airlines	

Key
=

Bonus Box: Find out the distance in miles from Louisville, Kentucky, to Honolulu, Hawaii. Based on a round-trip flight, how much per mile does it cost to fly to that location for each airline?

How To Extend The Lesson:

• Have students work in pairs to make pictographs using the following population data for the largest cities in the United States taken from the 1990 census. Instruct each pair to determine which symbol to use for its pictograph data, as well as the unit of measure each symbol represents. Provide students with construction paper from which to cut their symbols.

City	Population	City	Population
New York City	7,322,564	Los Angeles	3,485,398
Chicago	2,783,726	Houston	1,630,553
Philadelphia	1,585,577	San Diego	1,110,549
Detroit	1,027,974	Dallas	1,006,877

• Combine science and graphing by having your students make a pictograph of the average life expectancy of various animals.

Animal	Average Life Expectancy	Animal	Average Life Expectancy
opossum	1 year	cat (domestic)	12 years
mouse	3 years	camel	12 years
rabbit	5 years	lion	15 years
kangaroo	7 years	black bear	18 years
squirrel	10 years	gorilla	20 years
pig	10 years	horse	20 years
giraffe	10 years	Asian elephant	40 years
dog (domestic)	12 years	box turtle	100 years

• Challenge each student to consult the most recent almanac for specific data on a topic. Have the student use the data to construct a pictograph on the subject.

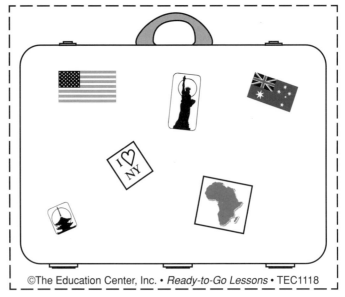

Note To The Teacher: Use suitcase pattern with Step 4 on page 166.

A Method To Your Madness

The scientific method is a great way to capture a child's interest in science. After conducting the following hands-on experiments, your class will be "mad" about science.

Skill: Learning to conduct an experiment using the scientific method

Estimated Lesson Time: 45 minutes

Teacher Preparation:
1. Make one copy of page 171 for each pair of students.
2. Make a transparency of page 171.

Materials:
1 blank transparency
1 transparency marker
1 hairpin for each pair of students
1 copy of page 171 for each pair

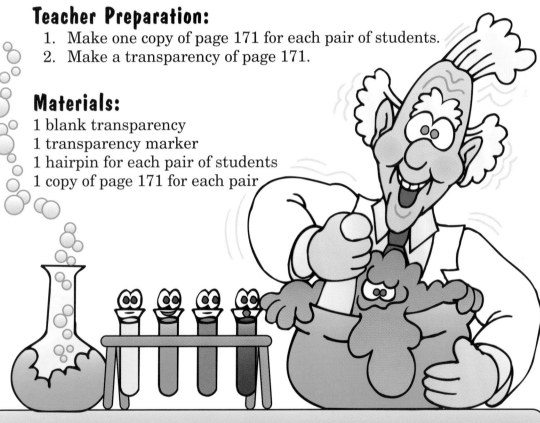

Background Information:
The *scientific method* is an orderly method used in scientific research. It consists of identifying the experiment's purpose, researching and collecting data, formulating a hypothesis, performing the experiment, observing, interpreting the results, and drawing a conclusion.

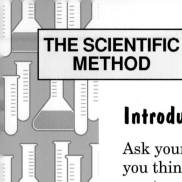

Introducing The Lesson:

Ask your students, "In which position—above your head or down by your sides—do you think the veins in your hands will be more visible?" Remind students that you want predictions only.

Steps:

1. Place the transparency of page 171 on the overhead projector. Identify each step of the scientific method. Tell students they will use the scientific method to find an answer to the question above. Have students help you complete the *purpose, hypothesis, materials,* and *procedure* sections of the lab report (transparency).

2. Instruct each student to hold her hands down by her sides for one minute, then observe the veins on the backs of her hands. Continue the experiment by having each student hold her hands over her head for one minute, then observe the veins on the backs of her hands.

3. Record students' *observations* and *conclusion* on the lab report. *(Holding your hands down by your sides causes the blood to fill the veins in your hands before going back to your heart. Holding your hands above your head causes less pressure on the veins, and they seem to disappear.)*

4. Divide students into pairs. Give each pair a copy of page 171 and a hairpin. Instruct each pair to follow the procedure below, then record its data on the lab report.

   A. Instruct your partner to close her eyes. Gently press one or both points of the hairpin on your partner's arm. Ask your partner to tell you if one or two points of the hairpin are touching her skin. Record the response on the back of this paper. Be sure to include how many points you used and if she guessed correctly.

   B. Repeat the process—touching the back of her hand, fingertip, and neck. Record your results.

   C. Try touching her skin in the same places again with the points of the hairpin farther apart. Record your results.

5. Discuss the results of the experiment. *(Skin is more sensitive in places on the body that have more nerve endings. Fingertips have more nerve endings than the back of the hand, the neck, and the arm. Therefore on the back of the hand, neck, and arm, it is impossible to feel if one or two points are touching the skin, unless the points are wide apart.)*

Name _____

Method To My Madness

Purpose: (Why are you conducting this experiment?) _____

Hypothesis: (What do you think will happen?) _____

Materials: (What items do you need?) _____

Procedure: (What steps will you take to prove or disprove your hypothesis?)

Observations: (What happened?)

Conclusion: (Was your hypothesis correct?)

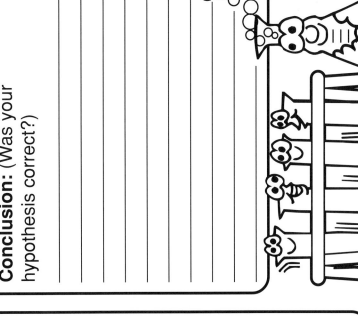

171

How To Extend The Lesson:

For more practice on the scientific method, have students conduct the following experiments:

Experiment 1

Purpose: What happens when the air pressure inside an object is not equal to the air pressure outside the object?

Materials: small plastic cup, index card (large enough to cover the opening of the cup), water, tray to catch spills

Procedure:

1. Hold the index card over the mouth of the cup and turn the cup over. Predict what you think will happen if you let go of the index card.
2. Let go of the index card. Observe and record what happens.
3. Fill the cup 1/2 full of water. Hold the index card over the cup by placing your palm over the card. Quickly turn the cup over. Predict what you think will happen if you let go of the index card.
4. Let go of the index card. Observe and record what happens.

(Since the air pressure inside and outside the empty cup is the same, gravity pulls the paper off the cup. In the cup half-filled with water, the air pressure inside and outside the cup starts out the same. When the cup is turned over, the water level in the cup drops. The amount of air pressure inside the cup, above the water, is less than the air pressure outside the cup. The outside air pressure pushes the paper in, holding the water in the cup.)

Experiment 2

Purpose: What happens when surface tension is broken?

Materials: ground black pepper, small bowl, water, liquid soap

Procedure:

1. Fill the bowl with water.
2. Sprinkle pepper on the surface of the water. Where is most of the pepper?
3. Place a drop of liquid soap on the water near the edge of the bowl.
4. Observe and record what happens.

(The pepper flakes fall to the bottom when the liquid soap is added. Adding the liquid soap reduces the lifting power or the surface tension of the water.)

Wide World Of Plants

Familiarize students with the ways scientists classify plants.

Skill: Classifying plants

Estimated Lesson Time: 45 minutes

Teacher Preparation:
Duplicate one copy of page 175 for each pair of students.

Materials:
(for each pair of students)
1 copy of page 175
1 large sheet of construction paper
yarn
scissors
glue

> A floating duckweed is the smallest flowering plant. Twenty-five of these plants would fit across your fingernail!

> The oldest seed plants are the ancestors of the ginkgo trees. They first appeared in China 180,000,000 years ago when dinosaurs roamed the earth!

Background Information:
- Plants can be divided into two groups—those that reproduce with seeds and those that do not.
- Plants that don't make seeds are *mosses, ferns, fungi,* and *algae*.
- Ferns have roots, stems, and leaves. Mosses, fungi, and algae do not.
- Plants that do make seeds can also be divided into two groups—*angiosperms,* or flowering plants, and *gymnosperms,* or naked seed plants.
- There are two types of angiosperms—*monocots,* those producing seeds with one seed leaf, and *dicots,* those producing seeds with two seed leaves.

Introducing The Lesson:

Ask students to brainstorm the different ways that the class could be divided into two groups.

Steps:

1. Have students stand on one side of the room or the other, according to an *attribute* (a natural characteristic or quality) that you specify. At first, keep the attributes simple; for example, divide boys and girls. Then begin to call out some of the attributes that your students named.

2. After several examples, direct students to return to their seats. Ask students which attributes are the best to use. *(Easily observable, physical attributes generally work best.)*

3. Ask students to name ways to subdivide the larger groups that you divided. Use students' suggestions to make a diagram on the chalkboard similar to the one shown.

4. Point out that scientists use attributes to classify living things. Ask students to name some ways that plants can be grouped. *(By their color, size, or shape of leaves, or by the way they reproduce.)*

5. Pair your students. Give each pair the materials listed on page 173 and one copy of page 175.

6. Instruct the pair to cut apart the cards on the reproducible. Then challenge each pair to use the information on the cards to arrange the cards on the construction paper to make a plant classification chart.

7. Go over the correct arrangement of cards using the answer key on page 317. Instruct each pair to glue the cards in place, connecting the cards with lengths of yarn.

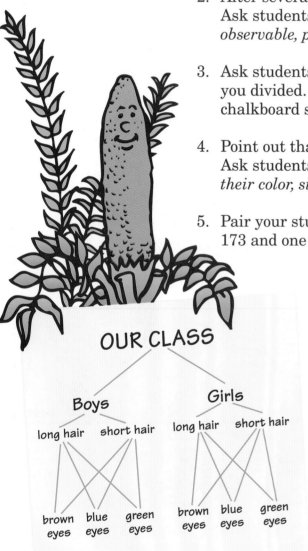

THE PLANT KINGDOM

Nonseed plants with roots, stems, and leaves

— example: ferns

Gymnosperms

— are seed plants that have cones
— are also called *conifers* or *evergreen trees*
— examples: pine, spruce, fir, cedar, bald cypress, hemlock, redwood, yew, and larch trees

Monocotyledons (monocots)

— are angiosperms that produce seeds having only one *cotyledon,* or seed leaf
— have petals in groups of three
— have leaves with parallel veins
— examples: grasses, palms, lilies, and orchids

Seed Plants

— plants that reproduce with seeds

Dicotyledons (dicots)

— are angiosperms that produce seeds having two *cotyledons,* or seed leaves
— have petals in groups of four or five
— have leaves with branching veins
— examples: roses, cacti, oak trees, and sunflowers

Nonseed Plants

— are plants that do not reproduce with seeds

Angiosperms

— are seed plants that have flowers
— include all garden and wildflowers, weeds, plants that produce fruits and vegetables, grasses, grains, and all trees and shrubs that lose their leaves in autumn

Nonseed plants without roots, stems, or leaves

— example: mosses, fungi, and algae

How To Extend The Lesson:

- Divide your class into five groups. Assign each group ten different states to research. Have the group find the names and pictures of the state flowers and trees for its assigned states. Challenge the group to use the pictures, what they've learned about plant classification, and reference materials, to identify each state tree as either an *angiosperm* or a *gymnosperm* and each state flower as a *monocot* or a *dicot*. Compile all researched information into a class chart.

- Encourage each student to take a walk through his yard or neighborhood to observe flowering plants. Instruct the student to write careful notes and make detailed drawings of three specimens that he finds. When he returns to school, challenge the student to use these observations and his research skills to find the scientific names of his three plants. Allow each student to share his findings with the class.

- Pair your students and assign the pair two different plant families, such as the rose and the lily. Challenge the pair to create a Venn diagram comparing and contrasting the two plant families. Have students include information on reproduction, growth, physical characteristics, and environment.

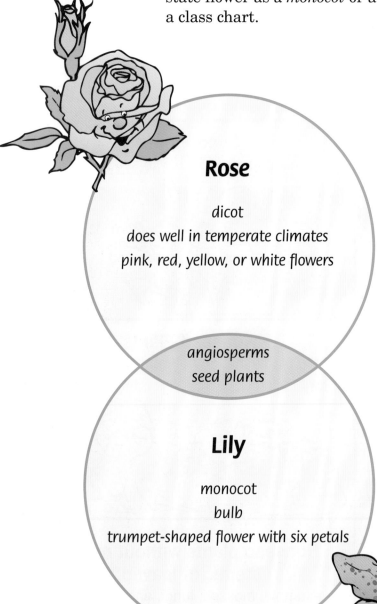

Rose

dicot
does well in temperate climates
pink, red, yellow, or white flowers

angiosperms
seed plants

Lily

monocot
bulb
trumpet-shaped flower with six petals

What's Blooming?

Watch your students' knowledge of flowering plants blossom with this hands-on lesson.

Skill: Identifying each part of a flower and its role in reproduction

Estimated Lesson Time: 1 hour

Teacher Preparation:
1. Duplicate one copy of page 179 for each student.
2. Make a transparency of page 179.

Materials:
1 copy of page 179 for each student
1 blank transparency
1 index card for each student
assorted craft materials such as pipe cleaners, yarn, bag ties,
    egg cartons, construction paper, tissue paper, and clay
tape, scissors, and glue

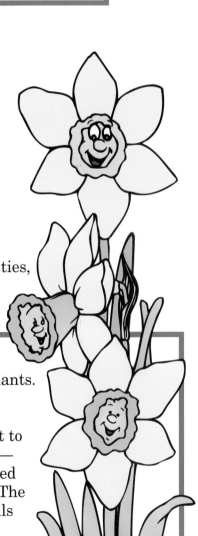

Background Information:
Flowers are the reproductive parts of *angiosperms* or flowering plants. A young flower bud is protected by green leaflike parts called *sepals.*

All flowers are made up of the same basic parts that allow a plant to produce a seed. Most flowers contain both a male part—the *stamen*—and a female part—the *pistil.* The stamen has an enlarged part called an *anther* that grows on the end of a long stalk called the *filament.* The anther produces pollen grains, which develop into sperm. Most pistils have three main parts: the *stigma, style,* and *ovary.*

The transfer of pollen from the anther to the stigma is called *pollination.* The surface of the stigma is sticky to catch pollen grains. A pollen grain will swell as it absorbs sugar and water from the stigma, and it will begin to grow a tube through the slender style down to the ovary. The ovary contains one or more ovules where egg cells are formed. *Fertilization* occurs when a pollen tube enters an ovule in the ovary. The fertilized egg then develops into a seed and the ovary grows into a structure called the *fruit.*

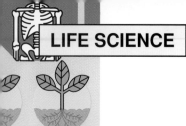

Introducing The Lesson:

To begin, have students name the main parts of a green plant—*roots, stem, seeds, leaves, flowers.* Ask students if they know the purpose of a flower. Explain to the class that the flower is the reproductive part of the plant.

Steps:

1. Display the transparency you created of page 179 and distribute one copy of page 179 to each child.

2. Use the Background Information on page 177 to name each flower part and explain its function in the reproduction of a plant. As you discuss each part, write its name on the line next to the appropriate definition. Have each student copy the information from the transparency onto his paper. Then instruct each student to write each numbered word in the appropriate numbered blank of the illustration at the top of page 179. Tell students to use this reproducible as a reference throughout their study of plants.

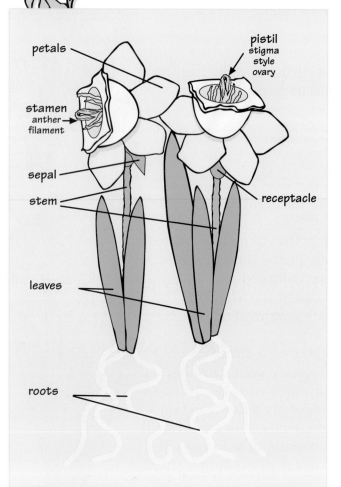

3. Divide the class into groups. Provide each group with scissors, tape, glue, index cards, and a variety of craft materials to choose from.

4. Tell each student to create a model of a flower using any materials that are on his group's table. Instruct him to include on the model all the plant parts that were discussed in this lesson. Have him use page 179 as a reference.

5. Have each student write a paragraph on an index card explaining what he used for each part of the flower. Attach the index card to the model flower and display it in the school media center.

Playing An Important Part

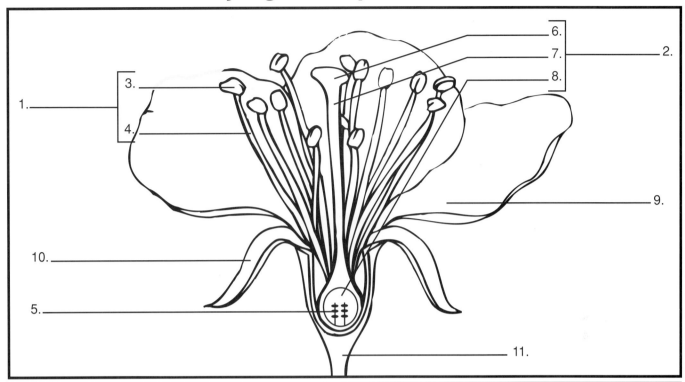

Parts Of A Flower

• anther	• ovules	• pistil	• sepal	• stigma	• ovary
• filament	• petal	• receptacle	• stamen	• style	

Use the diagram above and the clues to help you fill in the correct plant parts.

1. _____ —male reproductive part of a flower

2. _____ —female reproductive part of a flower

3. _____ —produces pollen grains which develop sperm

4. _____ —supports the anther

5. _____ —become the seeds when sperm cells fertilize the egg cells

6. _____ —sticky, pollen-receptive part of the pistil

7. _____ —the stalk of the pistil down which the pollen tube grows

8. _____ —contains the ovules and becomes the fruit

9. _____ —colorful part of a flower used to attract insects and birds

10. _____ —protects the bud of a young flower

11. _____ —reproductive parts of a plant are attached here

Bonus Box: What do you think is the most important part of the flower? Defend your answer on the back of this paper.

How To Extend The Lesson:

- Discuss the different agents of pollination—insects, birds, and wind. Divide the class into groups. Have each group create a poster using illustrations and labels to show how one of these agents aids in pollination. For example, have students illustrate the following sequence of events:
  1. A bee looks for nectar on a flower.
  2. Pollen collects on its body and legs.
  3. Pollen falls from the bee and sticks to the stigma of a flower.
  4. Pollen grains swell as they absorb sugar and water.
  5. A pollen tube begins to grow through the style.
  6. Fertilization occurs when a pollen tube enters the ovule.
  7. The ovary enlarges and seeds form.

- Have each student write a story about a typical day from the perspective of an insect or a bird that aids in the pollination of flowers.

- Have students research the work of Gregor Mendel and his impact on how plants are grown today. Mendel was a botanist who experimented in crossing plants—taking pollen from one flower and using it to pollinate a flower with an opposite trait.

Spotlight On Cells

Plant and animal cells are center stage with this helpful lesson.

> **Skill:** Identifying the parts of plant and animal cells

Estimated Lesson Time: 1 hour

Teacher Preparation:
1. Copy the diagram from page 182 onto a sheet of chart paper or a transparency.
2. Duplicate a copy of page 183 for each student.
3. Gather the materials listed below.

Materials:
1 sheet of chart paper or a blank transparency
1 copy of page 183 for each student
crayons or colored pencils, scissors, glue, and
   a 9" x 12" sheet of drawing paper for
   each student

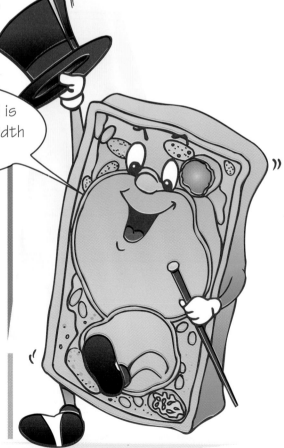

> An average animal cell is about one one-thousandth of an inch across.

Background Information:
All living things are made up of one or more cells. A cell is the basic unit of structure and function in an organism. There are billions of life forms that consist of a single cell and can be seen only with a microscope. Larger life forms have millions of cells. These larger organisms not only have a greater number of cells, but also have different kinds of cells within the same body. Each cell's structure and contents allow it to do a specialized job and contribute to the process of keeping the organism alive.

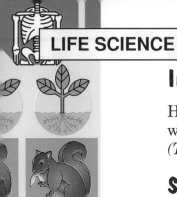

Introducing The Lesson:

Have students name the largest animal they can think of. Then ask them what the tiniest living organism and this large animal have in common. *(They are both composed of cells.)*

Steps:

1. Share the Background Information on page 181 with your students. Point out that cells, like all living things, are made up of parts.

2. Use the diagram and the definitions below to explain the structure and function of each cell part. Explain to students that these are the main parts of a cell, but not all of them.

3. Have students compare the two cells. Help students recognize that plant and animal cells are basically the same, except for two features. Have students identify these features. *(Plant cells have cell walls and chloroplasts; animal cells do not.)*

4. Distribute one copy of page 183, crayons or colored pencils, scissors, glue, and one 9" x 12" sheet of drawing paper to each student. Have the student complete the sheet as directed. Then check and discuss the completed sheets as a class.

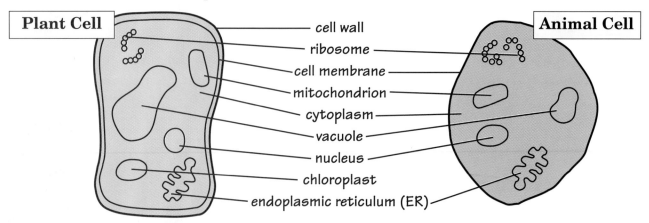

Cell Structures And Their Functions

- cell wall: nonliving structure surrounding a plant cell; provides shape and support
- cell membrane: encloses the cell; controls the inward and outward flow of materials
- chloroplasts: contain chlorophyll and are used by plants to make food
- cytoplasm: jellylike material where chemical processes take place
- mitochondria: rodlike structures that release energy from food and supply energy to other parts of the cell
- vacuoles: fluid-filled sacs that store different substances in liquid form
- nucleus: stores information and controls cell activities; is surrounded by a membrane that separates it from the rest of the cell
- ribosomes: particles in cytoplasm that look like small balls; build the proteins needed by a cell
- endoplasmic reticulum (ER): a network of membranes that run throughout the cytoplasm and form tubes through which materials move to all cell parts

Playing The Perfect Part

Each part of a cell has a special role to play. Color the pictures on the right-hand side of this page. Cut along the dashed lines of each picture at the right. Read each clue; then glue each circle onto the appropriate place of the diagram.

Plant Cell

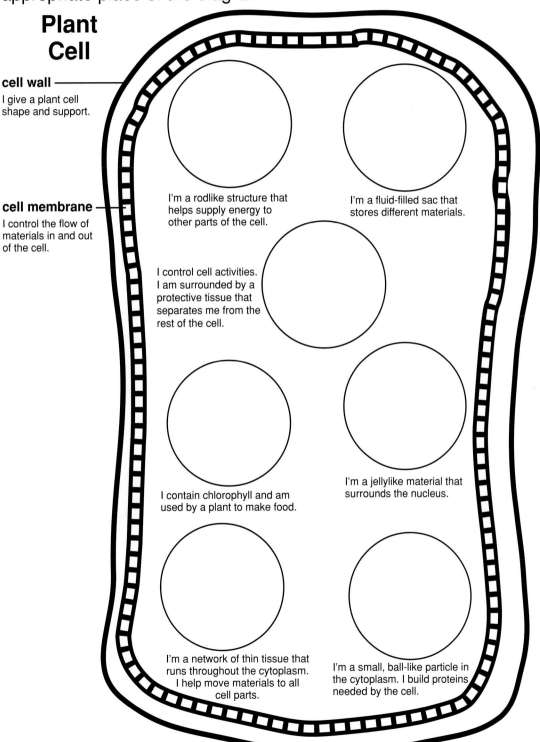

cell wall
I give a plant cell shape and support.

cell membrane
I control the flow of materials in and out of the cell.

I'm a rodlike structure that helps supply energy to other parts of the cell.

I'm a fluid-filled sac that stores different materials.

I control cell activities. I am surrounded by a protective tissue that separates me from the rest of the cell.

I contain chlorophyll and am used by a plant to make food.

I'm a jellylike material that surrounds the nucleus.

I'm a network of thin tissue that runs throughout the cytoplasm. I help move materials to all cell parts.

I'm a small, ball-like particle in the cytoplasm. I build proteins needed by the cell.

ribosome

nucleus

chloroplast

vacuole

endoplasmic reticulum (ER)

mitochondrion

cytoplasm

Note: These are the main parts of a cell, but not all of them. Drawings are not to scale.

Bonus Box: Draw an animal cell on another sheet of paper. Color and label each cell part.

How To Extend The Lesson:

- Review the parts of a plant cell and an animal cell with your students. Then have them suggest various everyday materials that they can associate with each cell part. *(Examples: cell membrane—a mesh bag, chloroplasts—green grapes, ribosomes—candy sprinkles)* Next provide each student with a light-colored, 12" x 18" sheet of construction paper. For homework, direct the student to create a three-dimensional picture of a plant or animal cell using arts-and-crafts supplies and/or odds and ends found around the home. Encourage students to be creative. The following school day, have students share their completed projects. Have them cast their votes for the most creative cells.

- Follow the directions below to prepare slides of plant and animal cells. Place the slides, a microscope, markers or colored pencils, and a supply of drawing paper at a center. In turn direct each student to the center. Instruct the student to use the microscope (at a high power) to observe the cells. Then have the student draw a labeled picture of what he observed about each cell.

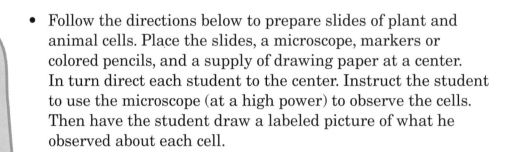

A muscle cell

A blood cell

A nerve cell

A fat cell

A skin cell is flat, hard, and tough. It protects the delicate body parts beneath it.

A bone cell

> **Materials:** 2 droppers, 2 slides and coverslips, iodine, toothpick, tweezers, 1 onion
>
> **Directions For Preparing Slides:**
> 1. Use a dropper to place a small amount of iodine on a slide. Using the toothpick, gently scrape the inside of your cheek. Place the scraping in the drop of iodine; then cover it with a coverslip.
> 2. Use a dropper to place a small amount of iodine on a slide. Use the tweezers to peel a thin, clear piece of skin from an inside section of an onion. Place the onion skin in the iodine. Add a coverslip.

- Draw a large outline of a human body and post it on a wall or bulletin board. Place a supply of markers or crayons and reference materials near the board. Remind students that the human body is a complex organism made of different types of cells. (Examples include muscle, blood, nerve, bone, skin, and fat cells.) Pair students and assign each pair a different type of body cell. Direct each pair to use the materials to illustrate a labeled picture of the cell and its parts. In turn have the pair draw its illustration on the body outline and write a caption beside the cell explaining the cell's function.

Spine-Tingling Science

Get "back" to the basics of classification with this exciting lesson!

Skill: Classifying animals as vertebrates and invertebrates

Estimated Lesson Time: 45 minutes

Teacher Preparation:
1. Duplicate the reproducible on page 187 for each student.
2. Collect several pictures of vertebrates and invertebrates from magazines.

Materials:
8–10 pictures of animals (including pictures of both vertebrates and invertebrates)
1 copy of page 187 for each student
2 metal rings for each student

Dr. Kyra Practer
Chiropractor

Background Information:
The scientific practice of classifying animals according to similar characteristics is known as *taxonomy.* All living things are divided into a series of groups and subgroups. The largest of these groups is known as a *kingdom.* Scientists classify most living things into two kingdoms—the plant kingdom and the animal kingdom.

The animal kingdom is broken down into subgroups, each of which is called a *phylum.* The phylum *Chordata* is made up of *vertebrates,* animals with backbones. There are about 40,000 species of vertebrates. The major classes of vertebrates include fish, amphibians, reptiles, birds, and mammals.

The remaining phyla are made up of *invertebrates,* animals that do not have backbones. There are more than one million species of invertebrates in the animal kingdom.

Fast Facts:
* Invertebrates make up more than 90 percent of the world's animal population, and vertebrates make up the remaining 10 percent.
* Some invertebrates are microscopic, whereas others, such as the giant squid, are large enough to take on a sperm whale!

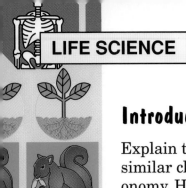

Introducing The Lesson:

Explain to students that scientists classify living things into categories based on similar characteristics. Point out that this classification process is known as taxonomy. Have ten student volunteers come to the front of the classroom. Challenge the remaining students to classify the student volunteers into categories based on a physical attribute such as hair color, eye color, or sex. Record the results on the board.

Steps:

1. Continue the classification activity by reclassifying the student volunteers using a different physical attribute. Encourage students to continue to divide each subgroup based on additional similarities and differences.

2. Show your students several pictures of animals that include examples of both vertebrates and invertebrates.

3. Challenge students to group the animal pictures into categories based on their similar characteristics or attributes.

4. On the board record the specific categories students used to classify the animals in the photos.

5. Share the Background Information on page 185 with your students. Explain that one way to classify animals is by determining if they have a backbone. Direct each student to stand and run his fingers up and down the center of his back. Explain that what he feels is his *vertebral column* or backbone.

6. Distribute one copy of page 187 to each student; then have him complete it as directed. Provide each student with two metal rings. Have him use a hole puncher to punch a hole in the upper left-hand corner of each cut-out card from page 187. Direct the student to place the vertebrate cards on one ring and the invertebrate cards on the other ring. Allow students to create other animal cards, placing each card on the appropriate ring.

Doctor, Doctor!

Dr. Kyra Practer has lost her patients' files and needs your help! Dr. Practer sees only patients that have backbones. Help Dr. Practer identify her patients by sorting the following animals using the directions provided.

Directions: Color the cards; then cut them apart. On the back of each card, write the animal's name, its classification (vertebrate or invertebrate), and one interesting fact about the animal.

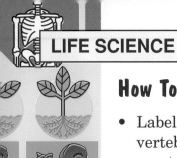

How To Extend The Lesson:

- Label a bulletin board with the heading "We've Got Class!" Record each of the five vertebrate classes—fish, amphibians, reptiles, birds, and mammals—on a separate construction-paper strip. Then divide the bulletin board into five sections and staple one of the labeled strips to the top of each section. Challenge students to look through old magazines to find examples of animals that fall into each of the five classes. Staple the animal pictures under the appropriate column to create an eye-catching display.

- Challenge students to learn more about invertebrates with this newsworthy idea! Discuss how an employment advertisement provides information on the credentials needed for a particular job. Divide students into groups; then assign each group one of the invertebrate phyla below. Have each group research information about its phylum and create an employment advertisement that includes the characteristics an organism needs to be successful in that phylum. Have each group share its ad with the rest of the class. Then assemble the ads into a class newspaper titled *Invertebrate Times.*

Protozoans: single-celled microscopic animals
Poriferons: animals with large pores
Coelenterates: water animals with stinging tendons
Ctenophores: animals with rows of little combs covering their bodies
Flatworms: animals that are thin and flat like ribbon
Nematodes: roundworms
Molluscs: soft-bodied animals that have shells to protect themselves
Annelids: segmented worms
Arthropods: animals with jointed legs and segmented bodies
Echinoderms: animals with many spines projecting from their bodies

- Give your students some additional practice with taxonomy by having them classify everyday items into categories based on similar characteristics. Bring in advertisements for automobiles, music CDs, toys, clothing, or any other product that might interest students. Then group students according to their interest in a particular product. Have each group classify the items featured in its advertisement into categories. For example, a group classifying music CDs might have categories for country, rock and roll, rap, and pop music. Direct the group to break down the categories even further based on criteria the group decides to use in its classification process. For example, rock and roll could be further broken down into heavy metal, alternative, and classic rock. Have each group create a chart or diagram to show how it chose to classify the items into categories.

It's All A Balancing Act

Help your students understand the delicate balance between plants, animals, and humans within our environment.

Skill: Recognizing the characteristics of different ecosystems

Estimated Lesson Time: 1 hour

Teacher Preparation:
1. Collect pictures of plants and animals within an ecosystem.
2. Gather research materials on ecosystems.
3. Duplicate one copy of page 191 for each student.

Materials:
pictures of plants and animals from an ecosystem
research materials on ecosystems
6 sheets of chart paper
6 large, light-colored sheets of bulletin-board paper or butcher paper
markers or colored pencils
1 copy of page 191 for each student
encyclopedias

Background Information:
An *ecosystem* includes the community of plants and animals that live within a certain area of our environment. These plants and animals rely on one another for survival: food, shelter, and protection. The earth supports a variety of ecosystems, including *deserts, forests, the tundra, oceans, grasslands,* and *wetlands.* Each ecosystem has its own unique characteristics, such as climate, terrain, and plant and animal life. The connection between the plants and animals within the ecosystem is so strong that any singular change can affect the balance of an entire ecosystem.

Introducing The Lesson:

Show students several pictures of various plants and animals within a particular ecosystem, such as wetlands or a desert. Ask students to explain any relationships between the plants and animals in these pictures. *(Example: The trees are supported by the soil, the coyote lives among trees, the coyote preys upon rabbits, rabbits eat plants, and plants are supported by the soil.)*

Steps:

1. Explain to students that plants, animals, and their surroundings are all linked together. They rely upon one another in what we call an *ecosystem.*

2. Tell students that the earth supports a variety of ecosystems including the following: *deserts, forests, the tundra, oceans, grasslands,* and *wetlands.* Each ecosystem has its own unique characteristics, such as climate, terrain, and plant and animal life. Ask students to name a specific characteristic of one of the ecosystems. *(Examples: The climate of the tundra is very, very cold. Oceans are composed of salt water.)*

3. Divide students into six groups and assign each group an ecosystem. Supply each group with research materials, a large piece of bulletin-board or butcher paper, and markers or colored pencils. Instruct each group to research the climate, terrain, and plant and animal life of its ecosystem. Then have each group draw a mural illustrating the characteristics of its ecosystem. Instruct each group to include at least five examples of interdependence among the inhabitants of its ecosystem. Finally have each group label and color its mural, then share its findings with the rest of the class.

4. Explain to your students that the connection between the plants and animals within an ecosystem is so strong that even a small change can affect the balance of the entire ecosystem. Appoint one member of each group as Recorder, giving each Recorder a piece of chart paper and a marker. Then have the class brainstorm as many changes as possible that would upset the balance of each ecosystem, including interference by humans. As each ecosystem is discussed, have that group's Recorder write the information on his piece of chart paper. Display the murals and the lists of changes in the hallway for all to view.

5. Give one copy of page 191 to each student. Have the student complete the page as directed.

Picture This!

Picture this—you're a world traveler studying the earth's numerous ecosystems: *deserts, forests, the tundra, oceans, grasslands, wetlands.* Each ecosystem has its own characteristics—such as climate, terrain, and plant and animal life—that make it unique.

Directions: Read each sentence below. Decide which ecosystem the sentence is describing. Then write the number of that fact in the appropriate snapshot. If you need help, use an encyclopedia. Bon voyage!

1. I'm a large expanse of land covered with tall grasses.
2. I'm also known as a *prairie* or *savanna.*
3. I cover one-seventh of the earth's land surface, but because of environmental changes, that amount is increasing.
4. My temperature range is from less than 0°C to never above 10°C.
5. I cover about 70 percent of the earth's surface.
6. I cover about 30 percent of the earth's land.
7. I receive less than ten inches of moisture a year.
8. I have a variety of plants and animals that live at different depths.
9. Most of my land in the United States has been plowed under and used for agricultural land.
10. I don't receive enough precipitation to support large trees.
11. I provide homes for birds, insects, and animals, as well as sources of medicines.
12. I can be located near an ocean and contain salt water, or in forests and contain freshwater.
13. I'm an area that helps absorb carbon dioxide, produce oxygen, and prevent erosion.
14. I can be located in very cold or very warm climates.
15. The ground below my surface stays frozen all year.
16. I'm the name for the plains of the arctic circle.
17. I'm primarily salt water.
18. Many plants and animals thrive in my hostile environment.
19. I provide homes for birds, fish, animals, and insects.
20. I include many species of fish and invertebrates.
21. My areas contain permanent moisture: bogs, swamps, marshes, estuaries, ponds, lakes, and rivers.
22. I contain tropical, temperate, coniferous, and deciduous trees.

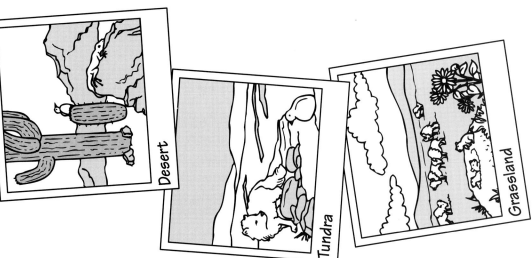

Desert

Tundra

Grassland

Ocean

Wetlands

Forest

How To Extend The Lesson:

- Challenge each student to go to an area in her backyard or a nearby park and to sit quietly for a period of time to observe. Instruct the student to take along a journal or a piece of paper and pencil with which to record her observations. Have the student record as many evidences as possible of interactions among the plants and animals. Have the students bring in their lists on a designated day to share with their classmates.

- Take a field trip to an ecosystem in your area. Instruct students to move through it quietly and to make observations without disturbing the balance of nature. If this is not possible, invite a local expert to your classroom to share photographs and information about a particular ecosystem.

- Have each student write a letter to a national environmental organization expressing his concern and asking how he can get involved in protecting our ecosystems.

- Post a large piece of bulletin-board paper on a wall. Divide this paper into bricklike sections. Then encourage students to find out more about ecosystems of the world by providing books and periodicals with inviting pictures and interesting information. As each student learns something new about an ecosystem, have her write this information in one of the bricks on the wall.

Go With The Flow

Expose your students to the wonders of the human circulatory system with this hands-on lesson.

Skill: Recognizing and identifying the components of the circulatory system

Estimated Lesson Time: 45 minutes

Teacher Preparation:

1. Make a copy of page 195 for each group of students.
2. Cut one 5-foot sheet of white bulletin-board paper for each group of students.

Materials:

1 empty one-quart milk or juice container
1 bucket (5 quarts or larger)
1 copy of page 195 for each group of students
blue and red yarn
one 5-foot sheet of white bulletin-board or butcher paper for each group of students
scissors and glue for each group of students

Background Information:

The circulatory system transports food and oxygen all over the body. The heart acts as a pump for the blood, which flows through a complex series of *arteries, capillaries,* and *veins.* The blood flowing through the arteries carries oxygenated blood and dissolved food. The arteries divide into smaller blood vessels called capillaries. Oxygen and food pass through the capillary walls into the cells of the body. Blood leaving the capillaries has lost its oxygen and carries waste products away from the body's cells. The capillaries join together to form larger vessels called veins. Veins carry deoxygenated blood and waste products back to the heart. The used blood then goes to the lungs, where it expels carbon dioxide and is refreshed with oxygen. It takes blood about one minute to make a complete circuit around the body.

Introducing The Lesson:

Show your students a one-quart carton. Explain that an average person's body contains nearly five quarts of blood, or five one-quart cartons. Demonstrate how much blood that is by filling up the carton with water and dumping it into a bucket five times.

Steps:

1. Ask students to volunteer information they know about how blood circulates through the body. Record students' responses on the board.

2. Share with your students the Background Information on page 193.

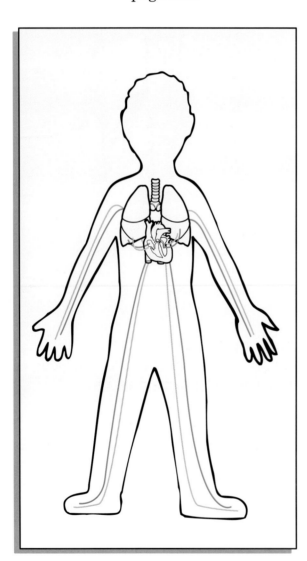

3. Remind students that this process takes place in a short amount of time and that the heart is a very strong muscle.

4. Divide your students into groups of four. Provide each group with a copy of page 195 and a five-foot piece of chart paper, blue and red yarn, scissors, and glue.

5. Direct each group to complete page 195 as directed to create a model of the human circulatory system.

6. Display the completed models in the hall for others to view.

Go With The Flow

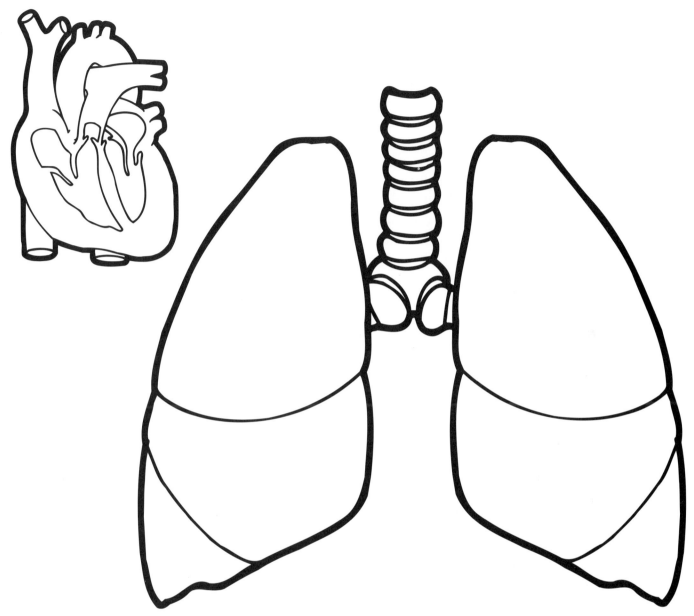

Directions for mapping the flow of blood in the human body:

1. Lay the paper provided by your teacher on the floor. Have one group member lie on the paper faceup. Use a pencil to carefully trace an outline of the student's body.
2. Cut out the heart and lungs on this sheet.
3. Glue the organs in the correct location on your group's paper outline.
4. Glue lengths of red yard, representing oxygenated blood, from the heart down to each hand and each foot.
5. Glue lengths of blue yarn, representing deoxygenated blood, going from each hand and foot back to the heart.
6. Glue additional lengths of blue yarn from the heart to the lungs to show the flow of blood as it moves to the lungs to be reoxygenated.
7. Finally, attach more red yarn from the lungs back to the heart to show the flow of reoxygenated blood from the lungs to the heart.
8. Have each group member sign his or her name at the bottom of your life-size diagram.

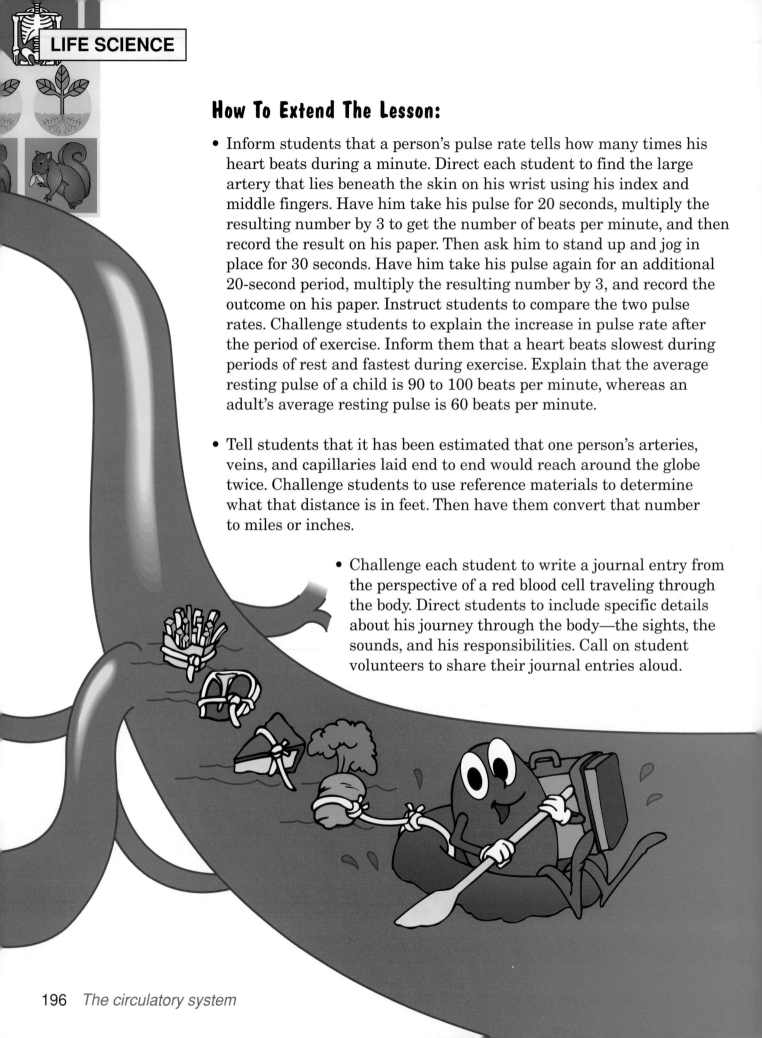

How To Extend The Lesson:

- Inform students that a person's pulse rate tells how many times his heart beats during a minute. Direct each student to find the large artery that lies beneath the skin on his wrist using his index and middle fingers. Have him take his pulse for 20 seconds, multiply the resulting number by 3 to get the number of beats per minute, and then record the result on his paper. Then ask him to stand up and jog in place for 30 seconds. Have him take his pulse again for an additional 20-second period, multiply the resulting number by 3, and record the outcome on his paper. Instruct students to compare the two pulse rates. Challenge students to explain the increase in pulse rate after the period of exercise. Inform them that a heart beats slowest during periods of rest and fastest during exercise. Explain that the average resting pulse of a child is 90 to 100 beats per minute, whereas an adult's average resting pulse is 60 beats per minute.

- Tell students that it has been estimated that one person's arteries, veins, and capillaries laid end to end would reach around the globe twice. Challenge students to use reference materials to determine what that distance is in feet. Then have them convert that number to miles or inches.

- Challenge each student to write a journal entry from the perspective of a red blood cell traveling through the body. Direct students to include specific details about his journey through the body—the sights, the sounds, and his responsibilities. Call on student volunteers to share their journal entries aloud.

Lights, Camera, Digestion!

Use this lesson to introduce your students to the star-studded cast responsible for human digestion.

Skills: Identifying the parts and function of the digestive system

Estimated Lesson Time: 45 minutes

Teacher Preparation:
1. Duplicate one copy of page 199 for each student.
2. Cut three lengths of yarn.

Materials:
1 copy of page 199 for each student
3 lengths of yarn cut to 1 foot, 3 feet, and 30 feet
scissors
glue

Background Information:
The digestive system is made up of a group of organs that break food down for use in the body. The broken-down food particles that result from the process of digestion provide the body with necessary nutrients.

The main part of the digestive system is the alimentary canal, a tube that begins at the mouth and continues on through the pharynx, esophagus, stomach, small intestine, large intestine, and rectum. An average human's alimentary canal is about 30 feet long.

Fast Facts:
- The human mouth makes about 1/2 quart of saliva a day. The body secretes more than 7 quarts of digestive juices daily.

- The appendix is a remnant of a longer intestine. Animals that graze for their food use the appendix for fermentation.

- The average person eats about 3 pounds of food each day or 1,095 pounds of food each year.

WOW! That's long!

Introducing The Lesson:

Have three student volunteers come to the front of the classroom. Give each volunteer a precut length of yarn and have him display it for the rest of the class. Challenge the remaining students to guess which length of yarn represents the length of the *alimentary canal,* the series of connected digestive organs that begins at the mouth and extends to the rectum.

Steps:

1. Have each student record his guess—1 foot, 3 feet, or 30 feet—on a scrap of paper.

2. Call on several student volunteers to share their answers and the reasons for the choices they make.

3. Explain that the answer is 30 feet. Tell your students that the human digestive system is made up of about 30 feet of connected organs known as the *alimentary canal.* Point out that the alimentary canal includes the mouth, pharynx, esophagus, stomach, small intestine, large intestine, and rectum.

4. Ask your students to explain how it is possible for 30 feet of organs to fit inside a human body. Guide the students into understanding that many of the organs must bend in order to fit into the body cavity. Coil up the yarn to demonstrate that point.

5. Explain to the class that when a person eats, he first places food in his *mouth.* Then the *pharynx* pushes the chewed food into the *esophagus.* The esophagus then moves in wavelike contractions and pushes the food into the *stomach.*

6. Share with students that special juices in the stomach help digest the food. Tell students that the resulting mixture is then emptied into the *small intestine,* where juices from the *pancreas, liver,* and the intestinal wall continue to digest the food. Point out that the remaining undigested food is then passed into the *large intestine* and then out of the body through the *rectum.*

7. To further investigate the digestive system, provide each student with scissors, glue, and a copy of page 199. Have him complete the activity as directed.

Meet The Cast

As food travels along the path to complete digestion, it comes into contact with a diverse cast of characters (organs), each of whom plays an important part in completing digestion.

Directions: Cut out each filmstrip square. Read the information on each square; then decide the order in which food meets the cast of characters as it flows through the digestive system. Glue the strips in order by placing each strip on the bottom of the one before it.

Cast Of Characters

The Small Intestine	The Esophagus
The Pharynx	The Mouth
The Large Intestine	The Stomach

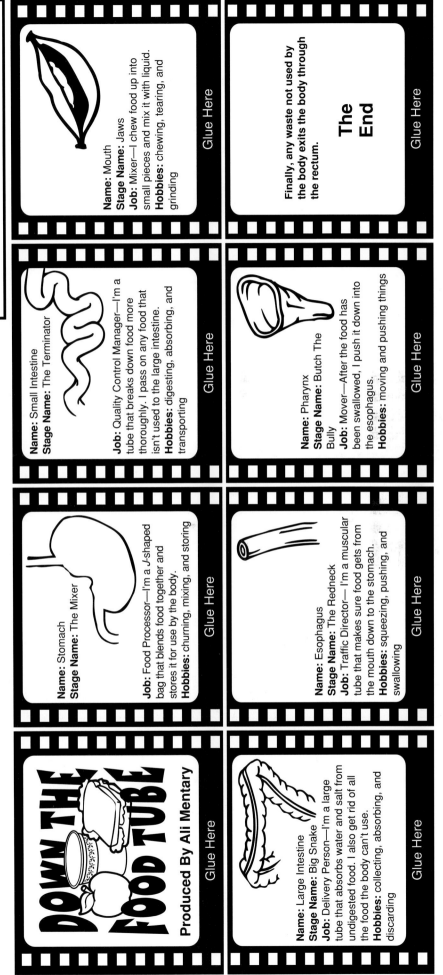

Name: Mouth
Stage Name: Jaws
Job: Mixer—I chew food up into small pieces and mix it with liquid.
Hobbies: chewing, tearing, and grinding
Glue Here

Name: Small Intestine
Stage Name: The Terminator
Job: Quality Control Manager—I'm a tube that breaks down food more thoroughly. I pass on any food that isn't used to the large intestine.
Hobbies: digesting, absorbing, and transporting
Glue Here

Name: Stomach
Stage Name: The Mixer
Job: Food Processor—I'm a J-shaped bag that blends food together and stores it for use by the body.
Hobbies: churning, mixing, and storing
Glue Here

DOWN THE FOOD TUBE
Produced By Ali Mentary
Glue Here

Finally, any waste not used by the body exits the body through the rectum.

The End
Glue Here

Name: Pharynx
Stage Name: Butch The Bully
Job: Mover—After the food has been swallowed, I push it down into the esophagus.
Hobbies: moving and pushing things
Glue Here

Name: Esophagus
Stage Name: The Redneck
Job: Traffic Director—I'm a muscular tube that makes sure food gets from the mouth down to the stomach.
Hobbies: squeezing, pushing, and swallowing
Glue Here

Name: Large Intestine
Stage Name: Big Snake
Job: Delivery Person—I'm a large tube that absorbs water and salt from undigested food. I also get rid of all the food the body can't use.
Hobbies: collecting, absorbing, and discarding
Glue Here

How To Extend The Lesson:

• Divide your students into groups of three or four. Give each group a large sheet of chart paper. Have each group trace the outline of one of its members onto the chart paper. Then direct the students to use construction paper, scissors, and glue to make a model of the digestive system for the outline. Post the completed outlines in your classroom and refer to them throughout your study of the digestive system.

Yum! This tastes sweet!

• Remind students that digestion begins in the mouth. Explain to students that saliva excreted in the mouth contains enzymes that help break food down. Point out that one of these enzymes, *amylase,* turns starches into sugars during the digestive process. Demonstrate the process of turning starches into sugars by giving each student a saltine cracker. Have the student bite the cracker and hold it in his mouth for several minutes before swallowing it. Then have the student describe how the cracker's taste changed. *(The starch in the cracker turns to sugar, and the cracker tastes sweet.)*

• Challenge each student to assume the identity of his favorite food. Have the student write a narrative as if he were the food being consumed by a fifth-grade student during lunch. Encourage the student to include specific details about the trip he takes through the fifth grader's digestive system. Have each student share his completed narrative with the rest of the class. Post the narratives on a bulletin board titled "Adventures In Digestion."

Presto Change-O!

Show your students the magic of matter with the following lesson on physical and chemical changes!

Skill: Identifying physical and chemical changes in matter

Estimated Lesson Time: 45 minutes

Teacher Preparation:
1. Make one copy of page 203 for each student.
2. Make an overhead transparency of the chart at the right (or copy the information onto a sheet of chart paper).

Materials:
1 blank transparency and a
   transparency pen or 1 sheet of
   chart paper and a marker
1 20-ounce plastic soda bottle
1/2 cup vinegar
2 tablespoons baking soda
1 medium-sized balloon
tape
1 cookie
knife
1 copy of page 203 for each student

	Definite Shape?	Definite Size?	Examples
Solid	yes	yes	wood iron glass
Liquid	no	yes	water gasoline milk
Gas	no	no	air oxygen carbon dioxide

Background Information:
   Everything in the universe is made up of *matter*. Matter comes in three different states: *solid, liquid,* and *gas*. The chart above shows characteristics and examples of each state of matter.
   There are two kinds of changes that occur in the matter around us all the time: *physical changes* and *chemical changes*. However, these two kinds of changes are very different from each other. A physical change takes place when only the physical characteristics of a substance are changed, and it is still the same substance. For example, wood is chopped, glass is broken, or ice is melted. Changing its state, such as from a solid to a liquid or a liquid to a gas, is also a physical change in matter. When a substance undergoes a physical change, it can usually be changed back to its original size, shape, or appearance. A chemical change takes place when the properties of one substance are changed so that a new substance with different properties is formed. Some examples of chemical changes are the burning of wood, the rusting of iron, or the digestion of food. For a chemical change to occur, energy is either needed or given off during the process.

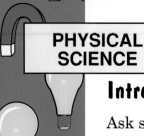

Introducing The Lesson:

Ask student volunteers to look around the room and give examples of matter—such as a chair, the chalkboard, the water fountain, and air. Next have each student volunteer tell what state of matter *(solid, liquid, or gas)* the thing is that he has named. Display the transparency or chart-paper drawing that you created of the chart on page 43. Briefly review the three states of matter and the characteristics and examples of each.

Steps:

1. Share with students the second paragraph in the Background Information on page 201.

2. Complete the teacher demonstration below for your students. Then ask students the following questions:
   • What two substances did I begin with? *(baking soda and vinegar)*
   • What happened when the two substances were mixed together? *(They bubbled. Then the balloon inflated.)*
   • What type of change occurred? *(a chemical change)*
   • Why? *(A new substance, carbon dioxide gas, was formed when the two original substances were mixed together.)*

Teacher Demonstration

Materials: 1 20-ounce plastic soda bottle, 1/2 cup vinegar, 2 tablespoons baking soda, 1 medium-sized balloon, tape

Directions:
1. Pour the vinegar into the soda bottle.
2. Have a student volunteer hold the mouth of the balloon open as wide as possible. Then carefully place the baking soda inside the balloon.
3. Without allowing any of the baking soda to escape into the bottle, place the mouth of the balloon over the mouth of the bottle. Use the tape to secure the balloon to the bottle.
4. Raise the balloon slowly to allow the baking soda to empty into the bottle.

3. Use a knife to cut a cookie into four pieces. Then ask students the following questions:
   • What substance did I begin with? *(a cookie)*
   • What happened to the substance when it was cut with the knife? *(It was divided into four separate pieces.)*
   • What type of change occurred? *(a physical change)*
   • Why? *(Only the shape and size of the cookie changed. No new substance was formed. It is still a cookie.)*

4. Distribute one copy of page 203 to each student. Instruct students to complete the reproducible as directed. After each student completes the activity, discuss the answers as a class.

Presto Change-O!

Each top hat contains a picture of a change in matter and a description of the picture. Wave your magic wand and decide whether the change is physical or chemical. Then write your answer on the line at the top of each hat.

1. _____

breaking a pencil lead

2. _____

tarnishing of silver

3. _____

digesting food

4. _____

melting of an ice cube

5. _____

crumpling a piece of paper

6. _____

slicing a loaf of bread

7. _____

burning a match

8. _____

making lemonade

9. _____

rusting of a nail

Bonus Box: On the back of this paper, draw three more examples of changes in matter, including both physical and chemical changes. Then label each.

How To Extend The Lesson:

• Provide your students with a better understanding of physical and chemical change by gathering a variety of the items mentioned on page 203. Then conduct a teacher demonstration or set up stations for students to observe firsthand the chemical and physical changes taking place.

• Give each student a sheet of drawing paper and crayons, markers, or colored pencils. Instruct her to illustrate an indoor or outdoor scene that shows several examples of physical and chemical changes. For example, she might draw the inside of her kitchen with physical changes taking place, such as water being boiled, bread being sliced, or spaghetti being cooked. Also, she might illustrate chemical changes, such as a pie being baked in the oven or an egg being scrambled on the stove. Direct the student to label each scene in her picture as a physical change or a chemical change; then have her color her picture.

• Supply each student with one 12" x 18" sheet of construction paper, scissors, and glue. Instruct him to divide the paper into two equal sections and then label the sections "Chemical Change" and "Physical Change." Next direct the student to search through magazines and newspapers for pictures that represent each kind of change. Have him cut out each picture and glue it to the appropriate section.

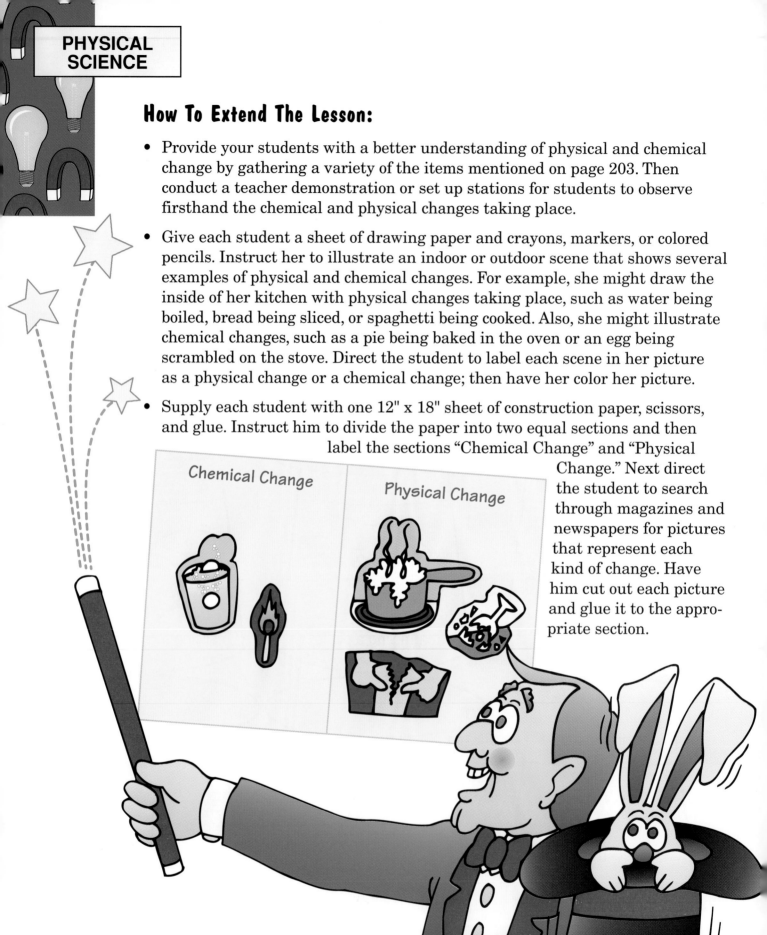

Feeling Hot, Hot, Hot!

*Familiarize your students with the hot topics of
conduction, convection, and radiation.*

Skill: Identifying heat, temperature, conduction, convection,
and radiation

Estimated Lesson Time: 45 minutes

Teacher Preparation:
Make one copy of page 207 for each student.

Materials:
1 copy of page 207 for each student
1 large, flat rubber band for each student
1 candle
3 or 4 wooden matches

Background Information:
- *Heat* is a form of energy that a substance has
  because of the motion of its molecules. The more
  heat a substance gains, the faster its molecules
  move. If a substance loses heat, its molecules
  will move slower.
- *Temperature* is a measure of how hot or cold
  something is. It is measured in degrees.
- Heat flows in three ways: *conduction, convection,*
  and *radiation.*
- *Conduction* is heat moving through a solid object.
  Example: heat traveling through the bottom of a
  cooking pot.
- *Convection* is the transfer of heat by a moving
  gas or liquid.
  Example: heat from a hair dryer.
- *Radiation* is heat moving through space as energy
  waves.
  Example: heat from the sun.

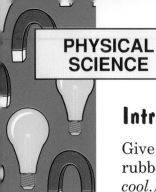

Introducing The Lesson:

Give each student one large, flat rubber band. Instruct the student to touch the rubber band to his forehead. Ask students how the rubber band feels. *(It should feel cool.)* Direct each student to stretch a small portion of the rubber band between two fingers as shown below and then touch it to his forehead again. Ask students how the rubber band feels now. *(The rubber band should feel warmer.)*

Steps:

1. Explain to students that they have just produced a little bit of *heat.* Share the definition of heat from the Background Information on page 205. Ask your students what they think will happen if they repeat the process above several times. Accept all student responses; then have each student try it. *(Each time the rubber band is stretched, it will produce heat and feel warmer.)*

2. Collect the rubber bands. Then tell your students that there are three ways heat can travel: *conduction, convection,* and *radiation.* Use the Background Information to define each method. Point out that heat can move only from a hotter area to one that has a lower temperature. Explain that the heat of the rubber band being transferred to skin is an example of conduction.

3. Demonstrate convection by first lighting a candle. Hold an unlit match next to the base of the flame and observe what happens. *(The match will not ignite.)* Next hold the match above the flame and observe what happens. *(The match will ignite.)* Ask students to explain what has happened. *(Heat rises, so the match can be lit from above the flame; however, if the match is held close to the bottom of the flame, it will not light.)* Repeat with the other matches held at varying heights above the flame.

4. Explain that the best example of radiation is the sun. The air above the earth is not warmed by the sun, but the earth's surface is.

5. Distribute one copy of page 207 to each student. Instruct students to complete the reproducible as directed.

Off To Some Place Cooler!

Did you know that heat travels only from a hotter area to one that is cooler? And there are only three ways that it can get there: conduction, convection, and radiation. *Conduction* is heat moving through a solid object. *Convection* is the transfer of heat by a moving gas or liquid. *Radiation* is heat moving through space as energy waves.

Identify each picture below as an example of conduction, convection, or radiation. Write your answers on the lines provided.

1. _____

2. _____

3. _____

4. _____

5. _____

6. _____

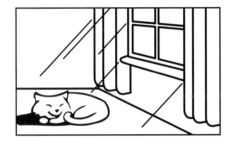

7. _____

8. _____

9. _____

10. _____

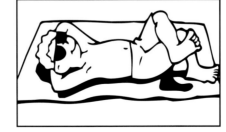

11. _____

12. _____

Bonus Box: On the back of this page, write examples of conduction, convection, and radiation that were not shown above.

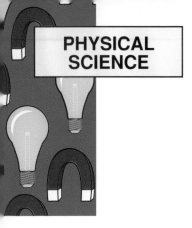

How To Extend The Lesson:

• Reinforce the concept of *conduction* with this hands-on project. Divide your students into groups of three or four. Tell each group that on the following day it will receive a tin can and an ice cube. Explain to each group that its mission is to design a container using materials from home and from school that will keep the ice cube from melting as long as possible. Instruct each student to bring any materials for his container to school the next day. Tell students that there are only three rules: no ice buckets, coolers, or ice may be used for the container; the tin can must be used in some way; and the ice cube must be accessible for periodic checks.

On the next school day, give each group time to construct its container. Provide additional materials such as plastic bags, tape, Styrofoam® pieces, empty cartons or boxes, tinfoil, and pieces of wood or plastic for each group to use. Once each container has been built, give each group an ice cube to place in its container. Place all the containers in the same area of the classroom. Plan for each group to check its cube once every hour (when the cubes become small, have them checked more frequently). Declare the team whose cube lasts the longest—the team that has reduced conduction the most—the winner.

HOT   TEPID   COLD

• Use this activity to demonstrate that a person's sense of hot and cold is not reliable. Fill three bowls with water, each with a different temperature—hot, tepid, and cold. Invite student volunteers one at a time to dip one hand in the cold water and the other in the hot water for one minute. Then have the student place both hands in the tepid water. Have the student describe how his hands feel. *(The water will feel warm to the hand that was in the cold water, but it will feel cold to the hand that was in the hot water.)* Have students discuss possible explanations for this outcome.

What's The Attraction?

Attract your students to the principles of magnetism with this hands-on lesson!

Skill: Identifying the principles of magnetic energy

Estimated Lesson Time: 45 minutes

Teacher Preparation:

1. Obtain two bar magnets and several other magnets of various shapes and sizes.
2. Select various metal and nonmetal classroom objects, such as keys, a filing cabinet, rubber bands, coins, a door, straight pins, paper clips, and plastic game pieces.
3. Make one copy of page 211 for each student.

Materials:

2 bar magnets
iron filings
paper
3 different-sized magnets, 1 sheet of paper, a small pile of paper clips, 1 pencil, and 1 ruler for each group of students
1 copy of page 211 for each student

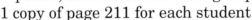

Background Information:

Magnetism is the force that causes something to attract or repel something else. A magnet is usually made of iron or steel and attracts only magnetic materials (such as iron, steel, nickel, and cobalt). Magnets do not attract materials such as plastic, paper, wood, and certain metals such as aluminum, copper, tin, and lead.

A magnet has a magnetic field (an area around the magnet in which the force can be detected) and two poles, a north-seeking pole and a south-seeking pole. Also, a magnet is attracted to another magnet only if the two opposite poles are brought together (north and south). Two like poles repel or push each other away (north and north or south and south).

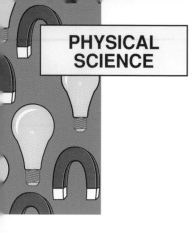

Introducing The Lesson:

Place a magnet on different objects around the room, such as a globe, blackboard, file cabinet, window, door, and student desk. Direct the students to note which objects the magnet sticks to and which objects the magnet does not stick to.

Steps:

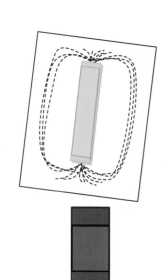

1. Ask your students why the magnet stuck only to certain objects. *(Students should be able to generalize that a magnet is attracted only to material with metal in it.)* Share the first paragraph of the Background Information on page 209 with your students.

2. Share the second paragraph of the Background Information with your students. Then show students two bar magnets with the north and south poles labeled. Next place one of the bar magnets on a lighted overhead projector. Sprinkle some iron filings on a sheet of white paper and place the paper on the bar magnet. Gently tap the paper with your finger. Ask students what they see happening. *(The iron filings curve around the poles.)* Explain to students that this is the magnetic field around the magnet.

3. Remove the labels from the two bar magnets; then put two ends of the magnets together. Ask students what they can figure out about the north and south poles based on the attraction of the magnets. *(If the ends attract, one is north and one is south. If the ends repel, they are either both north or both south.)*

4. Divide students into five or six groups. Distribute one copy of page 211 to each student. Provide each group with the materials listed on page 209. Instruct each group to complete each activity on the reproducible as directed.

5. Have each group present its findings to the class.

Pulling Power!

Magnetism: although its energy can't be seen or heard, its force is all around us. To find out more about this "magical" magnetic force, follow the directions for the experiment below.

Materials:

• 3 different-sized magnets	• small pile of paper clips	• sheet of paper	• pencil	• ruler

Procedure:

Step 1: Lay a sheet of paper on a flat surface. Put a paper clip on it and make a mark where you place the clip.

Step 2: Set a magnet several inches away from the paper clip. Slowly move the magnet toward the clip. Make a mark where the magnet was when it pulled the clip to itself. Measure and record the distance between the marks.

Step 3: Dip the magnet in a pile of paper clips. Note which part of the magnet picks up the most clips.

Step 4: Repeat Steps 1–3 with the remaining two magnets.

Observations:

1. What conclusions can you draw about the strength of each magnet?

   _____

   _____

2. Does the size of the magnet affect its strength?

   _____

   _____

3. What part of the magnet seems stronger? Is it the middle or the ends?

   _____

   _____

How To Extend The Lesson:

• Divide your students into groups of three. Supply each group with a shoebox, various paper and craft supplies, paper clips, glue, scissors, and several magnets. Direct each group to create a short animated skit about a favorite day, such as a day at the beach or a birthday party. Instruct the group to decorate the inside of the shoebox and create several cutouts to illustrate the story. Tell the group to fasten a paper clip to the back of each cutout and place the cutouts in the shoebox scene. Then have the group press a magnet against the back of the box behind the paper clip and let go of the cutout. Students will find that the force of the magnet keeps the cutouts from falling, and they will be able to share a *moving* story.

• Brainstorm with your students the many everyday uses of magnets. For example, magnets are used to post papers, keep doors and containers closed, and keep paper clips in place. Next challenge each student to think of a new and different way to use a magnet. Have the student draw, label, and color a picture of her new invention. Display the creations on a wall or bulletin board titled "Magnificent Magnets."

• Bury several metallic objects—such as paper clips, nails, tacks, and coins—in a container filled with sand. Place the container and a large magnet at a center. Invite each student to go to the center during free time. Challenge the student to find as many buried objects as possible using the magnet.

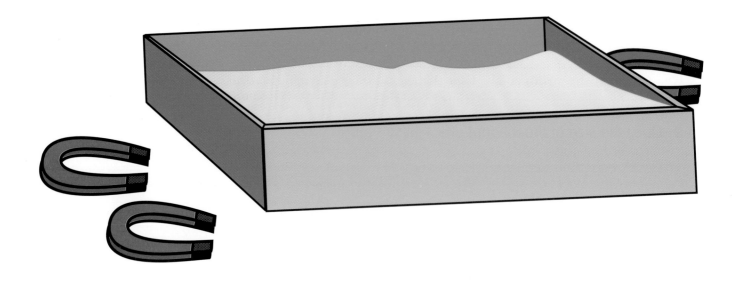

May The Forces Be With You!

Familiarize your students with the fantastic forces of push, pull, gravity, and friction with a lesson that's out of this world!

Skills: Identifying the forces of push, pull, gravity, and friction

Estimated Lesson Time: 1 hour

Teacher Preparation:
1. Copy the Background Information on this page onto a transparency or the chalkboard.
2. Gather a tennis (or another) ball and a book for a class demonstration. Also gather various items—such as a coin, a length of string, an eraser, and an empty plastic bottle or can—for each pair of students.
3. Duplicate a copy of page 215 for each pair of students.

Materials:
1 tennis (or another) ball and a book for a class demonstration
various items, such as a coin, a length of string, an eraser, and an empty plastic bottle or can for each pair of students
1 copy of page 215 for each pair of students

Background Information:
Forces are all around us. Forces allow us to breathe, throw a ball, or ride a bicycle.
- A *force* is a push or pull that makes an object move, or change direction or shape.
- *Push* is force pressed against something to make it move forward, outward, or upward.
- *Pull* is a force that moves something toward or nearer.
- *Gravity* is the earth's pulling force that makes things fall and gives things weight.
- *Friction* is a force that occurs when two objects rub against each other. It slows or stops moving objects.

Fantastic Facts About Force!
- The British scientist, Sir Isaac Newton, was able to describe the force of gravity after being hit on the head by a falling apple!
- In order to break through the earth's gravitational pull, rockets and space shuttles must reach speeds of 25,000 miles per hour!
- The longest recorded pull in a tug of war took place between Ireland and England during the World Championships in 1988. It lasted 24 minutes and 45 seconds!
- You would weigh almost three times as much on Jupiter as you weigh on Earth!
- Some racing cars travel so fast that when their brakes are put on, they glow red because of the friction between the disc pads on the discs!

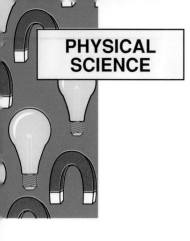

Introducing The Lesson:

Gather the tennis ball and the book. One at a time, throw the tennis ball into the air, pick up the book, roll the tennis ball along the floor, and drop the book on the floor. As you put each item into motion, direct your students to observe what type of movement is occurring.

Steps:

1. Explain to students that in order to move an object or put it into motion, you have to give it a *push* or a *pull*. Scientists call this push or pull a *force*. Share with your students the definitions of push and pull from the Background Information on page 213.

2. Ask students what type of movement occurred with each action—a push or a pull. *(throwing/pushing the ball into the air, picking up/pulling the book, rolling/pushing the ball along the floor, and dropping/pushing the book)*

3. Use the Background Information to discuss *gravity* and *friction*. Then throw the ball back up into the air. Ask students which force they think brings the ball back down. *(gravity)* Explain that without gravity, things would not stay on the ground. Next slowly roll the tennis ball along the floor. Ask students to identify which force makes the ball's speed decrease and eventually stop. *(friction)* Explain that the friction is caused by the floor pushing against the ball and reducing its movement or motion. Further explain that without friction, things would slip and slide away from each other.

4. Share the Fantastic Facts About Force on the bottom of page 213.

5. Pair students and provide each pair with various objects, such as a coin, a length of string, an eraser, and an empty plastic bottle or can. Direct each pair to use the objects to demonstrate each type of force. Have the group create a chart like the one shown to describe its force demonstrations.

6. Afterwards have each pair share its demonstrations and information on its chart with the class. Then give each pair a copy of page 215. Instruct the pair to follow the directions on the sheet for completing the activity.

Object(s)	Action	Force	Reason
coin	We rolled the coin along the floor.	push	Pushing the coin makes it move forward.
string	We used the string in a tug of war.	pull	Pulling the string brings it toward our bodies.
eraser	We threw it into the air.	push/gravity	We pushed the eraser upwards into the air, then gravity brought it back down.
coin, eraser, plastic bottle	We put the eraser and coin into the bottle. We rolled the bottle across the floor.	friction	The bottle slowed and stopped moving because of the friction caused by the objects rubbing against the bottle and the bottle rubbing against the floor.

May The Forces Be With You!

Force isn't just something found in science fiction movies—it's all around us! Forces allow us to breathe, walk, and even sing! Below is a list of everyday activities. Identify the force—*push, pull, gravity,* or *friction*—being demonstrated in each activity; then explain your answer. Write your answers in the spaces provided.

Activity	Force	Reason
1. bike skidding on road		
2. jumping off diving board		
3. skiing downhill		
4. shooting a basketball		
5. getting out of chair		
6. opening a can of soda		
7. brushing your hair		
8. riding a seesaw		
9. drinking out of a straw		
10. sliding into a baseball base		
11. tractor stopping in a muddy field		
12. opening a door		
13. sliding down a slide		
14. removing a nail from a wall		
15. paddling in a paddleboat		

Bonus Box: On the back of this sheet, list an example of four different forces found in your classroom.

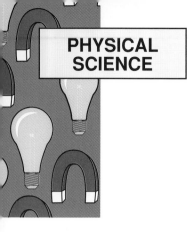

How To Extend The Lesson:

- Get your students to identify forces in action—firsthand—with this first-rate idea! On a sheet of loose-leaf paper, have each student create a chart like the one shown. Direct the student to observe her family, friends, and community members in action for one week. Have the student record her observations on the chart, identifying at least four different actions for each force—push, pull, gravity, and friction. Afterwards divide students into groups of four. Have group members share their findings with one another. Then have each group choose one example for each force to share with the class.

Date	Time	Persons Involved	Action	Force	Explanation
Nov. 2	4:25 P.M.	stock person at grocery store	stocking canned food	push and gravity	The stock person was putting the cans on the shelf (push) when all of a sudden, he knocked a can and they all started falling on the floor (gravity).

- Have your students create a class scrapbook of the forces found in their favorite activities. Provide each student with a sheet of drawing paper. Direct each student to bring in photographs of himself participating in various activities. Have the students bring in one photograph for each force. (Be sure to get parental permission for using the photos. Or, vary the activity by having each student search through magazines and newspapers for an example of each force.) Instruct the student to glue or tape each picture to the drawing paper and caption each picture with the name and explanation of the force. Afterwards, collect all the pages. Use two 9" x 12" sheets of construction paper as front and back covers. Use a hole puncher to make holes on the left side of the pages; then bind the pages together using yarn or brads. Finally have a student volunteer title and decorate the front cover. Display the scrapbook, having each student share his page.

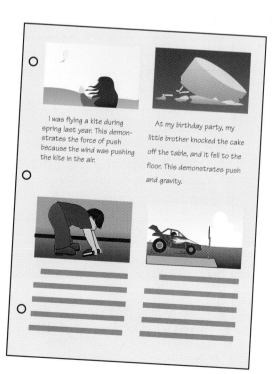

I was flying a kite during spring last year. This demonstrates the force of push because the wind was pushing the kite in the air.

At my birthday party, my little brother knocked the cake off the table, and it fell to the floor. This demonstrates push and gravity.

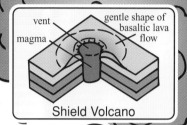

It's Going To Blow!

Help your students understand the awesome power and wonder of volcanoes with the following activity.

Skill: Researching the different types and classes of volcanoes

Estimated Lesson Time: 1 hour

Teacher Preparation:
1. Make one copy of page 219 for each team of students.
2. Gather reference materials on volcanoes (see list of volcanoes on page 220).
3. Post a world map on a bulletin board.

Materials For Each Team Of Students:
1 copy of page 219
reference materials on volcanoes
2 pushpins
1 length of yarn

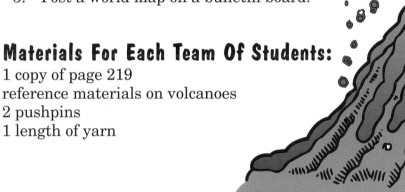

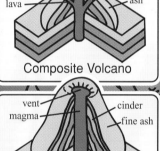

Shield Volcano

Composite Volcano

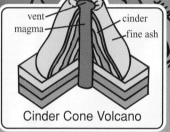

Cinder Cone Volcano

Background Information:
The word *volcano* comes from the Roman god of fire, *Vulcan*. The ancient Romans believed that a volcano was a hot forge where Vulcan made swords and armor for the other gods.

Most volcanoes are found where the earth's crust is weak. Scientists believe that volcanoes begin with *magma* or melted rock deep beneath the earth's crust. The melting rock creates a gas that mixes with the magma, causing it to rise. Pockets of this gas/magma mixture are formed in the earth's crust about two miles below the surface. Pressure begins to build as more and more magma fills these pockets. Eventually the magma is forced up through the crust. Once hot magma reaches the surface, it is called *lava*. This hot lava pours out onto the surface of the earth. When the lava cools, it hardens into rock.

More that 1,500 active volcanoes can be found on the earth. Many volcanoes are found in the Pacific Ring Of Fire, which circles most of the Pacific Ocean.

Scientists classify volcanic activity by how often a volcano erupts. Volcanoes are classed into the following groups:

Active—a volcano that erupts constantly.

Intermittent—a volcano that erupts at regular periods.

Dormant—a volcano that has become inactive but not long enough to know if it will ever erupt again.

Extinct—a volcano that has been inactive since the beginning of recorded history.

Scientists have also divided volcanoes into the three main groups shown below.

Shield Volcano—broad, shallow cones made when free-flowing lava pours from the top and spreads widely.

Cinder Cone Volcano—very explosive, formed when mainly *tephra* (cinders) erupts from a vent, then falls back around the vent, forming a cone-shaped mountain.

Composite Volcano—formed when alternate layers of lava and tephra erupt from one central vent.

Introducing The Lesson:

Amaze your students with the following facts:

- Gases in the air we breathe come from volcanoes that erupted billions of years ago.
- The ground we walk on is partly made of molten rock from ancient volcanoes.
- All water on the earth began as steam from volcanoes.
- Much of the soil on the earth consists of volcanic ash, which makes it very rich in minerals.

Steps:

1. After reading the information above, continue to amaze your students by reading the Background Information at the bottom of page 217.
2. Next tell your students that they are going to work in teams of two or three to research an assigned volcano.
3. Distribute one copy of page 219 to each team of students. Assign each team a different volcano to research. (See list of suggested volcanoes on page 220.)
4. Make available to each team various reference materials on volcanoes.
5. Instruct each team to fill in the missing data on page 219 for its assigned volcano.
6. Have each team present its findings to the rest of the class. Then post a world map on a bulletin board and tack each team's "Mountains Of Fire" page around the map. Connect each page to the location of the appropriate volcano on the map using pushpins and lengths of yarn so that students can see the location of each volcano researched.

- Gases in the air we breathe come from volcanoes that erupted billions of years ago.
- The ground we walk on is partly made of molten rock from ancient volcanoes.
- All water on the earth began as steam from volcanoes.
- Much of the soil on earth consists of volcanic ash, which makes it very rich in minerals.

Mountains Of Fire

Directions: Your teacher will assign your research team a specific volcano to investigate. Use reference books, maps, and other sources of information to fill in the missing data below.

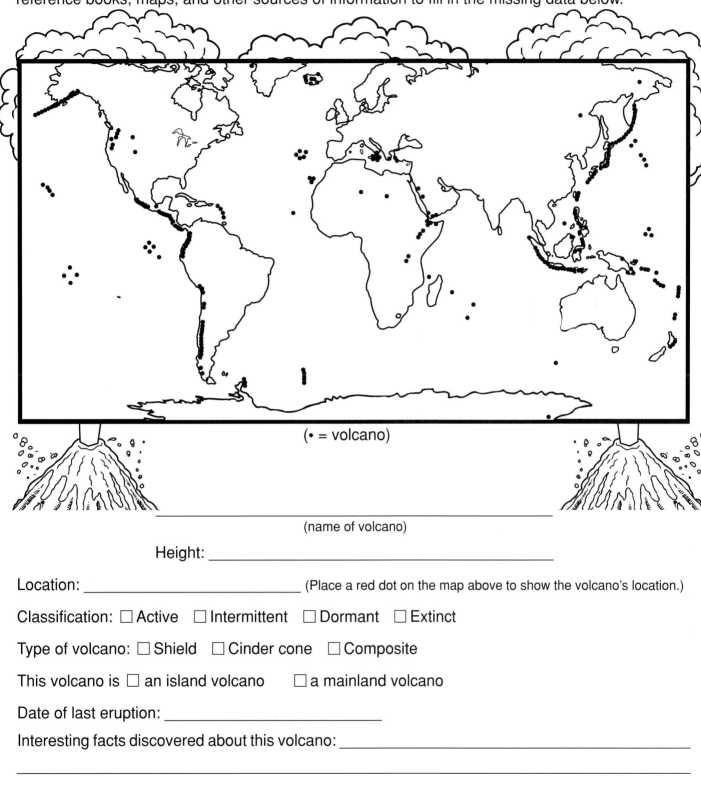

(• = volcano)

_____
(name of volcano)

Height: _____

Location: _____ (Place a red dot on the map above to show the volcano's location.)

Classification: ☐ Active ☐ Intermittent ☐ Dormant ☐ Extinct

Type of volcano: ☐ Shield ☐ Cinder cone ☐ Composite

This volcano is ☐ an island volcano   ☐ a mainland volcano

Date of last eruption: _____

Interesting facts discovered about this volcano: _____

_____

_____

_____

_____

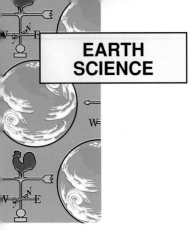
How To Extend The Lesson:

- Help your students experience volcanic activity by working in small groups to complete the experiment below. After each group has completed its experiment, have each group hypothesize why the eruption occurred. *(When you mix vinegar and baking soda, there is a chemical reaction. It makes carbon dioxide gas. Carbon dioxide makes bubbles, and the bubbles build up in the soda bottle. The bubbles take up space, and when there is no more room inside the bottle, the liquid comes out of the top of the volcano.)*

  Materials For Each Group:
  6 cups flour, 2 cups salt, 4 tablespoons cooking oil, 2 cups warm water, a 20-ounce plastic soda bottle, red flood coloring, liquid detergent, 2 tablespoons baking soda, vinegar, a funnel, a baking pan, newspaper

  Directions:
  1. Put some newspaper over the table and floor where you are working.
  2. Mix the flour, salt, oil, and warm water together. Mix it with your hands until the mixture is smooth. If it is too dry and crumbly, add a little more water.
  3. Stand the soda bottle in the middle of a baking pan. Press the dough up against and around the bottle. Shape the dough to look like a volcano. Do not cover or get dough inside the opening of the bottle.
  4. Mix together some warm water and a few drops of red food coloring. Using the funnel, pour the red water into the opening so the bottle is filled almost to the top. Dry the funnel.
  5. Add six drops of liquid detergent to the bottle. Pour the baking soda through the funnel. Next slowly pour some vinegar into the bottle.

- Share with your students the following books about volcanoes:
  The Magic School Bus Blows Its Top: A Book About Volcanoes by
    Joanna Cole (Scholastic Inc., 1996)
  Mountains And Volcanoes by Barbara Taylor (Kingfisher, 1993)
  Shake, Rattle, And Roll: The World's Most Amazing Natural Forces
    by Spencer Christian and Antonia Felix (John Wiley & Sons, Inc.;
    1997)
  Volcano & Earthquake by Susanna Van Rose (Alfred A. Knopf, Inc.;
    1992)
  Volcanoes & Earthquakes by Patricia Lauber (Scholastic Inc., 1991)
  Volcanoes: Earth's Inner Fire by Sally M. Walker (Carolrhoda Books,
    Inc.; 1994)

Major Volcanoes And Their Locations	
Volcano	**Location**
Mauna Loa	Hawaii
Mount Fuji	Japan
Mount Pinatubo	Philippines
Vesuvius	Italy
Mount Saint Helens	United States
Cotopaxi	Ecuador
Krakatau	Indonesia
El Misti	Peru
Hekla	Iceland
Kilimanjaro	Tanzania
Popocatepetl	Mexico

Are You Ready To Rock?

Get your students rockin' and rollin' with this cool lesson on rocks and minerals!

Skill: Classifying rocks and minerals

Estimated Lesson Time: 45 minutes

Teacher Preparation:
1. Duplicate one copy of page 223 for each student.
2. Have each group of students bring in five rock samples and the bottom portion of an egg carton. (See Step 3 on page 222.)

Materials:
1 copy of page 223 for each student
hammer
several rocks for classroom demonstration
5 rocks for each group
1 bottom portion of an egg carton for each group
1 unglazed ceramic tile for each group
1/4 cup vinegar for each group
1 eyedropper for each group
1 permanent marker for each group
scissors
stapler
safety goggles

Background Information:
Minerals are made up of simple chemical substances called *elements*. Some minerals are made up of a single element, and others are made up of more than one element.

Most *rocks* are made up of a combination of minerals. The eight major characteristics used to identify and classify rocks are:
- *Hardness*—measured using *Moh's Scale of Hardness*, which orders ten minerals from softest to hardest
- *Color*—the color of the rock
- *Streak*—the color that results when a rock is rubbed against something
- *Texture*—the size of the grains or crystals in the rock
- *Luster*—how the rock reflects light, which can be metallic, glassy, or dull
- *Cleavage*—how a rock breaks when hit by a hammer or another object
- *Chemical*—the chemical composition of the rock. For example, if a rock contains lime (calcium carbonate), it will fizz when acid is placed on it.
- *Density*—the amount of matter in a unit volume of any substance

Introducing The Lesson:

Explain to students that rocks and minerals are identified and classified based on eight major characteristics. Point out that one of these characteristics is *cleavage,* or the way a rock sample breaks when hit by a hammer. Wearing safety goggles, demonstrate cleavage by breaking a rock sample with the hammer. Have students describe how the rock breaks. Then break another rock and have students compare the breakage.

Steps:

1. Explain that *hardness* is another characteristic used to identify and classify rocks and minerals. Geologists use a hardness scale invented by Friedrich Mohs of Germany. This scale orders ten minerals from softest to hardest, with talc being the softest mineral and diamond being the hardest. Share with students the following scale:

Hardness	Rock	Test Sample
1	talc	soft, greasy flakes on fingers
2	gypsum	scratched by fingernail
3	calcite	scratched slightly with penny
4	fluorite	scratched easily by knife
5	apatite	not scratched easily by knife
6	orthoclase	scratched by a file
7	quartz	scratches glass easily
8	topaz	scratches glass easily
9	corundum	scratches glass easily
10	diamond	scratches all other materials

2. Share with students the remaining characteristics used to identify and classify rocks found in the Background Information on page 221.

3. Divide your class into small groups. Provide each group with a ceramic tile, 1/4 cup of vinegar, a permanent marker, and an eyedropper. Have each group place five rock samples in the bottom of the egg carton, each in a different section. Direct each group to label each rock sample 1–5 by writing the appropriate numeral on the egg carton in permanent marker.

4. Distribute one copy of page 223 to each student. Have each group work together to further explore the characteristics of color, streak, texture, luster, and chemical composition of each rock sample.

Are You Ready To Rock?

Get jammin' to the beat of rocks and minerals with this cool activity!

Directions: Cut out the six notebook sheets below and place them in order with the cover on top. Staple the sheets together along the top edge. Observe the characteristics of the five rock samples; then record your information in the spaces provided.

ROCK LOG

Color is a rock's color.
Streak is the color that results when a rock is rubbed against something. To find the streak for your rock sample, rub it against the tile.
Texture describes the size of the grains or crystals in a rock. These grains are classified as coarse, fine, or nonexistent.
Luster refers to how the rock reflects light. A rock can have a metallic luster, a glassy luster, or it can be dull.
Chemical composition is the rock's chemical makeup. Use the eyedropper to place a small amount of vinegar on the rock sample. If it bubbles, the rock sample contains lime.

SAMPLE 1
SKETCH

COLOR _____

STREAK _____

TEXTURE
☐ coarse
☐ fine
☐ nonexistent

LUSTER
☐ dull
☐ glassy
☐ metallic

CHEMICAL
Does the rock contain lime?
☐ yes
☐ no

1

SAMPLE 2
SKETCH

COLOR _____

STREAK _____

TEXTURE
☐ coarse
☐ fine
☐ nonexistent

LUSTER
☐ dull
☐ glassy
☐ metallic

CHEMICAL
Does the rock contain lime?
☐ yes
☐ no

2

SAMPLE 3
SKETCH

COLOR _____

STREAK _____

TEXTURE
☐ coarse
☐ fine
☐ nonexistent

LUSTER
☐ dull
☐ glassy
☐ metallic

CHEMICAL
Does the rock contain lime?
☐ yes
☐ no

3

SAMPLE 4
SKETCH

COLOR _____

STREAK _____

TEXTURE
☐ coarse
☐ fine
☐ nonexistent

LUSTER
☐ dull
☐ glassy
☐ metallic

CHEMICAL
Does the rock contain lime?
☐ yes
☐ no

4

SAMPLE 5
SKETCH

COLOR _____

STREAK _____

TEXTURE
☐ coarse
☐ fine
☐ nonexistent

LUSTER
☐ dull
☐ glassy
☐ metallic

CHEMICAL
Does the rock contain lime?
☐ yes
☐ no

5

How To Extend The Lesson:

- Sponsor a Celebrity Rock Contest in your classroom. Begin by asking each student to bring in a rock. Provide an assortment of art supplies, such as yarn, movable craft eyes, and paint. Have each student decorate his rock to look like a well-known celebrity. Then have each student write a short biography about his celebrity. After the student shares his celebrity rock and biography with the rest of the class, have him display his creation on a table labeled "Celebrity Rock Hall Of Fame." Conclude the activity by asking a panel of judges to view the celebrity rocks, then select winners in categories, such as most creative, most interesting biography, and most realistic.

- Gather several reference guides on rocks and minerals from your school's media center. Challenge each student to collect several rock samples from the area around her home. Have the student place each sample in a plastic sandwich bag, then number each bag. Direct the student to record the number of each rock sample in a notebook along with information about the rock, such as the specific location and type of soil in which it was found. Then have students work in groups to identify the type of each rock sample.

- Explain to students that some minerals form regular, flat-sided shapes called *crystals*. Demonstrate how crystals form with the following two ideas:
  — Begin by mixing as much alum in a beaker of hot water as you can. Keep adding alum until no more will dissolve in the water. Place the beaker in a bed of crushed ice. Observe the mixture during the next few hours. Have students use magnifying glasses to view the newly formed crystals.
  — For a similar activity, fill a clear jar with very hot, but not boiling, water. Stir in salt or sugar until no more will dissolve in the water. Tie one end of a string to the center of a craft stick and the other end of the string to a button. Lower the button end of the string into the mixture, resting the craft stick on the mouth of the jar. Place the jar in a safe, draft-free location for a week or two. Have students use magnifying glasses to view the crystals.

Biome Buddies

Swing into the study of land biomes with this group booklet activity!

Skill: Examining the major land biomes and the plants and animals that live within each

Estimated Lesson Time: 45 minutes

Teacher Preparation:
Duplicate one copy of page 227 for each group of three or four students.

Materials:
(For each group of three or four students)
1 copy of page 227
4 sheets of 8 1/2" x 11" drawing paper cut in half
1 sheet of 9" x 12" construction paper
scissors
reference books
glue
access to a stapler

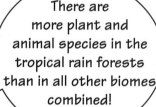

There are more plant and animal species in the tropical rain forests than in all other biomes combined!

Background Information:

A *biome* is a plant and animal community that covers a large geographic area. A biome has the same general climate throughout the area. The eight major land biomes include the following:

- *Chaparral*—region with shrubs and small trees
- *Desert*—region with little plant life because of its scarce rainfall and dry soil
- *Grassland*—region covered with short or tall grass
- *Savanna*—grassland with scattered trees and shrubs
- *Temperate coniferous forest*—region with pinecone-bearing evergreen trees
- *Temperate deciduous forest*—region with trees that lose their leaves
- *Tropical rain forest*—region with a forest of tall trees, year-round warmth, and lots of rain
- *Tundra*—cold, dry region where trees cannot grow

Introducing The Lesson:

Ask students to name some types of plants and animals that live around their homes. Then choose an animal that does not live in your area, and ask students if they have ever seen that animal around their homes. *(For example, if you live in the southeast United States, ask students if they have ever seen a polar bear in their community.)* Pose a similar question, this time choosing a plant.

Steps:

1. Question students as to why they haven't seen the types of plants and animals that you've mentioned in their area of the country.

2. Guide students to realize that plants and animals need particular living conditions, such as the appropriate climate and food supply, in order to survive.

3. Use the Background Information on page 225 to explain the term *biome* to your students. Point out that different biomes have varying rainfall amounts and temperatures. Tell students that these differences help determine which plants and animals survive in each biome.

4. Introduce the eight major biomes listed on page 225.

5. Divide your class into groups of three or four students. Provide each group with the materials listed on page 225 and access to reference materials.

6. Explain that page 227 contains some information on each of the eight biomes. Challenge the group to use reference materials to find and write two more general facts about each biome: one about the plant life and the other about the animal life. Have the group record these facts on the lines provided on each card.

7. Direct the group to cut apart the cards and glue each onto a different half-sheet of drawing paper.

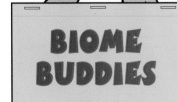

8. Have the group draw on each paper at least one plant and one animal that live in that particular biome.

9. Instruct each group to bind its papers into a booklet by placing the pages inside a folded sheet of construction paper titled "Biome Buddies" and stapling along the folded edge.

10. Place the completed booklets in a science center.

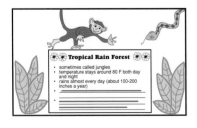

Tropical Rain Forest
- sometimes called jungles
- temperature stays around 80 F both day and night
- rains almost every day (about 100-200 inches a year)

Grassland

- deep and rich soil
- averages 10–40 inches of rainfall a year
- _____
  _____
  _____
- _____
  _____

Tundra

- very cold, dry region where trees cannot grow
- region lies on top of a layer of ice that never melts
- receives only about 4–6 inches of precipitation a year
- _____
  _____
  _____
- _____
  _____

Coniferous Forest

- sometimes called a _needle-leaf forest_
- mild winters and heavy rainfall in coastal areas
- cool, moist mountain slopes
- _____
  _____
  _____
- _____
  _____

Deciduous Forest

- has four distinct seasons
- has rich, moist soil
- averages about 40 inches of rain each year
- _____
  _____
  _____
- _____
  _____

SAVANNA

- long dry season
- warm temperatures
- _____
  _____
  _____
- _____
  _____

Tropical Rain Forest

- sometimes called _jungles_
- temperature stays around 80°F both day and night
- rains almost every day (about 100–200 inches a year)
- _____
  _____
  _____
- _____
  _____

DESERT

- extremely hot temperatures during the days and cool, even freezing, nights
- less than 10 inches of rain per year
- _____
  _____
  _____
- _____
  _____

Chaparral

- coastal biome sometimes called _scrubland_
- cool and moist in winter; hot and dry in summer
- averages around 10 inches of rain a year
- _____
  _____
  _____
- _____
  _____

How To Extend The Lesson:

- Direct each student to choose one of the biomes discussed in this lesson and write a story about living in that biome. Have the student write the final copy of his story on a cut-out shape of a plant or animal that lives in that particular biome. Post these completed writings on a bulletin board titled "Life In The Biomes."

- Divide your students into pairs. Provide each pair with a large outline map of the world. Challenge each pair to use reference materials to label its map with the locations of the eight biomes. Have each pair include a legend or map key on its map.

- Assign each student a different biome. Give the student one 5" x 8" unlined index card and either colored pencils or crayons. On one side of his card, instruct the student to create a postcard illustration of his assigned biome. On the other side of the card, have him write the name of his assigned biome and a brief description of what he illustrated on the front of the card. Use a pushpin to display the illustrated side of each postcard on a bulletin board. Invite students to visit this board and identify the biome that is represented on each card. To reveal the correct answers, simply have students flip the cards over.

Tropical Rain Forest

The toucan lives in the canopy level of the rain forest. At this level the branches of trees grow close together, forming an umbrella over the forest.

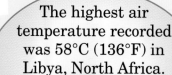

Clue In To Climate

Get your young "investi-gators" thinking critically about climate with this creative lesson.

Skill: Identifying factors that affect climate

Estimated Lesson Time: 1 hour

The highest air temperature recorded was 58°C (136°F) in Libya, North Africa.

Teacher Preparation:
1. Obtain a large world map or globe.
2. Make one copy of page 231 for each student.

Materials:
weather forecast from local newspaper
large world map or globe
1 copy of page 231 for each student

The lowest air temperature recorded was –88°C (–127°F) in Antarctica.

Background Information:

Climate is the average weather in one place over a long period of time. Sunlight, temperature, precipitation, and wind are factors that affect climate in any given area. Temperature and precipitation are the most important factors affecting climate.

Since the earth is tilted, the sun's rays strike it at different angles. The equator receives the most direct sunlight, and the poles receive the least direct sunlight. Air and water currents produced by the interaction between the sun's heating patterns and the earth's rotation and orbit are major factors in the distribution of heat and precipitation.

Introducing The Lesson:

Share with your students the day's weather forecast from a local newspaper. Point out the temperature, wind speed, precipitation, and amount of sunlight. Then have students describe the past week's weather conditions.

Steps:

1. Explain to students that *weather* is the condition of the air at any given time and place. *Climate* is the average weather in one place over a long period of time. Share the first paragraph from the Background Information on page 229. Then have students describe the climate of your area.

2. Have a student volunteer find the equator on a map or globe. Then have different volunteers find Venezuela, Egypt, and the North Pole. Guide students in describing the typical climate of each of these three areas *(Venezuela: lowland areas are warm and wet, higher elevations are cool and dry; Egypt: hot and dry; North Pole: cold and dry).*

3. Ask students whether there is a relationship between climate and location on the earth's surface *(yes).* Share the second paragraph from the Background Information. Emphasize that land areas nearest the equator generally receive the most sunlight, so these areas have higher temperatures. Land areas farther away from the equator receive less sunlight, so these areas have lower temperatures.

4. Explain to students that scientists divide the earth into six major regions, called *biomes,* based on climate and plant and animal life. Use a map or globe and the diagram below to point out these regions to students.

5. Distribute one copy of page 231 to each student. Instruct students to complete the activity as directed; then have them share their findings about each biome's climate.

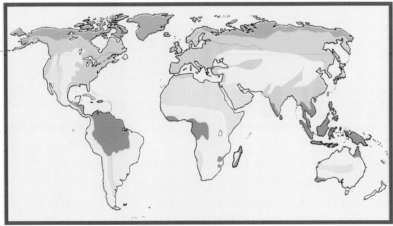

Biomes

- Tundra
- Temperate Forest
- Grassland
- Taiga
- Tropical Rain Forest
- Desert

Reading a graph

Climate Is The Key

The earth is divided into six major land regions called *biomes.* Each region's climate is different. The differences in climate affect the kind of plant and animal life found in each region.

Directions: Read the temperature and precipitation ranges on the graphs below. Use the information to answer the questions that follow. Record your answers on the back of this sheet.

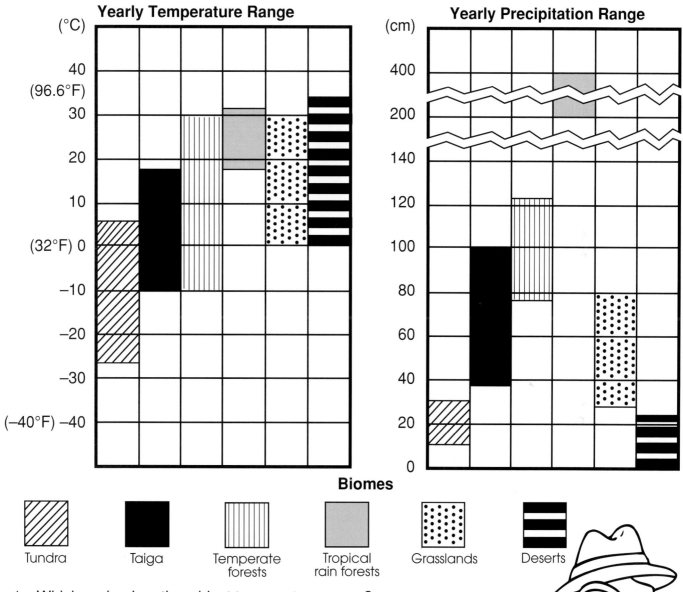

Biomes

Tundra   Taiga   Temperate forests   Tropical rain forests   Grasslands   Deserts

1. Which region has the widest temperature range?
2. Which region has the narrowest temperature range?
3. Which region has the coldest temperatures? Why do you think this is so?
4. Which region has the most precipitation in one year? Which has the least precipitation in one year?
5. If a city has very high temperatures and very little precipitation throughout the year, in which region is it most likely to belong?
6. Which region's temperature is about −10°C in the winter and about 17°C in the summer?
7. Use the graphs to describe the yearly climate of each region.
8. What do you think would happen to plants and animals living in a tropical rain forest if the climate changed to that of a tundra?

How To Extend The Lesson:

- Divide students into six groups and assign each group a different biome: tundra, taiga, temperate forest, tropical rain forest, grassland, or desert. Direct the group to research the climate and native plant and animal life of its assigned biome. Then have each group imagine it is a team of scientists exploring the area. Direct each group member to write a journal entry describing its area, including weather conditions and plant and animal life. Afterward, have each group share its journal entries with the rest of the class.

> With my long snout and sticky tongue, I find my food: tasty termites and ants that live in the undergrowth. The canopy of trees under which I live protects me from the heavy rains and strong sunlight.

anteater

tropical rain forest

- Place reference materials on the different biomes, a supply of 5" x 7" index cards, and markers or colored pencils at a center. Direct each student using the center to choose a biome to research. Then, on the front of an index card, have the student write a riddle about an animal living in that biome. Direct the student to include information about its physical characteristics, food requirements, and immediate habitat. On the back of the card, have the student write the name of the animal and the biome in which it lives. After each student completes a riddle, collect the cards. Post a different riddle each day, challenging students to guess the animal and its biome home.

- Pair students; then assign each pair a different U.S. city from the list shown. Direct each pair to use encyclopedias and atlases to research its city's average yearly weather conditions: sunlight, temperature, precipitation, and wind. Then have each pair use a newspaper to find that city's forecast. Have the pair decide whether the forecast is normal for that area based on its research. Afterward, have each pair share its findings and conclusion. Follow up the activity by having the class group the cities into regions based on similar climates.

Boston	Memphis
Chicago	Milwaukee
Charlotte	New York City
Denver	Orlando
Houston	San Francisco
Los Angeles	Seattle
New Orleans	St. Louis
Las Vegas	

Star Style

Add some sparkle to your classroom with this lesson on stars!

Skill: Comparing different types of stars

Estimated Lesson Time: 1 hour

Teacher Preparation:

1. Make a transparency of the diagram on page 234, or draw the diagram on the chalkboard.
2. Duplicate page 235 and the materials list and directions on page 236 for each student.
3. Gather the materials listed below for each student.

Materials:

1 blank transparency (optional)
1 copy of page 235 and 1 copy of the materials list and directions on page 236 for each student
one 9" x 12" sheet of white construction paper or tagboard, one 12" and five 6" lengths of yellow yarn, markers or colored pencils, scissors, and a hole puncher for each student

Background Information:

A star is a huge ball of glowing gas in the sky. Although there are trillions of stars, only about 6,000 can be seen from the earth without using a telescope. During the day, sunlight brightens the sky and keeps us from seeing the stars, so we can see them only at night when the sky is dark and clear. These stars are so far away that they look like tiny points of light in the sky, but they are actually quite large. Stars vary in size from the smaller *neutron* stars to *supergiants,* which are much larger than the sun. Stars also vary in color and brightness depending on their size and temperature. Colors vary—red, orange, yellow, white, or blue—and temperatures range from 5,000°F to 50,000°F.

Scientists predict that in about five billion years, our aging sun will swell into a red giant and ultimately eliminate life on Earth. Later, this giant will cool down into a cold, burned-out ember.

Comparing different types of stars 233

Introducing The Lesson:

Draw a large star on the chalkboard. Then have students tell you what words come to mind when they think of a star, such as *bright, far away, small, twinkling,* and *pointed.* Record their responses inside the star.

Steps:

1. You will probably need to explain to students that some of their ideas about stars are true, but others are not. Share the Background Information on page 233.

2. Discuss how scientists divide stars into five main groups based on size: *neutron stars, white dwarfs, dwarf stars, giants,* and *supergiants.* Display the star diagram transparency or chalkboard drawing. Have students use the diagram to compare the relative sizes of stars.

3. Point out to students that a star changes during its lifetime. For example, a large giant may grow into a huge supergiant, or if it uses up all its fuel, it may shrink down to a white dwarf. The greater a star's mass (the amount of matter of which it's made), the higher its temperature and brightness, and the faster it changes.

4. Distribute a copy of page 235 and a copy of the materials list and directions on page 236 to each student. Then distribute the materials listed on page 236 to each student. Read "The Story Of Stars" together as a class. Then guide each student in completing the activity as directed on page 236. Have several student volunteers share their descriptions; then display the resulting star groups by hanging them from the ceiling.

Our Sun
The sun is a medium-sized dwarf star. Its diameter is about 865,000 miles (109 times the diameter of the earth).

Star Groups

Neutron Stars
Diameter = about 12 miles.

White Dwarfs
Diameter = about 5,200 miles.

Dwarfs
Diameter = about one-tenth the sun's diameter to ten times the sun's diameter.

Giants
Diameter = about 10 to 100 times the sun's diameter.

Supergiants
Diameter = about 330 to 1,000 times the sun's diameter.

Note: Drawings are not to scale.

The Story Of Stars

When you look up into the night sky, stars look like tiny pinpoints of light. Actually, the smallest type of star is the size of a small city! Read the story below. Then follow the directions on page 236 to create your own star-studded mobile.

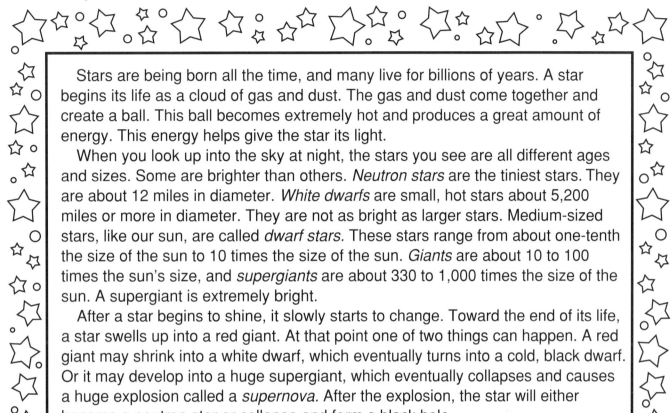

Stars are being born all the time, and many live for billions of years. A star begins its life as a cloud of gas and dust. The gas and dust come together and create a ball. This ball becomes extremely hot and produces a great amount of energy. This energy helps give the star its light.

When you look up into the sky at night, the stars you see are all different ages and sizes. Some are brighter than others. *Neutron stars* are the tiniest stars. They are about 12 miles in diameter. *White dwarfs* are small, hot stars about 5,200 miles or more in diameter. They are not as bright as larger stars. Medium-sized stars, like our sun, are called *dwarf stars.* These stars range from about one-tenth the size of the sun to 10 times the size of the sun. *Giants* are about 10 to 100 times the sun's size, and *supergiants* are about 330 to 1,000 times the size of the sun. A supergiant is extremely bright.

After a star begins to shine, it slowly starts to change. Toward the end of its life, a star swells up into a red giant. At that point one of two things can happen. A red giant may shrink into a white dwarf, which eventually turns into a cold, black dwarf. Or it may develop into a huge supergiant, which eventually collapses and causes a huge explosion called a *supernova.* After the explosion, the star will either become a neutron star or collapse and form a black hole.

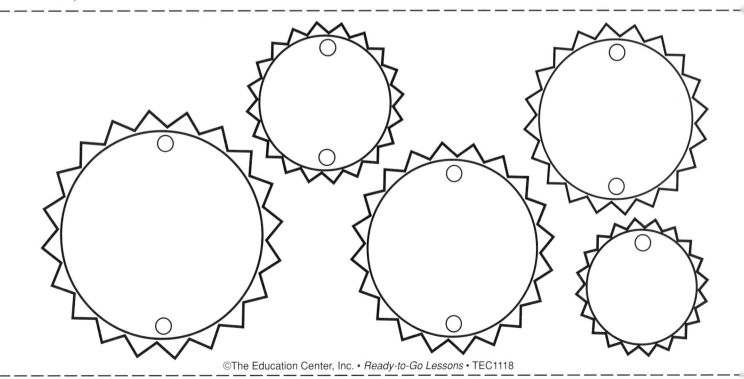

Note To The Teacher: Drawings are not to scale.

How To Extend The Lesson:

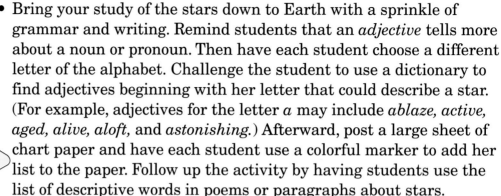

- Bring your study of the stars down to Earth with a sprinkle of grammar and writing. Remind students that an *adjective* tells more about a noun or pronoun. Then have each student choose a different letter of the alphabet. Challenge the student to use a dictionary to find adjectives beginning with her letter that could describe a star. (For example, adjectives for the letter *a* may include *ablaze, active, aged, alive, aloft,* and *astonishing.*) Afterward, post a large sheet of chart paper and have each student use a colorful marker to add her list to the paper. Follow up the activity by having students use the list of descriptive words in poems or paragraphs about stars.

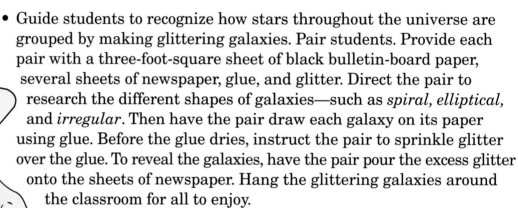

- Guide students to recognize how stars throughout the universe are grouped by making glittering galaxies. Pair students. Provide each pair with a three-foot-square sheet of black bulletin-board paper, several sheets of newspaper, glue, and glitter. Direct the pair to research the different shapes of galaxies—such as *spiral, elliptical,* and *irregular.* Then have the pair draw each galaxy on its paper using glue. Before the glue dries, instruct the pair to sprinkle glitter over the glue. To reveal the galaxies, have the pair pour the excess glitter onto the sheets of newspaper. Hang the glittering galaxies around the classroom for all to enjoy.

Materials: five star patterns, a 9" x 12" sheet of white construction paper or tagboard, one 12" and five 6" lengths of yellow yarn, markers or colored pencils, scissors, and a hole puncher

Directions:
1. Cut out the star patterns on the bottom of page 235. Use the patterns to trace an outline of each star onto construction paper or tagboard. Cut out each new pattern.
2. Read the paragraphs at the top of page 235. Then write the name of a different type of star on each cutout. (Make sure each cutout matches the size of the star you are describing.) Color each cutout.
3. On the back of each cutout, write a sentence describing the star.
4. Punch the holes where shown.
5. Connect all the cutouts using lengths of yarn. Use the 12" piece for the top cutout.

Note To The Teacher: Use with "The Story Of Stars" on page 235.

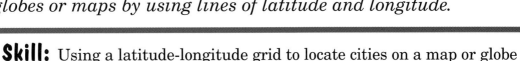

Where In The World Am I?

Help your students accurately locate their town and other U.S. cities on globes or maps by using lines of latitude and longitude.

Skill: Using a latitude-longitude grid to locate cities on a map or globe

Estimated Lesson Time: 45 minutes

Teacher Preparation:
Duplicate a class set of page 239.

Materials:
1 copy of page 239 for each student
crayons

Background Information:
The *latitude-longitude grid* is a system used by mapmakers all over the world to pinpoint exact locations on maps and globes.
- **Lines of Latitude**—run east–west; measure distances north and south
- **Lines of Longitude**—run north–south, crossing at the North and South Poles; measure distances east and west
- **Hemisphere**—half of a sphere or half of the earth
- **Degree**—unit of measurement for latitude and longitude (°)
- **Equator**—line of latitude dividing the earth into the Northern and Southern Hemispheres
- **Prime Meridian**—line of longitude located at 0°; divides the earth into the Eastern and Western Hemispheres

Introducing The Lesson:

Have students brainstorm ways early mapmakers made maps of the world. Then tell students that today mapmakers use a grid system known as the *latitude-longitude grid* to pinpoint exact locations.

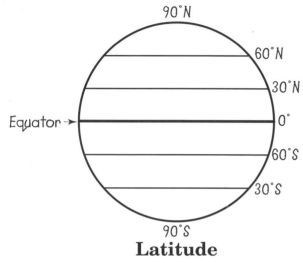

Latitude

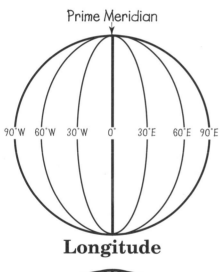

Longitude

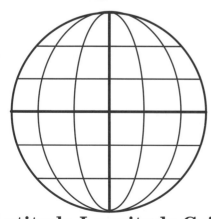

Latitude-Longitude Grid

Steps:

1. Draw these diagrams on the board or on a transparency.

2. Explain that the *equator* is a line of *latitude* located halfway between the North Pole and the South Pole that divides the earth into the Northern and Southern Hemispheres.

3. Inform students that lines of *latitude* are parallel lines that run east and west and measure distances in *degrees* north or south of the equator. Tell students the equator is located at 0° latitude, the North Pole at 90°N latitude, and the South Pole at 90°S latitude.

4. Next explain that lines of *longitude* run north and south (crossing at the poles) and measure distances east and west. Tell students that the *prime meridian* is located at 0° longitude and divides the earth into the Eastern and Western Hemispheres.

5. Tell students that each line of longitude crosses each line of latitude, creating a grid. By using this grid you can pinpoint any location on earth.

6. Distribute crayons and one copy of page 239 to each student. Instruct each student to complete the reproducible as directed.

Latitude-Longitude Grid

Directions: Use the map and the latitude-longitude grid to complete the activities below.

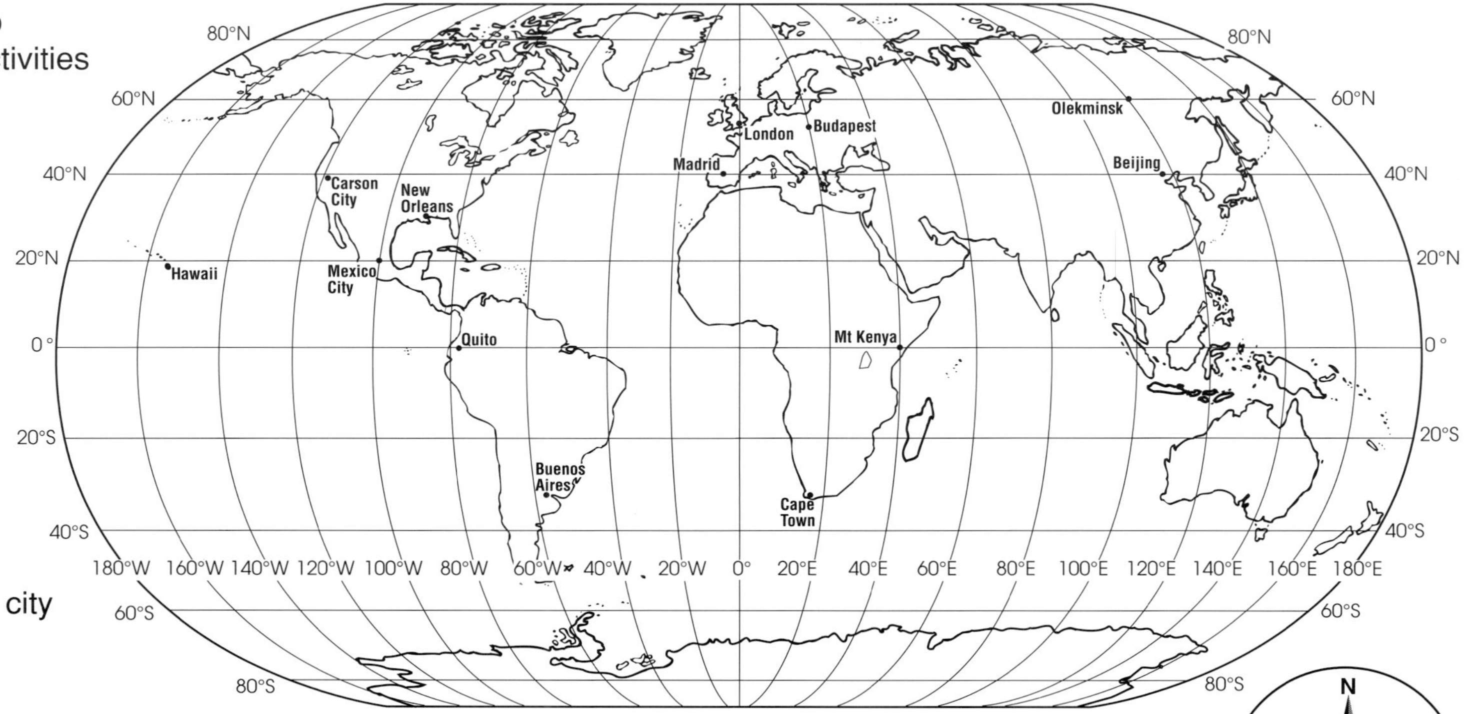

1. Locate and color the equator blue.

2. Locate and color the prime meridian red.

3. Draw an orange box around the city and the landform located on the equator.

4. Draw a green circle around the city located on the prime meridian.

5. What city is located near 40°N latitude, 0° longitude? _____

6. Give the location of the Asian city of Olekminsk.
   _____ latitude, _____ longitude

7. Name two cities located on or near 20°E longitude.
   _____ and _____

8. Name the North American city located at 20°N latitude, 100°W longitude. _____

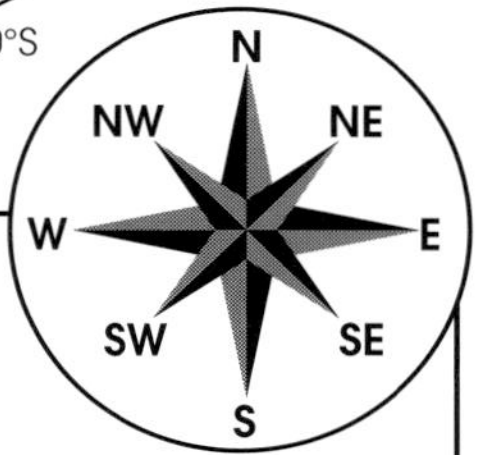

Bonus Box: The climate at the equator is very warm and tropical. The closer to the equator, the warmer the climate. The farther away from the equator, the cooler the climate. Locate Buenos Aires, New Orleans, and London on the map above. Which two of these three cities have similar climates? Explain your answer. _____

Map labels: 80°N, 60°N, 40°N, 20°N, 0°, 20°S, 40°S, 60°S, 80°S

Longitude labels: 180°W, 160°W, 140°W, 120°W, 100°W, 80°W, 60°W, 40°W, 20°W, 0°, 20°E, 40°E, 60°E, 80°E, 100°E, 120°E, 140°E, 160°E, 180°E

City/landform labels: Olekminsk, Beijing, Budapest, London, Madrid, Mt Kenya, Cape Town, Buenos Aires, Quito, New Orleans, Carson City, Mexico City, Hawaii

Compass: N, NE, E, SE, S, SW, W, NW

©The Education Center, Inc. • *Ready-to-Go Lessons* • TEC1118 • Key p. 319

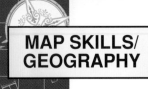
How To Extend The Lesson:

- June through November marks the hurricane season for the United States. Contact the weather department of a local television station and request a class set of hurricane tracking maps—many stations distribute the maps free of charge. Inform students that meteorologists use lines of latitude and longitude to track hurricanes. Have students use the latitude-longitude grid and the tracking maps to plot the movements of hurricanes and tropical storms during the first few months of school. Also have students explore reasons why so many hurricanes develop in the north Atlantic Ocean and the Gulf of Mexico.

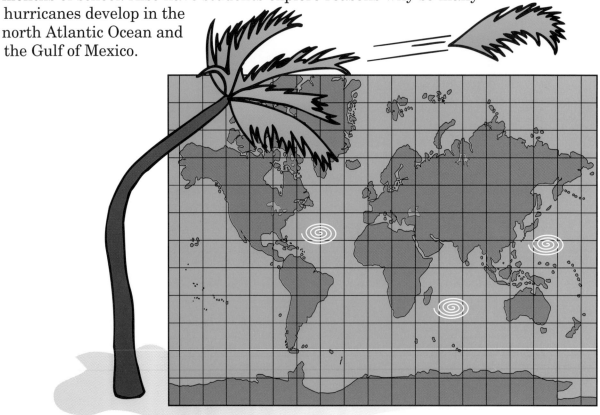

- Have each student plan a trip around the world. Instruct each student to create a travel journal of his trip. Direct the student to visit at least one city in each continent. Have the student include the name of each city, country, and continent visited. Also direct him to give the location of each city using the latitude-longitude grid. Have each student research interesting information on the climate and physical features of each city. Encourage the student to include maps, illustrations, and magazine clippings for each city.

Direction Detection!

*Create a class full of direction detectives with this hands-on
lesson about map-reading.*

Skill: Using cardinal and intermediate directions

Estimated Lesson Time: 45 minutes

Teacher Preparation:
1. Duplicate one copy of page 243 for each student.
2. Make a large construction-paper model of a
   compass rose.

Materials:
1 copy of page 243 for each student
1 U.S. map with a compass rose
1 large construction-paper model of
   a compass rose
crayons or colored pencils

Background Information:
Mapmakers use special marks and symbols to show direction on a map. A map's
compass rose shows these directions. The four main directions are called *cardinal
directions*. They are north (N), south (S), east (E), and west (W). The directions in
between these main directions are called *intermediate directions*. They are northeast (NE), southeast (SE), southwest (SW), and northwest (NW). To remember the
clockwise order of north, east, south, and west, a mnemonic sentence such as "**N**ed
Eats **S**hredded **W**heat" is helpful.

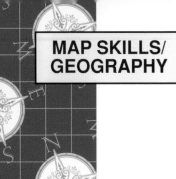

Introducing The Lesson:

Begin by challenging a student volunteer to give you directions for going from your classroom to the cafeteria. Ask another student to tell how to get from school to his home. Next have yet another student explain how to get from your school to your state capital. (Expect this student to hesitate.) Then ask your class to name a tool that would provide accurate directions to your state capital. Help your students conclude that a map is designed to help people find their way from one place or location to another.

Steps:

1. Display a large map of the United States that features a compass rose. Have a student volunteer point out the compass rose on the map and offer several ways that it could be useful to a traveler.

2. Write the sentence "Ned Eats Shredded Wheat" on your chalkboard. Underline the first letter of each word: the *N*, *E*, *S*, and *W*.

3. Use this sentence to help your students learn the clockwise order of directions on a compass rose. Explain that each word represents a specific direction on the compass rose: the *N* in Ned stands for north, the *E* in Eats represents east, the *S* in Shredded stands for south, and the *W* in Wheat indicates west.

4. Ask a student to point out the locations of northeast, southeast, southwest, and northwest on the large construction-paper compass rose that you made.

5. Ask another student to locate your state on the U.S. map. Direct different volunteers to point out other states, major landforms, or bodies of water that are located directly north, south, east, and west of your state.

6. Give a copy of page 243 to each student. Instruct the student to follow the directions on the sheet for completing the activity.

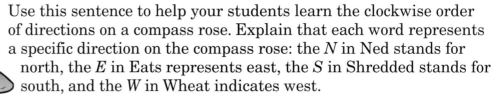

Fly two miles south, then . . .

Direction Detection

Directions: The postal abbreviations for each of the fifty states are shown on the map below. Use your map-reading skills to answer the questions on this sheet. When you finish, color your map. Then draw a star on the state in which you live.

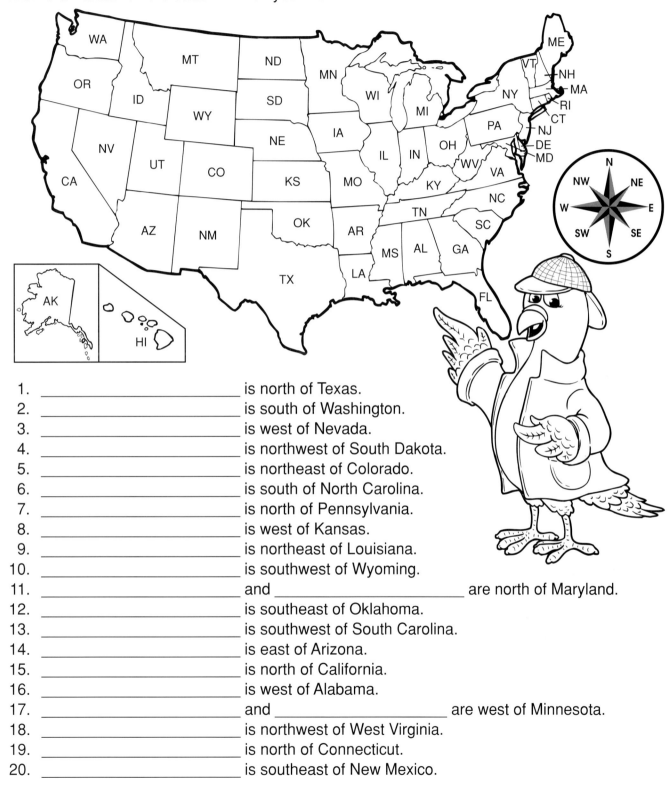

1. _____ is north of Texas.
2. _____ is south of Washington.
3. _____ is west of Nevada.
4. _____ is northwest of South Dakota.
5. _____ is northeast of Colorado.
6. _____ is south of North Carolina.
7. _____ is north of Pennsylvania.
8. _____ is west of Kansas.
9. _____ is northeast of Louisiana.
10. _____ is southwest of Wyoming.
11. _____ and _____ are north of Maryland.
12. _____ is southeast of Oklahoma.
13. _____ is southwest of South Carolina.
14. _____ is east of Arizona.
15. _____ is north of California.
16. _____ is west of Alabama.
17. _____ and _____ are west of Minnesota.
18. _____ is northwest of West Virginia.
19. _____ is north of Connecticut.
20. _____ is southeast of New Mexico.

Bonus Box: Which state in the United States is bordered by the most states? How many states border it? Write the names of these bordering states on the back of this sheet.

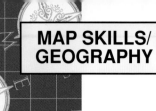

How To Extend The Lesson:

- Allow students to experience the terrain of the United States first-hand by making a class relief map. Follow the recipe below to make several batches of salt clay. Afterward instruct your students to draw an outline of the United States on a large piece of corrugated cardboard and cover it with salt clay. Then have them use the rest of their clay to form major geographic features and make their map as topographically accurate as possible. Before the clay dries, direct your students to label these features with flags made from tooth-picks and strips of paper. After the relief map has dried, allow your students to paint it with tempera paint.

Salt Clay

3 cups flour
1 cup salt
1 cup water

1. Mix together three cups of flour and one cup of salt in a large mixing bowl.
2. Add one cup of water and stir.
3. Knead the mixture until it is well blended.

- Request an area map and several travel brochures that feature local tourist attractions from your local Chamber of Commerce. Post this map on a bulletin board. Pair your students; then give each pair a travel brochure. Challenge the pairs to locate one or more attractions featured in these travel brochures on the displayed map. Afterward, have each pair post its travel brochure on the bulletin board with a length of yarn that matches each attraction to its location on the map. Allow each pair to name the direction they would need to travel if they wanted to visit the local attraction.

- Have each student in your class design a unique compass rose by drawing or tracing objects of his choice. For example, a student could make a compass rose from a drawing that uses arrows, pencils, flowers, etc. Remind each student that his compass rose drawing must have cardinal and intermediate directions that are clearly labeled. Then display your students' creative compass roses in your classroom.

Let's Get Physical!

Your students will be in top form after taking part in this fun physical geography lesson!

Skill: Identifying major geographic features of the United States

Estimated Lesson Time: 45 minutes

Teacher Preparation:

1. Duplicate one copy of page 247 for each student.
2. Gather several pictures or postcards of landforms found in the United States.

Materials:

pictures or postcards of landforms
1 copy of page 247 for each student
1 physical map of the United States for each student
reference materials, such as an encyclopedia or atlas

Background Information:

Physical geography is the study of the land, water, and climate of the earth. A few of the types of physical features found in the United States are defined below.

- *island*—a body of land completely surrounded by water
- *peninsula*—land surrounded by water on three sides
- *volcano*—a hill or mountain formed by molten rock forced through the earth's surface
- *mountain*—a part of land that rises abruptly to at least 1,000 feet above the land around it
- *mountain range*—a group or chain of mountains
- *valley*—low land between mountains or hills
- *canyon*—a narrow valley with high, steep sides
- *gulf*—a large area of ocean partly surrounded by land
- *plain*—a large area of flat or gently rolling land
- *lake*—a body of water, usually freshwater, surrounded by land
- *river*—a large stream that flows from a source to a larger body of water

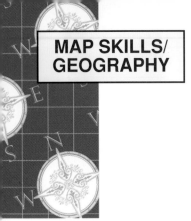

Introducing The Lesson:

Ask several student volunteers to share one of their prominent physical features with the class, such as a nose, a birthmark, hair color, eye color, or a scar. Guide students in understanding that, like people, the earth has a variety of physical features that make it unique.

Steps:

1. Explain to students that *physical geography* is the study of the earth's physical features.

2. Display several postcards or photographs of physical features of the United States; then ask students to try to identify the physical feature presented in each picture.

3. Record the following headings on the chalkboard: *island, peninsula, volcano, mountain, canyon, mountain range, river, lake, valley, plain,* and *gulf.*

4. Use the Background Information on page 245 to define any physical features that are unfamiliar to students.

5. Ask students to brainstorm the names of specific landforms and bodies of water within the United States that they have seen pictures of or have visited. Direct students to decide under which heading you should record each name.

6. Pair students; then provide each student with a copy of page 247. Have the pair work together to complete the page as directed.

7. Afterward, give each pair a physical map; then challenge the pair to locate each physical feature from page 247.

Rocky Mountains

Mount Rainier

Lake Okeechobee

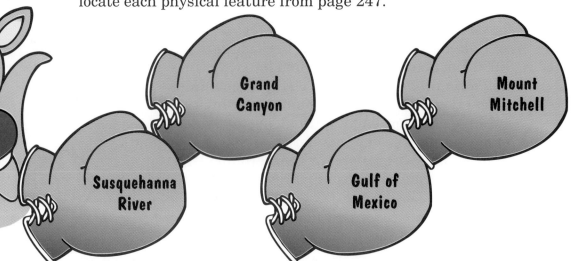

Grand Canyon

Mount Mitchell

Susquehanna River

Gulf of Mexico

Let's Get Physical!

Does your knowledge of U.S. geography really pack a punch? Follow the directions below to find out!

Directions: Work with a partner to find the name of each landform or body of water described below. Use an encyclopedia or other reference materials if necessary. After your paper has been graded, check the scoring chart to see what kind of expert you are.

1. This river flows 2,540 miles from southwestern Montana to its mouth on the Mississippi River.

_____

2. This volcano, located in the Cascade Mountains, erupted on May 18, 1980.

_____

3. This famous waterfall is actually two waterfalls: Horseshoe Falls in Ontario and American Falls in New York.

_____

4. This largest cave system ever explored by man is located in central Kentucky.

_____

5. Known as the lowest point in the United States, this valley lies 282 feet below sea level.

_____

6. This second-longest U.S. river flows from northwestern Minnesota to the Gulf of Mexico.

_____

7. This river forms part of the boundary between the United States and Mexico.

_____

8. This 277-mile-long canyon contains the Colorado River and cuts through northwestern Arizona.

_____

9. This inland saltwater sea is the largest lake in the western United States and is saltier than the oceans.

_____

10. This mountain system extends from northern Alaska to northern New Mexico.

_____

Scoring Chart

10 correct = Knockout Know-It-All

9 correct = Power Puncher

8 correct = Big-Time Boxer

Bonus Box: On the back of this sheet, name the five Great Lakes.

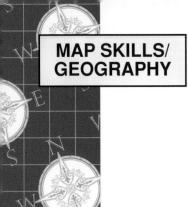

How To Extend The Lesson:

- Cut a supply of 8 1/2" x 11" sheets of paper in half. Provide each student with 11 half-sheets. Direct the student to record, define, and illustrate one physical geography term on each half-sheet of paper. Then have the student make an attractive cover for his booklet. Direct the student to put his sheets in alphabetical order with the cover page on top. Bind each booklet with brads or staples.

- Challenge each student to create a model that shows at least three landforms and two bodies of water from the booklet he created in the above activity. Allow the student to choose his own materials for this project, such as clay, salt dough, recycled materials, cardboard, papier-mâché, or a combination of these materials. Instruct the student to label each landform on his map. If desired, have the student attach index card labels telling how each landform was formed and where examples of each can be found in the United States.

- Post the chart below on the overhead. Point out that the chart provides information on the world's largest physical features: landforms and bodies of water. Divide your class into pairs. Then have each pair use a variety of reference materials to find the largest of each physical feature listed below found in the United States. Instruct student pairs to compare the largest physical features of the world to the largest physical features of the United States. Post the information on a bulletin board titled "The United States And The World."

The World's Largest

Physical Feature	Location	Size
Island	Greenland	840,000 square miles
Peninsula	Arabia	1,254,000 square miles
Volcano (largest)	Mauna Loa	30,000 feet from ocean floor; 60 miles wide
Mountain	Mt. Everest	29,028 feet
Mountain range (longest)	Andes	4,500 miles
River (longest)	Nile	4,145 miles
Lake	Caspian Sea	143,244 square miles
Waterfall (tallest)	Angel Falls	3,212 feet
Desert	Sahara	3,500,000 square miles
Swamp	Basin of Pripyat River	29,174 square miles

Eye On Colonial America

Give your students an inside view of colonial life in America.

Skill: Identifying characteristics of colonial life

Estimated Lesson Time: 45 minutes

Teacher Preparation:

1. Enlarge the map of the 13 colonies on page 250 and then post it.
2. Gather reference materials on the 13 colonies.
3. Duplicate one copy of page 251 for each group of students.

Materials:

1 enlarged map of the 13 colonies
1 copy of page 251 for each group of students
markers, crayons, or colored pencils
scissors
paper clips
string

Background Information:

The British-American colonial period began in the late 1500s with England's attempts to settle off the coast of North Carolina, and ended with the start of the Revolutionary War in 1775. The first permanent English settlement was Jamestown, founded in 1607.

Large numbers of people from many European countries, including England, Scotland, Wales, France, Germany, and the Netherlands, left Europe and made the treacherous journey across the Atlantic Ocean to the New World. Most came in search of a more prosperous life or religious freedom.

The 13 colonies are often divided into three geographic regions. They include *New England*—New Hampshire, Massachusetts, Connecticut, and Rhode Island; the *Middle colonies*—New York, New Jersey, Delaware, and Pennsylvania; and the *Southern colonies*—Maryland, Virginia, North Carolina, South Carolina, and Georgia. (Some historians consider Maryland and Virginia a fourth geographic area known as the *Chesapeake colonies.*)

Introducing The Lesson:

Ask students to imagine what it would be like to have no electricity or running water, grow their own food, make their own clothes, and learn to read and write in a one-room schoolhouse. Tell students that this is what life was like in colonial days.

Steps:

1. Share the Background Information on page 249 with your students.

2. Post an enlarged copy of the map below. Ask students to identify the original 13 colonies. Explain that present-day Maine was once part of Massachusetts, and present-day Vermont was once part of New Hampshire.

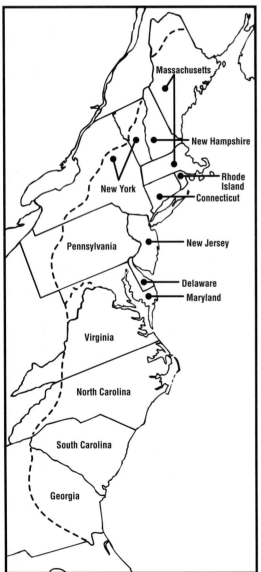

3. Ask students how each region is different today. (Students may note differences in climate, terrain, food, clothing, and shelter.)

4. Point out that the New England colonies consisted of small farms and villages. The Middle colonies had larger farms that produced surpluses of agricultural products for export, making it a center of trade. Southern colonies mainly consisted of large farms and plantations. Life here was rural and towns developed slowly. Encourage students to imagine what life was like in each region. Guide students to recognize that like today, environmental differences had an impact on how people lived.

5. Divide students into small groups. Distribute one copy of page 251 to each group. Assign each group one of the 13 colonies to research; then instruct the group to complete page 251 as directed. If desired, direct the group to cut out its completed sign.

6. Have each group present its information to the rest of the class. Using paper clips, attach the signs in geographic order (north to south) to a length of yarn. Attach both ends of the yarn to the ceiling like a clothesline. Title the display "Signs Of The Times."

It's The Sign Of The Times

What was life like during colonial times? What kinds of foods were eaten? What did people do for fun? Research to find information on each topic below. Record your findings in the space provided. After researching each topic, turn your paper over and trace the outline of the sign below using a black marker, crayon, or pencil; then draw and color simple illustrations that represent your colony.

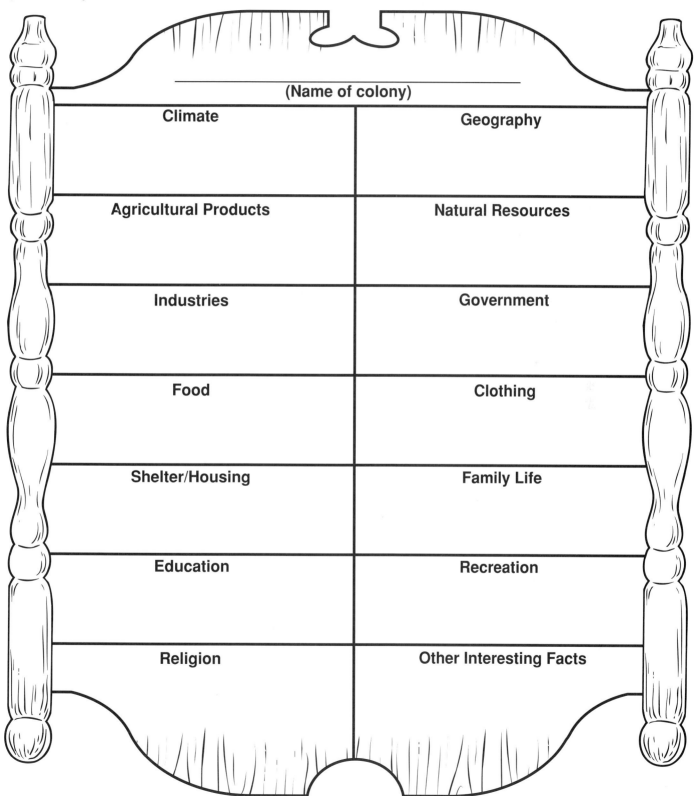

_____
(Name of colony)

Climate	Geography
Agricultural Products	Natural Resources
Industries	Government
Food	Clothing
Shelter/Housing	Family Life
Education	Recreation
Religion	Other Interesting Facts

How To Extend The Lesson:

- After researching information about colonial life, divide students into small groups. Then have each group create and present a puppet show describing a day in the life of a colonist. Instruct each group to create stick puppets using tagboard and straws. Have students dress the puppets using various materials such as fabric, ribbon, and buttons. Also encourage students to use realistic colonial names for their puppets such as Abigail, Caleb, Constance, or Miles.

- Have small groups of students search for data on colonial life, such as the total population in each colony, the ethnic population within each colony, natural resources available, and crops produced. Then have each group create a graph (bar graph, pictograph, or pie graph) presenting the data collected.

- Provide each student or pair of students with a colonial quotation from the chart below. Guide each student in determining the meaning of the quotation. Then supply the student with a sheet of drawing paper and markers or crayons. Have the student write the quotation at the bottom of his paper, then illustrate its meaning with a colored drawing. Finally, on the back of his paper, have the student write why he thinks the quotation was popular at the time and whether it is still used today.

Make hay while the sun shines.	Where there's a will, there's a way.
Nothing ventured, nothing gained.	Everything comes to him who waits.
Never put off until tomorrow what can be done today.	Birds of a feather flock together.
All that glitters is not gold.	A new broom sweeps clean.
Curiosity killed the cat.	It takes two to make a quarrel.
Handsome is as handsome does.	The early bird catches the worm.
Idleness is the mother of evil.	A rolling stone gathers no moss.
A place for everything and everything in its place.	A fool and his money are soon parted.
	Two wrongs do not make a right.

Tension Brews In Boston

Help students investigate the reasons behind the Boston Tea Party with this thought-provoking lesson.

Skill: Identifying and understanding the reasons behind the Boston Tea Party

Estimated Lesson Time: 1 hour

Teacher Preparation:

1. Duplicate one copy of page 255 for each pair of students.
2. Gather various resources and references on the American Revolution.

Materials:

1 copy of page 255 for each pair of students
reference materials

Background Information:

In December 1773, the British ships *Dartmouth, Eleanor,* and *Beaver* sailed into Boston harbor loaded with tea. The patriots of Boston were tired of paying English taxes on tea and gave their governor a deadline, December 16, 1773, to send back the tea. When that day arrived, the ships were still in the harbor. Patriot leaders gave the governor one last chance to send back the tea. When he refused, the patriots disguised themselves as Indians and hurried to the ships. Upon reaching the wharf, they divided into three groups, led by Samuel Adams, John Hancock, and Paul Revere. As a protest, the men dumped more than 300 chests of tea into the harbor.

Shortly thereafter, Paul Revere took to his horse and spread the news to other colonists. Patriots were questioned, but nobody talked. The colonists were punished with the Boston Port Bill, which stated that no ship was allowed to enter the harbor after June 1, 1774, until the patriots had paid for all the tea. People in the other 12 colonies also had tax problems with the British. So when word spread that the Boston harbor had closed, the other colonies sent rye and flour to help the people of Boston. Wagons came from South Carolina piled with rice. Maryland sent wheat. Although the Boston colonists were often hungry, they refused to give in to the king's orders.

Introducing The Lesson:

Begin this lesson by sharing the facts surrounding the Boston Tea Party found in the Background Information on page 253.

Steps:

1. Point out that there are often two sides to a situation. Have students identify the two conflicting sides of the Boston Tea Party *(the patriots and the British)*. Then explain that both sides had their own specific reasons for what they were doing.

2. Hold a class discussion in which students give examples of times when they were told to do something that they didn't support or believe in and weren't able to express their points of view on the situation. For example, maybe a student's parents made him take piano lessons even though he would have rather played on the soccer team.

3. Pair students and assign each pair a side, either British or patriot. Using a social studies text and/or other reference materials, have each pair research its respective side of the taxing of tea and the Boston Tea Party.

4. Give each pair one copy of page 255.

5. Instruct each pair to use its reproducible to outline its reasons for and feelings about either taxing the tea, if British, or tossing the tea overboard, if a patriot.

6. Select a British pair and a Patriot pair to present their cases in a debate in front of the class. Challenge pairs to argue their points, using their sheets as guides. Be sure to establish some debating rules, such as no interruptions and time limits for each pair's responses. After the debate, have the two pairs answer questions from the audience. Continue the debating process with other pairs if time allows.

Boston Tea Party: research, debating

Two Sides To Every Story

The Boston Tea Party was one of America's first acts of independence. The British, however, had their reasons for taxation, too. Using the new identity your teacher has assigned to you, fill out this sheet and explain your actions during the famous Boston Tea Party.

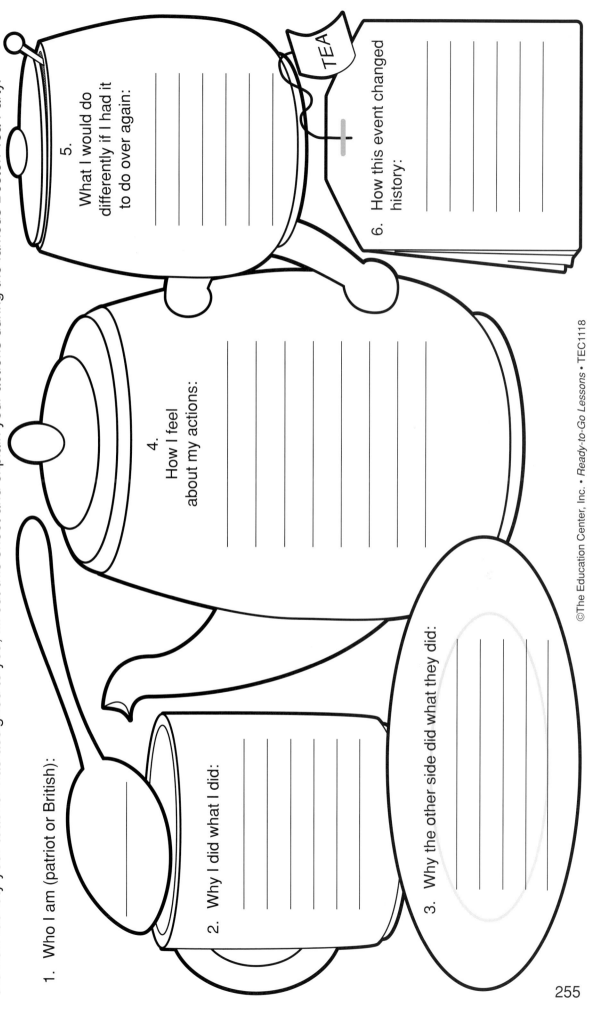

1. Who I am (patriot or British): _____

2. Why I did what I did:

3. Why the other side did what they did:

4. How I feel about my actions:

5. What I would do differently if I had it to do over again:

6. How this event changed history:

How To Extend The Lesson:

- Share some of the following literature with your students during your study of the Boston Tea Party:
  — *Boston's Freedom Trail* by Terry Dunnahoo (Dillon Press, 1995)
  — *Book Of The American Revolution* by Howard Egger-Bovet and Marlene Smith-Baranzini (Little, Brown And Company; 1994)
  — *Colonial People* by Sarah Howarth (The Millbrook Press, Inc.; 1994)
  — *Colonial Places* by Sarah Howarth (The Millbrook Press, Inc.; 1994)
  — *And Then What Happened, Paul Revere?* by Jean Fritz (Coward McCann, Inc.; 1998)
  — *The Boston Tea Party* by Steven Kroll (Holiday House, Inc.; 1998)

- Students often have a hard time realizing the impact of taxation on food items simply because they don't buy their own groceries. Collect grocery store flyers from several newspapers and pass one out to each of your students. Write a monetary amount on the board, such as $10.00. Next have each of your students go through his flyer and pick out as many items as he can up to that amount. Have him list the items on a sheet of notebook paper. When his list is complete, add a twist by telling him that you'd forgotten about the state sales tax! Now have him multiply his fictional purchase by your state's food tax or by 5 to 10 percent. Direct him to add this figure to his total. *(He will now have to give up one or two food items to make up the difference.)* Now have him multiply his purchase by an exorbitant tax, such as 20 or 30 percent! How many items will he have to give up now? Remind him that this is exactly what was happening to the patriots.

- Personalize the Boston Tea Party for your students with this writing activity. Write the following story starter on the board: "It is December 1773, and my brother William desperately needs hot tea to soothe his pneumonia. Yet the British tax on tea makes it too expensive for us to afford. But those crafty patriots have a plan…" Give each of your students an opportunity to finish the story for herself. Stipulate that the climax of each story must take place on one of the three ships involved in the Boston Tea Party. Bind the completed stories in a class book titled "British Colonist, What Would You Do?" Then place the book in your reading center for all to enjoy.

A Fight For Independence

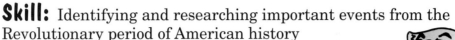

Help your students catch the spirit of '76 as they study this classic conflict with the following Revolutionary lesson!

Skill: Identifying and researching important events from the Revolutionary period of American history

Estimated Lesson Time: 45 minutes

Teacher Preparation:
Duplicate one copy of page 259 on heavyweight paper for each student.

Materials:
1 copy of page 259 for each student
crayons
reference materials

Background Information:

From 1775 to 1783 the Revolutionary War was fought between Great Britain and its 13 American colonies. The American colonies were successful in their battle for independence. As a result, the United States of America was formed.

Important Events Of The American Revolution

April 19, 1775 Redcoats and minutemen fight at Lexington and Concord.
June 15, 1775 George Washington is named commander-in-chief of the Continental Army.
June 17, 1775 The Battle of Bunker Hill takes place.
July 4, 1776 The Declaration of Independence is adopted.
August 27, 1776 British defeat Americans on Long Island.
December 26, 1776 Washington leads a surprise attack on Hessian troops at Trenton.
January 3, 1777 Americans win the battle at Princeton.
September 11, 1777 British defeat Americans at Brandywine.
September 26, 1777 Philadelphia is occupied by the British.
October 4, 1777 American troops are defeated in the Battle of Germantown.
December 19, 1777 Washington and troops move to winter quarters at Valley Forge.
February 6, 1778 France signs an alliance with the Americans.
February 25, 1779 British troops at Vincennes surrender to George Rogers Clark.
June 21, 1779 Spain declares war on Great Britain.
May 12, 1780 Charleston falls after a British attack.
August 16, 1780 British defeat Americans at Camden.
March 15, 1781 Cornwallis battles Greene at Guilford Courthouse.
September 5, 1781 British fleet is heavily damaged by French naval fleet at Chesapeake Bay.
October 19, 1781 Cornwallis's forces surrender at Yorktown.
November 30, 1782 British and Americans sign a preliminary peace treaty in Paris.
April 15, 1783 U.S. Congress ratifies preliminary peace treaty.
September 3, 1783 Final peace treaty between Great Britain and the United States is signed in Paris.

Introducing The Lesson:

Explain to students that an *effect* is the result of a cause or set of causes. Tell students that the Revolutionary War was an effect; then ask them to think about possible causes of the war. Invite students to share several causes aloud; then record students' responses on the board.

Steps:

1. Point out to students that while there were many key events that caused the Revolution, there were also many important events that occurred during the war.

2. Divide your class into pairs. Ask each pair to use a variety of reference materials to find important events that occurred during the Revolution. Have each pair record its findings on a sheet of paper. Combine each pair's responses to make a large list of important wartime events.

3. Assign each student a specific event from your class list or the list on page 257 to research. Then provide each student with one copy of page 259.

4. Instruct each student to follow the directions as written on page 259 to complete the activity.

5. Display your students' frames in chronological order on a bulletin board or wall to create a timeline of the Revolutionary War.

Causes Of The American Revolution
- 1763—Parliament issued the Proclamation of 1763.
- 1765—Parliament passed the Stamp Act.
- 1767—Parliament passed the Townshend Acts.
- 1768—British soldiers moved into Boston, which eventually triggered the Boston Massacre in 1770.
- 1773—Boston colonists took part in the Boston Tea Party.
- 1774—The British passed strict laws that colonists called the Intolerable Acts.

A Time Of War

Directions: Illustrate an important event from the Revolutionary War inside the frame below. Record the title and date of the event in the ribbon; then write a short summary of the event on the lines provided.

Event _____

Date _____

_____
_____
_____
_____
_____
_____
_____
_____
_____

Name _____

How To Extend The Lesson:

- Have students locate sites of major Revolutionary War battles listed below on a large map of the United States. Direct students to label the location of each battle won by the Americans with a miniature model of the American flag, *Old Glory.* Likewise, direct students to label each battle won by the British forces with a miniature model of the British flag, the *Union Jack.*

British Victories	American Victories
Montreal (Canada)	Ticonderoga (NY)
Bunker Hill (MA)	Saratoga (NY)
Germantown (PA)	Lexington (MA)
Jamestown (VA)	Princeton (NJ)
Long Island (NY)	Trenton (NJ)
Brandywine (PA)	Cowpens (SC)
Camden (SC)	Chesapeake Bay (MD/VA)
	Yorktown (VA)
	Guilford Courthouse (NC)

Famous Figures Of The American Revolution
Abigail Adams
John Adams
Samuel Adams
Ethan Allen
Crispus Attucks
Jean-Baptiste Mars Belley
George Rogers Clark
Lydia Darragh
William Flora
Benjamin Franklin
Nathanael Greene
John Hancock
Mary "Molly Pitcher" Hays
Patrick Henry
Thomas Jefferson
John Paul Jones
Marquis de Lafayette
Sybil Ludington
Saul Matthews
Thomas Paine
Paul Revere
Betsy Ross
Baron von Steuben
George Washington
Phillis Wheatley

- Familiarize students with some important people involved in the American Revolution with this activity. Assign each student a famous figure from the list at the left; then give each student an enlarged copy of the bell pattern below. Direct each student to find out about the person's life, accomplishments, and role in the Revolution. Then have the student record his findings on the pattern. Display the bell patterns on a bulletin board titled "Let Freedom Ring!"

- Divide your students into groups of four; then provide each group with an 11" x 14" sheet of tagboard, a die, and 20 blank 2" x 3" tagboard cards. Direct each group to use its knowledge of the Revolutionary War to create an original board game with a Revolutionary theme. Instruct students to record questions pertaining to the war and its personalities on the cards. Remind each group to include an answer key with its game as well as a set of rules. Invite each group to exchange its game with another group to test each group's knowledge of the era.

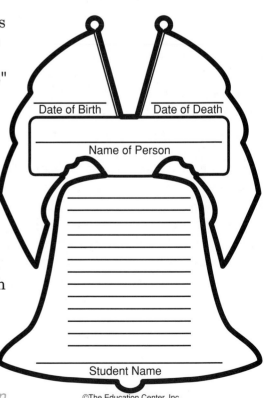

Date of Birth   Date of Death

Name of Person

Student Name

Westward Ho!

Get the wheels turning on your study of America's westward expansion with the following lesson.

Skill: Categorizing supplies needed on the Oregon Trail

Estimated Lesson Time: 45 minutes

Teacher Preparation:
Duplicate one copy of page 263 for each student.

Materials:
1 copy of page 263 per student
chart paper
markers
a supply of scrap paper, counters, or game
    chips per student

Background Information:
    Heading west was not an easy job. A family packed possessions, a supply of food, and themselves into a *Conestoga* (covered) wagon. Together families headed west on one of several main trails. The 2,000-mile Oregon Trail took settlers to Oregon's Willamette Valley. The Oregon Trail also had a southern branch that took settlers to the area of Sacramento, California. Others traveled the Old Spanish Trail, which ended in the area of Los Angeles, California.

    Pioneers ready to travel the Oregon Trail arrived in Independence or St. Joseph, Missouri, with only their most prized possessions; family heirlooms; and essential supplies, such as food, clothing, and firearms. Pioneers had to pack their wagons very carefully, making room for all the items needed to start their new homes out west. The chart at the right shows the food supplies needed for *each* adult traveling the Oregon Trail.

**Supplies
Needed Per Adult**
200 pounds of flour
1/2 bushel of dried beans
10 pounds of rice
75 pounds of bacon
25 pounds of sugar
2 pounds of baking soda
30 pounds of flatbread
2 pounds of tea
1 bushel of dried fruit
10 pounds of salt
1/2 bushel of cornmeal
5 pounds of coffee

Introducing The Lesson:

Begin the lesson by taking a poll of how many students have ever moved from one city to another, one state to another, and/or one country to another. Then ask students to describe what was involved in moving all their possessions to a new location. Now have your students close their eyes and try to imagine cramming all their possessions and the necessary supplies for a six-month, 2,000-mile trek aboard a 10' x 4' wooden wagon. Then explain that that's exactly what pioneer families did in the 1800s when they decided to move westward along the Oregon Trail.

Steps:

1. Share with students the Background Information on page 261. Then have students explain which were the most important items to be packed in each family's wagon in order to survive the 2,000-mile journey *(food and supplies)*.

2. Explain to your students that it was a hard task for families to select what to bring along on the westward trip. They needed to be prepared not only for the trip but for life as settlers once they reached their destination.

3. Have your students brainstorm a list of supplies, including food, clothing, tools, and cooking gear, that might have been taken on the trip (see the list at the left for possible supplies). Write the students' responses on a sheet of chart paper or on the chalkboard.

4. Give each student one copy of page 263 and a supply of counters or game chips. *(If counters or game chips are not available, have students tear off a supply of small scrap-paper squares.)*

5. Instruct each student to write a different supply from the class list in each square underneath the appropriate category heading.

6. Tell your students that they are going to play a game called Westo. To play the game, follow the same rules used for playing bingo. Call out a category heading and one supply item from the class list. If the student has written down the supply item underneath the correct category, he may cover that square with a counter or game chip. Once a student has five items in a row, he yells out "Westo!" Be sure to check that the student has marked the correct items.

Supplies

flour
yeast
crackers
cornmeal
bacon
eggs
dried meat and fruit
potatoes
rice
beans
coffee
sugar
salt
water
cows for milk and meat
cloth
needles
thread
pins
scissors
leather
saws
hammers
axes
nails
string
knives
soap
wax for making candles
lanterns
washbowls
tents
medicines
cooking supplies
eating utensils and cups
pots and pans
weapons

Name _____

WESTO

Food	Tools	Clothing	Household Goods	Cooking Gear
		FREE		

©The Education Center, Inc. • *Ready-to-Go Lessons* • TEC1118

How To Extend The Lesson:

• Have your students pack their own Conestoga wagon for an imaginary trip along the Oregon Trail. Cut two ten-foot lengths of yarn and two four-foot lengths of yarn. Tape the lengths of yarn to the floor to create a 4' x 10' rectangle. Inform your students that this is the actual size of a Conestoga wagon used by many settlers to move their entire family, food, supplies, and household goods to Oregon. Have students list items that families may have packed in their wagons (see supply lists on pages 261 and 262). Then have students find other objects in the classroom—a desk, books, cardboard boxes, etc.—to represent the needed supplies. Have students pack the items inside the 4' x 10' rectangle. After students have packed their wagon, have them discuss whether they got all the items inside the wagon. Is there enough room for family members? After students have evaluated their packing, have each student write about what it would be like to be a member of a family in the 1800s heading west along the Oregon Trail and to be able to take only the barest essentials.

• Many men and women braved the westward trails. Have each student in your class select a different person listed below to research. Instruct each student to write at least a one-page paper describing his person's contributions to the westward movement of the 1800s. Also have the student include an illustration with his writing. Post each student's work on a bulletin board titled "Headin' West!"

Mary Achey	Marie Dorion	John McLoughlin
Antonio Armijo	William George Fargo	Esther Morris
William Becknell	John Charles Frémont	Carrie Roach
Catharine Beecher	James Gadsden	Sacajewea
Daniel Boone	Mary Anna Hallock	Jedediah S. Smith
James Bowie	Sam Houston	Eliza Spalding
Jim Bridger	Thomas Jefferson	Robert Stuart
Evelyn Jephson Cameron	Mary Jemison	Tecumseh
Kit Carson	Meriwether Lewis	Marcus Whitman
William Clark	Abraham Lincoln	Narcissa Prentiss Whitman
Davy Crockett	James Marshall	Sarah Winnemucca
	Biddy Mason	

• Display the following books about westward expansion in your classroom for students to enjoy:
— *Caddie Woodlawn* by Carol Ryrie Brink (Aladdin Paperbacks, 1990)
— *Only The Names Remain: The Cherokees And The Trail Of Tears* by Alex W. Bealer (Little, Brown And Company; 1996)
— *Daily Life In A Covered Wagon* by Paul Erickson (Puffin Books, 1997)
— *The Pioneers Go West* by George Rippey Stewart (Random House, Inc.; 1997)
— *Wagon Train: A Family Goes West In 1865* by Courtni Crump Wright (Holiday House, Inc.; 1995)

A House Divided

Guide your students' independent research into the Civil War with this simple graphic organizer.

Skill: Understanding basic facts about the Civil War

Estimated Lesson Time: 1 hour

Teacher Preparation:

1. Duplicate one copy of page 267 for each student.
2. Gather resources depicting life in America during the Civil War.
3. Display a large map of the United States.

Materials:

1 copy of page 267 for each student
Civil War resources

Background Information:

Slavery was an issue long before the Civil War began in 1861. In 1820, Thomas Jefferson wrote that the issue of slavery was "like a firebell in the night [that] awakened and filled me with terror." That firebell sounded for all Americans in 1860 when Northerners believed the election of Abraham Lincoln would end slavery. Some Southerners, worried that the Northerners were right, decided that if Lincoln was elected, their states would *secede,* or withdraw, from the Union. Before Lincoln could take office in March of 1861, 11 states seceded, leading to the Civil War.

When the fighting began on April 12, 1861, it seemed that the North, with its superior fighting force, industrial power, and larger population, would easily overcome the smaller, more agricultural South. Yet many Northerners were shocked when the Southern attack on Fort Sumter caused a Northern retreat two days later. The North then realized that it faced a long fight.

The North was right. The Civil War lasted four years, and when it ended with Confederate General Robert E. Lee's surrender to Union General Ulysses S. Grant on April 9, 1865, more than 6 million soldiers were dead, missing, or wounded.

Introducing The Lesson:

Begin this lesson by sharing the Background Information on page 265 with your students.

Steps:

1. Using a large map of the United States, help students identify the two conflicting sides of the Civil War: the Northern states (or the Union) and the Southern states (or the Confederacy). Then explain that each side of the struggle had its own president, generals, successful battles, and uniforms.

2. Give each student a copy of page 267. Then pair students and assign each partner a side of the Civil War to research, either Union or Confederate.

3. Using social studies texts, encyclopedias, the Internet, and other reference materials you've gathered, have each student research his side of the Civil War using the reproducible as a guide.

4. Instruct the students in each pair to exchange their completed copies of page 267 with each other. Using his partner's sheet as a guide, have each student write a brief paper summarizing what he learned from his partner's research. In this way, both students learn about both sides of the Civil War. Then collect the students' summaries and bind them together in a notebook titled "Understanding The Civil War."

A House Divided

At the time of the Civil War, Abraham Lincoln called the nation "a house divided."
Use the graphic organizer below to guide your research into the Civil War.

_____
(Union or Confederate)

States

Famous Generals

Causes Of The War: Your Side's Point Of View

President

Famous Battle Victories

Bonus Box: Add another room to your "house divided." Choose one of your side's famous battles and research it more thoroughly.

How To Extend The Lesson:

- Share some of the following literature with your students during your study of the Civil War:
  — *Who Comes With Cannons?* by Patricia Beatty (Greenwillow, 1992)
  — *Running For Our Lives* by Glennette Tilley Turner (Holiday House, 1994)
  — *Christmas In The Big House, Christmas In The Quarters* by Patricia C. McKissack and Frederick L. McKissack (Scholastic Trade, 1994)
  — *Gentle Annie: The True Story Of A Civil War Nurse* by Mary Francis Shura (Scholastic Inc., 1994)
  — *A Separate Battle: Women And The Civil War* by Ina Chang (Puffin, 1996)
  — *A Nation Torn: The Story Of How The Civil War Began* by Delia Ray (Puffin, 1996)

- Read aloud from Lincoln's Gettysburg Address, second inaugural speech, or the Emancipation Proclamation as found in your social studies text or other resources. As you read, have each student write down ten important words he hears. After each student has compiled his list, call on volunteers to share their words and then have them write the words on the board. Provide magazines, scissors, glue, and construction paper; then instruct each student to find pictures that represent several of the key words listed on the board. Instruct each student to use his pictures to make a collage. Display the completed collages. Then invite students to visit each other's work and guess which words are represented by the pictures.

- The Civil War so divided the country that in many cases brother fought against brother. Share this fact with students and discuss what impact this might have had on a family facing such a tragedy. Then instruct each student to imagine that his brother or sister is fighting for the opposing side during the Civil War. Have each student write a letter to this sibling explaining his reasons for fighting for his side during the struggle. Collect the letters and bind them in a book titled "Brothers And Sisters In Battle."

Dear Brother,
  I now resume my seat to write you a few lines to let you know I am still in the land of the living.
  We had but one big battle that was at Gettysburg, Pennsylvania. This was said to be the hardest fight that has been fought during the war, and great slaughter was on both sides. The ground lay covered with the dead and wounded for miles...

Wheels Of Change

*Start your students down the road to understanding the
Industrial Revolution with this hands-on lesson.*

Skill: Understanding the impact of the Industrial Revolution
on American society

Estimated Lesson Time: 45 minutes

Teacher Preparation:

1. Duplicate one copy of page 271 for each student pair.
2. Gather resources depicting life in America in the late 1700s.
3. Display a map of the United States.
4. Gather one paper-towel tube and one toilet-paper tube for each pair of students.

Materials For Each Pair Of Students:

1 copy of page 271
1 empty paper-towel tube
1 empty toilet-paper tube
two 3" x 5" index cards
scissors
tape
1 large rubber band
1 unsharpened pencil

Background Information:

The Industrial Revolution changed the way Americans lived in the late 1700s and the 1800s. It began in the early 1700s when the British invented power-driven machinery and developed factories. By the late 1700s, power-driven factories began to appear all along the free-flowing rivers of northeast America.

American manufacturing no longer depended on people working by hand or in their own homes. Cities experienced rapid growth as families left their farms and moved near factories to work. Women and young children made up a large part of this workforce. Many immigrants moved to the United States to work in the factories. Workers eventually formed labor unions to help improve their dangerous working conditions and poor wages.

Transportation grew as industry needed greater amounts of raw materials and finished goods carried over long distances. The United States moved from a farming society to a more industrial country.

Introducing The Lesson:

Share the Background Information on page 269 with your students. Then ask them the following question: "How would your life change if you no longer had electricity or power-driven machines?" Write a list of their responses on the board. *(Include changes in recreation, work, products, transportation, and industry.)* Tell students that they now have an idea of what life was like in early America.

Steps:

1. Show a map of the United States. Explain how the total U.S. population in 1780 was only 2,780,400. Emphasize that 1,681,000 people, or 61% of the country, lived in the Northeast. The United States only extended to the Mississippi River, but many pioneers were already heading west.

2. Ask students what major event had just taken place in our country in the early 1780s. *(America had just gained its independence from Great Britain.)*

3. Next ask students how people traveled and worked in the late 1700s. *(People traveled by foot, horse, wagon, coach, or boat. Most people lived on farms and all manufacturing was done by hand.)* If available, show students pictures depicting life during that period.

4. Tell students that today's activity will show them how life in America changed dramatically after 1790.

5. Divide the class into pairs. Distribute one copy of page 271 to each pair and the materials listed on page 269. Direct students to carefully read the background information and follow the directions on the reproducible.

6. After they are finished with the activity, invite students to share their responses to the question at the bottom of the reproducible.

Wheels Of Change

Samuel Slater was a British textile worker who used waterpowered spinning machines. In 1790, he left England and came to work in a cotton-spinning mill in Pawtucket, Rhode Island. Slater built a machine like the one he had worked with in England. The water of the Blackstone River powered the waterwheel. The waterwheel, in turn, operated a series of belts and gears that ran the machinery.

Directions: Follow the steps below to make a waterwheel with your partner.

1. Cut both index cards in half horizontally (see Figure 1).

Figure 1

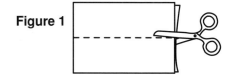

2. Make a 1/2" fold on the long edge of each card (see Figure 2). Figure 2

3. Make the waterwheel's paddles by taping the folded edge of each card to the paper-towel tube. Leave a 1" border from the end of the tube (see Figure 3).

Figure 3

4. Attach the rubber band to the other end of the paper-towel tube. Hold the band open and place the toilet-paper tube inside the rubber band. Place the pencil inside the toilet-paper tube (see Figure 4).

Figure 4

5. Have your partner hold each end of the pencil and gently stretch the rubber band until it feels tight (see Figure 5). Then turn the paper-towel tube with your hand.

Figure 5

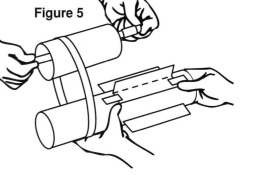

6. As you turn the paper-towel tube, what happens to the rubber band? _____ _____ What happens to the toilet-paper tube? _____ In a real waterwheel, how would this action operate the machinery? _____ _____

Bonus Box: With your partner, think about the ways life changed after power-driven machinery began to be used. List your ideas on the back of this paper and be prepared to share them with the class.

How To Extend The Lesson:

• The Industrial Revolution caused environmental problems, such as air and water pollution. Raise your students' awareness of this issue by reading aloud the beautifully illustrated book by Lynne Cherry, *A River Ran Wild: An Environmental History* (Harcourt Brace & Company, 1992). Set in the Northeast, it tells the history of the Nashua River. Its pristine condition, when only Native Americans lived on the land, changed through the years to a state of pollution. Restoration of the river began in the 1960s. After hearing and discussing the story, challenge each student to become the river. Direct him to tell the story of the river's life from the river's point of view. Encourage each student to illustrate his work and then share his story aloud.

• Many Americans' lives were affected by the Industrial Revolution. Cities became overcrowded as families left rural areas and moved near the factories to work. Most of the factories employed women and children. Samuel Slater's mill, for example, hired children between the ages of 7 and 14 to run machinery. The workdays were long, and the working conditions were dangerous. Have each student imagine that she has a pen pal her age who worked at Slater's mill in the early 1790s. Have her first write a letter from the pen pal's point of view, telling about that child's life in the 1790s. Then have the student respond to her imaginary pen pal with a letter telling about her own life in the present.

• Transportation grew as industry needed greater amounts of raw materials and finished goods carried over long distances. Post the outline below on a bulletin board, leaving space under each category. Divide the class into small cooperative groups and assign each group a category to research. Direct each group to collect facts about its category to complete the outline. Then have each group write its facts on a sentence strip and add the strip to the bulletin board.

America On The Move: 1750–1875

1. Natural waterways

2. Canals

3. Roads

4. Railroad

5. Steamboats and steam engines

Coming To America

Celebrate America's rich cultural diversity with this
thought-provoking lesson that explores immigration.

Skill: Interpreting graphs and maps to identify immigrant populations

Estimated Lesson Time: 45 minutes

Teacher Preparation:

1. Duplicate one copy of page 275 for each student.
2. Obtain a picture of the Statue of Liberty.

Materials:

1 copy of page 275 for each student
picture of the Statue of Liberty
1 sheet of chart paper
marker

Background Information:

Immigration is the act of entering into a foreign country for residence. An *immigrant* is a person who comes from one country to live in another country. Although there are many reasons why people leave their home-land and move to another country, the main reason for immigration has long been economic opportunity. Religious persecution has forced many people to move to a new land. Wars, revolutions, and political unrest have also driven millions to find new homes.

The majority of immigrants who came to America during the peak period between 1880 and 1920 landed at Ellis Island in New York City. Ellis Island welcomed over 12 million immigrants of various cultures to the United States.

Today the United States continues to admit more immigrants than any other nation. In 1990, amendments to the Immigration and Nationality Act of 1952 raised the total number of immigrants entering the United States to approximately 700,000 each year. Experts predict that America's population will continue to become more heterogeneous in the future.

Introducing The Lesson:

Begin this activity by showing your students a picture of the Statue of Liberty. Explain to students that the majority of immigrants who came to America during the peak period (1880–1920) landed in New York City. There to welcome them as they entered the harbor stood a majestic greeter, the Statue of Liberty. Ask students what they think these immigrants thought and felt as they passed by her.

Steps:

1. Share the Background Information on page 273 with your students. As you do, write the definition of *immigrant* and *immigration* on the chalkboard.

2. Explain to students that over 37 million immigrants entered the United States between 1901 and 1990. Further explain that these immigrants came from many different countries.

3. Conduct a survey of your students to find out who is a descendant of immigrants. Ask students who have ancestors from European countries to raise their hands. Record the data on the board.

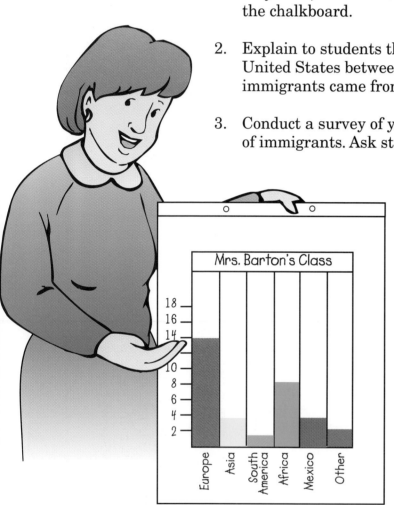

4. Next ask students who have ancestors from Asian countries to raise their hands; then record the data on the board.

5. Continue surveying students by asking for descendants of South America, Mexico, Canada, Africa, and so on.

6. Use the data collected from the survey to create a bar graph on chart paper showing the number of students from the various countries.

7. Finally, provide each student with a copy of page 275 for further exploration of the population of immigrants.

Interpreting graphs and maps

Coming To America

An *immigrant* is a person who comes from one country to live in another country. Use the map and the graphs below to learn about the immigrants who have come into the United States during the past century.

A. The graphs below show the countries of origin for immigrants during 1900 and 1990. Use the graphs to answer the questions that follow.

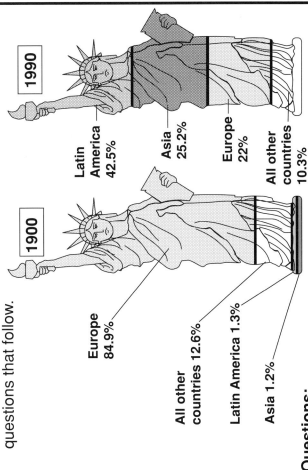

1900

Europe 84.9%

All other countries 12.6%

Latin America 1.3%

Asia 1.2%

1990

Latin America 42.5%

Asia 25.2%

Europe 22%

All other countries 10.3%

Questions:

1. Where were most immigrants from in 1900? _____

2. From which two places did the fewest immigrants come in 1900? _____

3. Where were most immigrants from in 1990? _____

4. In 1990, what percentage of immigrants came from Europe? _____

5. Use the information from questions 1–4 to write a sentence on the back of this sheet explaining how immigration has changed since 1900.

B. Use the map and map key below to answer the following questions about where immigrants live in the United States.

Total Percent Of Foreign Born By State (1990)

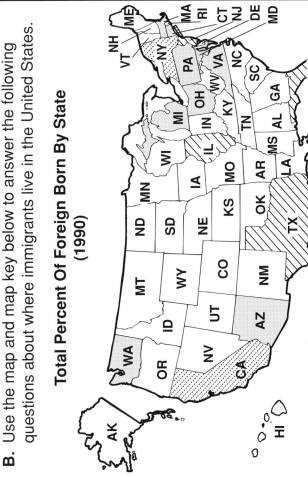

Map Key

☐ Less than 1%	▨ 3% to 9.9%
▨ 1% to 2.9%	▦ 10% or more

1. Which two states have the largest share of the immigrant population? _____

2. Which states have the next highest numbers of immigrants? _____

3. How many states have less than 1% of immigrants? _____

4. What percentage of people in your state are foreign born? _____

©The Education Center, Inc. • *Ready-to-Go Lessons* • TEC1118 • Key p. 319

How To Extend The Lesson:

- Display the following books about immigration in your classroom for students to enjoy:
  — *Immigrant Kids* by Russell Freedman (Puffin, 1995)
  — *The Night Journey* by Kathryn Lasky (Viking Press, 1986)
  — *Journey To America* by Sonia Levitin (Aladdin Paperbacks, 1987)
  — *If Your Name Was Changed At Ellis Island* by Ellen Levin (Scholastic Trade, 1994)
  — *My Grandmother's Journey* by John Cech (Aladdin Paperbacks, 1998)
  — *The Cat Who Escaped From Steerage* by Evelyn Wilde Mayerson (Atheneum, 1990)

- Some of the most important threads in the patchwork of American progress are famous immigrants to the United States. Have your students find out more about these famous immigrants with the following activity. Divide your class into pairs; then assign each pair an immigrant to research from the list provided. Direct the pair to find out information about the famous immigrant, such as birthplace, birthdate, date of death (if applicable), date of immigration, and contributions to American society. If desired, have each student pair record its findings on a quilt square pattern as shown and post them on a bulletin board titled "America's Immigrants: A Patchwork Of Colorful People."

Famous Immigrants

Luis Aparicio	Harry Houdini
John Jacob Astor	Ann Lee
John J. Audubon	Jan Matzeliger
George Balanchine	I. M. Pei
Alexander Graham Bell	Joseph Pulitzer
Ingrid Bergman	Jacob A. Riis
Irving Berlin	Knute Rockne
Elizabeth Blackwell	Haym Salomon
Wernher von Braun	Margarethe Schurz
Mother Cabrini	Igor Sikorsky
Andrew Carnegie	Isaac Bashevis Singer
E. I. Du Pont	Levi Strauss
Albert Einstein	Maia Wojciechowska
Greta Garbo	John Peter Zenger

Radio News Of World War II

Tune your students in to World War II history through the use of radio news broadcasts.

Skill: To learn about the role and importance of radio news broadcasts used during World War II

Estimated Lesson Time: 1 hour

Teacher Preparation:

1. Duplicate one copy of page 279 for each group of students.
2. Obtain an audiotape of one of Franklin Delano Roosevelt's fireside chats or a World War II radio news broadcast (optional).

Materials:

1 copy of page 279 per group
encyclopedias and other reference books
audiotape of World War II radio news
    broadcast or a fireside chat (optional)
1 tape recorder per group (optional)
1 audio cassette tape per group (optional)
1 screen or curtain

"The D-Day invasion is a success!"

Background Information:

World War II was the biggest war in history. Battles were fought in almost every part of the world—in Europe, Asia, Africa, and the islands of the Pacific. The United States, Great Britain, France, and their partners were known as the Allies. There were about 50 Allied nations. Germany, Italy, and Japan were the Axis nations. The Axis nations were also supported by Rumania and Bulgaria.

The 1930s and 1940s were known as the Golden Age of Radio. Americans not only listened to the radio, but they watched it in their minds. During World War II, millions of Americans depended on radio newscasts daily for the latest war news. Many governments of countries that fought in the war began to make widespread use of radio broadcasts for propaganda. The Voice of America, a U.S. government agency, began broadcasting overseas in 1942 to let the world know of America's role in the war.

Introducing The Lesson:

Begin the lesson by asking your students, "How do we get news?" Write students' responses on the board *(newspapers, magazines, television, radio, the Internet)*. Then have your students brainstorm ways Americans might have received news during World War II, which took place in the 1930s and 1940s, before the age of television. List their responses on the board beside the first list.

Steps:

1. Share with students the Background Information on page 277. Explain that the radio was not only a means of getting news, but it was also a major form of entertainment. Tell your students that families would often gather around the radio, which was often as big as many television sets today, to listen to the big bands play or to listen to a favorite program.

2. Ask your students to raise their hands if they've ever heard a mystery program or play on the radio. Then ask them what makes listening to a story on the radio even more fun and mysterious than seeing it on television? *(The listener has to use sound to help him visualize the entire scene.)*

3. Tell your students that President Franklin Delano Roosevelt broadcast live informal talks called *fireside chats* on the radio during the 1930s and 1940s. He did this to gain the confidence of the American people and inform them of government policies. Further explain that during WWII, many people depended on radio news broadcasts to keep them informed of the war in Europe and Asia.

4. If possible, play an audiotape of one of FDR's fireside chats or of a radio news broadcast aired during WWII. (Check with your public library for audiotapes on this topic.)

5. Divide students into small groups. Distribute one copy of page 279 to each group. Also, if desired, supply each group with a tape recorder and one audiocassette tape.

6. Instruct each group to use page 279 as a guide to help it create a radio news broadcast from the World War II era. Have each group research a different event of the war for its radio news broadcast *(see the list of events on page 280)*. If you are planning to use tape recorders, have each group record its final version of the broadcast for the rest of the class to hear. If tape recorders are not available, have each group simulate a radio news broadcast by reading aloud its broadcast while standing behind a screen or curtain.

"Stay tuned for 'The Lone Ranger' and 'The Green Hornet'!"

Let's Hear It For News Radio!

Directions: Use the form below to record data about your group's assigned World War II event. Use the data to help your group write, on another sheet of paper, a script for your news radio broadcast. Rehearse your broadcast; then tape the broadcast on an audio cassette or perform the broadcast live in front of your class.

Event: _____

 Who?	 What?	 When?	 Where?	 Why?	 How?

How To Extend The Lesson:

- Take a poll of the number of television sets in each student's household. Record the results on a chart on the board. Then have your students brainstorm a list of ways that television has helped and hindered the ability of Americans to stay informed and up-to-date on U.S. and world news. Finally, have your students discuss the question "Is more (news) always better?"

- Sound effects are very important to radio plays. It helps the listener to better visualize the performance. Today most sound effects used are recordings of the actual sounds needed. However, back in the early days of radio, many sound effects were created right in the studio using some quite unusual items. Have your students experiment with creating their own sound effects. Listed below are some suggested sound effects to get them started.

> **rain**—roll a handful of dried beans around on a cookie sheet or pie pan
> **running water**—pour water from a pitcher into another container
> **fire**—crinkle cellophane or plastic wrap in your hands
> **phone conversation**—talk into a box
> **strong wind**—blow with force directly into the microphone
> **gentle breeze**—from a distance, blow gently into the microphone
> **engine**—use the sound of a kitchen blender

- At home on the Mighty Mo! The USS *Missouri* saw action from the first days of the United States' involvement in World War II to the end. In fact, the Japanese surrendered right on the deck of this mighty battleship. Moored permanently now in Pearl Harbor, Hawaii, as a museum, information about her involvement in the war is easily available on the Internet at http://www.ussmissouri.com or by writing USS *Missouri* Memorial Association Inc., P.O. Box 6339, Honolulu, HI 96818. Have your students research this famous battleship and others like it that served and protected the United States so fiercely during World War II.

Note To The Teacher: Use the list of events below with Step 6 on page 278.

World War II Events

- Germany invades Poland, marking the beginning of World War II.
- Italy declares war on France and Great Britain.
- Germany invades the Soviet Union.
- Japan attacks Pearl Harbor in Hawaii.
- The United States, Great Britain, and Canada declare war on Japan.
- The United States bombs Tokyo in the Doolittle raid.
- Allies defeat Japan in the Battle of Midway.
- Hitler orders his troops to capture Stalingrad.
- Allied troops land in Normandy in the D-Day invasion of northern France.
- Germany is defeated and surrenders to the Allies in Reims, France.
- An atomic bomb is dropped on Hiroshima.
- Japan agrees to surrender.

By The People And For The People!

Use the Preamble to the Constitution to help your students better understand the meaning of democracy.

Skill: To understand the importance and significance of the Preamble to the Constitution of the United States

Estimated Lesson Time: 45 minutes

Teacher Preparation:

1. Duplicate one copy of page 283 for each student pair.
2. Make a transparency of the Preamble found on this page (optional).

Materials:

1 copy of page 283 per student pair
1 dictionary per student pair
1 blank transparency (optional)

"We the people of the United States, in order to form a more perfect Union, establish justice, insure domestic tranquility, provide for the common defense, promote the general welfare, and secure the blessings of liberty to ourselves and our posterity do ordain and establish this Constitution for the United States of America."

Background Information:

The present government of the United States was created by a document called the Constitution. It was written in 1787, but didn't go into effect until 1789. The Constitution established three main branches of government: the *executive* (the president), the *legislative* (Congress), the *judiciary* (the Supreme Court and other federal courts). The Constitution established a system of separation of powers in which the three branches of government can keep a check on each other so that no one branch gains more power than another.

The 52-word sentence above is known as the Preamble. It is the introductory statement to the Constitution. This statement declares that our government was established by the people.

Introducing The Lesson:

Write the word *democracy* on the board. Then ask your students to raise their hands if they've ever heard the word. Next have students volunteer possible definitions for the word. Write their responses on the board underneath the word *democracy*. Continue the lesson with the steps below.

Steps:

1. Explain that a democracy is a government by the people.

2. Share with your students the Background Information on page 281.

3. Tell your students that our founding fathers wanted a powerful statement to introduce the Constitution; therefore, the Preamble was written. Tell your students that this 52-word sentence clearly states that the government of the United States of America was created by the people.

4. Show the transparency of the Preamble or read it aloud to your students. Then ask your students if the sentence is easy to understand. *(Most students will say no.)* Explain to your students that many words used in the Preamble may be difficult to understand.

5. Divide your students into pairs. Give each pair one copy of page 283 and a dictionary. Instruct each pair to complete the reproducible as directed. Then have each pair read its version of the Preamble aloud to the rest of the class.

6. Post each pair's work on a bulletin board titled "The Preamble: An Update."

Name _____

The Preamble

The Preamble is the introductory statement to the United States Constitution. It consists of one sentence that contains 52 words! This statement declares that our government was established by the people.

Directions: The Preamble was written at the Constitutional Convention of 1787. Some of the words used during that time period may be difficult to understand. Read the original Preamble below. Look up each boldfaced word in a dictionary and write its definition on the back of this sheet. Then, using your own words, rewrite the Preamble on the sheet of notebook paper below.

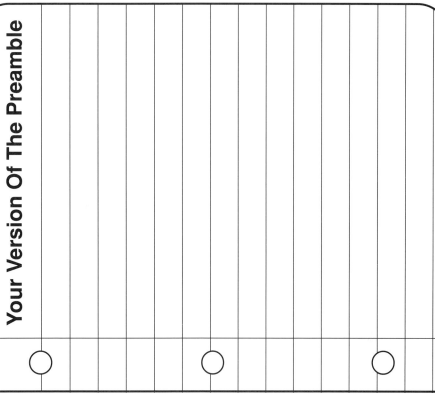

The Preamble

"We the people of the United States, in order to form a more perfect **Union**, establish **justice**, insure **domestic tranquility,** provide for the **common defense,** promote the **general welfare,** and **secure** the blessings of **liberty** to ourselves and our **posterity** do **ordain** and **establish** this Constitution for the United States of America."

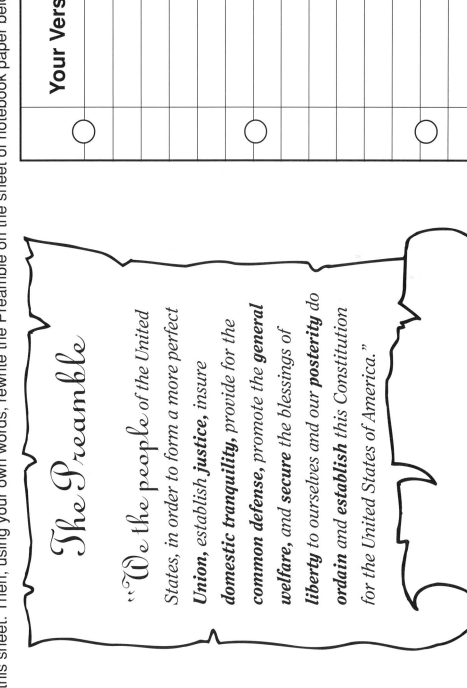

Your Version Of The Preamble

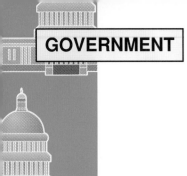

How To Extend The Lesson:

- Extra! Extra! Read all about it! Have students pretend that they are news reporters who have been sent to report on the events of the Constitutional Convention of 1787. Instruct each student to write a brief news article telling the *who, what, when, where,* and *why* of the convention.

- Help your students see how the Constitution is applied to everyday life. Have students locate newspaper and magazine articles about new laws, elections, voting, the judicial system, specific trials, etc. Supply students with colored construction paper, scissors, and glue. Have each student cut out at least one article and mount it to a sheet of construction paper. Post the articles on a bulletin board titled "Our Living Constitution."

- Hold your own Constitutional Convention in which your students write a class constitution. Use the U.S. Constitution as a model. Have your students decide and vote on various issues of organization, such as how decisions are made, how disputes are settled, how a class president is selected, etc. Write the class constitution on chart paper; then have each student sign it. For a special touch have the students sign it with a quill pen and ink! Keep it posted throughout the year and refer to it often when making decisions or settling disputes in the classroom.

Checks And Balances

Help your students develop an understanding and appreciation for the system of checks and balances with this simulation activity.

Skill: Recognizing the three branches of the U.S. government and the roles of each

Estimated Lesson Time: 1 hour

Teacher Preparation:
1. Duplicate one copy of page 287.
2. Make a transparency of the Background Information below.

Materials:
1 copy of page 287
1 blank transparency
overhead projector pen

Executive

Legislative

Judicial

Background Information:

For more than 200 years, the Constitution has provided the framework for the federal government. It created a system of *checks and balances* to keep any one branch from becoming too powerful. Each branch can stop another branch from abusing its powers. For example, the president (executive branch) can *veto,* or refuse to pass, a law proposed by Congress (legislative branch). However, if two-thirds of the members of Congress agree, they can override the veto and pass the law.

Executive Branch
President
* manages the government
* appoints government leaders
* makes treaties
* is commander in chief of the armed forces

can appoint Supreme Court justices, can grant pardons

can rule whether a president's actions are unconstitutional

can pass laws over a veto, can reject a president's appointments can charge a president with wrong doing

can veto laws passed by Congress

Judicial Branch
Supreme Court and Federal Courts
* explains the meanings of laws and treaties
* decides if laws are constitutional

determines the number of Supreme Court justices, can reject appointments to the Supreme Court

decides if laws passed by Congress are constitutional

Legislative Branch
Congress: the Senate and the House of Representatives
* writes new laws
* passes taxes
* approves treaties made by the president
* declares war

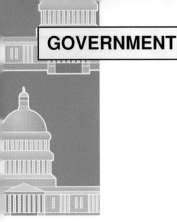

Introducing The Lesson:

Show your students the transparency of the Background Information on page 285. Ask your students who they think "runs" the country. Explain to your students that there are actually hundreds of people who work together to run the country. Read aloud the information contained in the Background Information paragraph and chart. Point out on the transparency that the president is actually the head of only one branch of the government—the executive branch.

Steps:

1. Inform your students that they are going to be divided into the three branches of government and that they will be adopting a new classroom rule following the system of checks and balances.

2. Have each student write his/her name on a slip of paper. Collect the names in a hat or container. Draw two names from the hat to be the president and vice president of the executive branch. Then draw four or five names from the hat to represent the Supreme Court justices of the judicial branch. For the legislative branch, draw four or five names to represent the Senate and the remaining names to represent members of the House of Representatives.

3. Have each branch meet in a separate area of the classroom. Have the Senate and House members meet separately within the legislative area.

4. List several potential classroom rules on the board, such as no homework on Fridays or 20 minutes of extra free time for each week that everyone turns in all homework. Inform your students that these are proposed new bills and that the members of the House of Representatives will be voting on whether one of the bills should become a law in the classroom.

5. Give the House approximately 15 minutes to vote on the bill. Inform the House members that the bill has to pass by a majority vote. After the House passes the bill, have one of the members write it on the copy of page 287 to pass along to the Senate.

6. Next have the Senate vote on the bill. If it passes, send the bill on to the executive branch. If the bill doesn't pass in the Senate, return the bill to the House and instruct the House to work on the bill and vote again.

7. Inform the executive branch that the president can sign the bill, which makes it law, or he or she can veto the bill and send it back to Congress. If the president decides to veto the bill, Congress can override the veto by revoting on the bill and passing it by a two-thirds margin in each house.

8. Send the new law on to the judiciary branch. Have the members of this branch evaluate the new law to see if it is constitutional.

9. Post the new law in the classroom and begin enforcing it immediately!

New Classroom Rule

A homework checklist will be marked each day. Each Friday the members of the class will participate in a popcorn party if every student has a check mark for each assignment given that week.

Emily Carpenter
9/15/00

New Classroom Rule

We, the students of Mr./Mrs./Ms. _____'s class, in order to form a more perfect learning atmosphere and establish fairness in classroom discipline and procedures, do hereby declare the following rule legal and applicable to all students in the class. Failure to comply with the rule will be dealt with by the Supreme Court of the classroom.

New Rule:

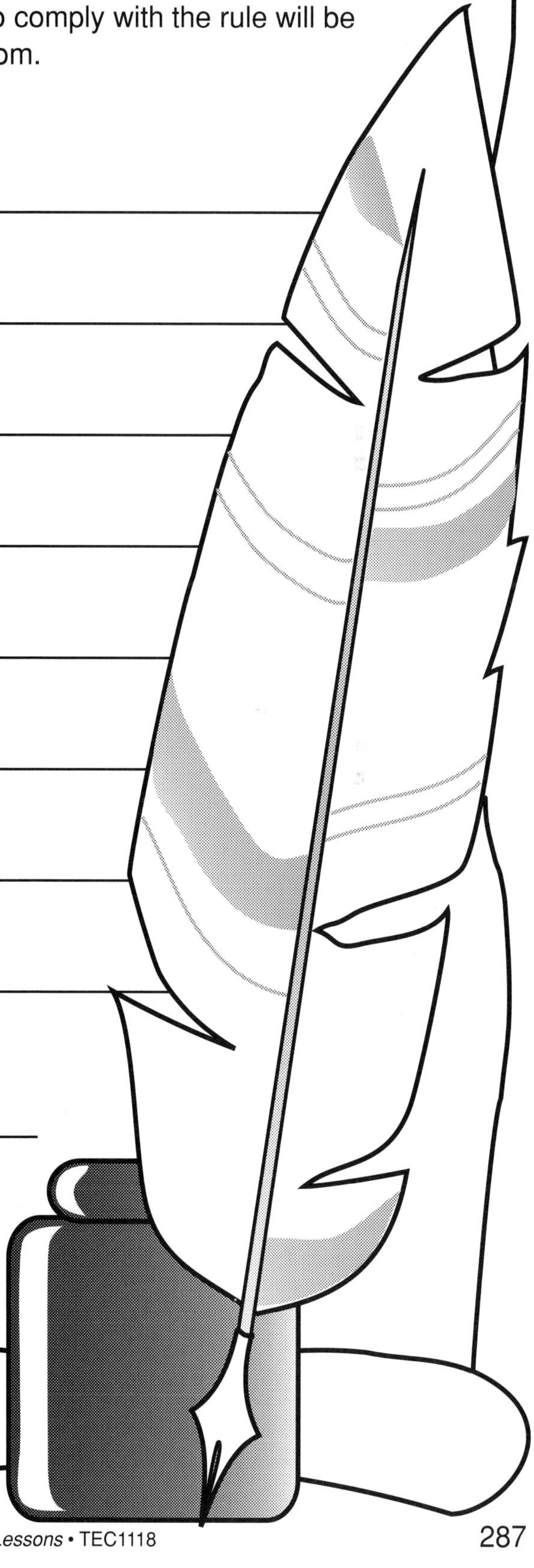

_____

_____

_____

_____

_____

_____

_____

_____

_____
(President's Signature)

_____
(Date)

How To Extend The Lesson:

• Inform your students that during two weeks of each month the Supreme Court hears cases. Then they recess for two weeks to write their opinions on the cases heard. Each Monday at noon, the Supreme Court hands down its opinion on the cases. Monday in Washington, DC, has become known as Opinion Monday or Judgment Day. Tell your students that once the Supreme Court delivers its verdict, a case cannot be retried. Begin a similar tradition in your classroom each Monday by allowing students to express their opinions about various topics in the news. Have each student write down his opinion on a strip of paper. Tack the opinion strips to a board titled "Opinion Monday." Before long, the board will be overflowing with student opinions.

• Have your students research the names of the senators representing your state in Washington, DC. Instruct students to find out the length of a senator's term in office. Next, have your students find out to which political party each senator belongs. Then, have your students research to see what bills have been introduced by your state's senators and whether they have passed. Present your students' findings on a bulletin board titled "Our Sensational Senators."

• Help students investigate the jobs of government officials with this newsworthy center activity. Cover three shoeboxes with construction paper. Decorate each box with either executive, legislative, or judicial symbols; then label each box accordingly. Enlarge and duplicate a class supply of the pattern on this page. Challenge each student to find a magazine or newspaper article relating to an official's job in one of the branches of government. Have the student summarize his article on the form, staple the article to the back of the form, and then place it in the appropriate box. At various times throughout your study of U.S. government, allow a student to pull a paper out of a box to share.

Newsworthy Work

Name:_____

Article Title:_____ Article Date:_____

Name of the official:_____
Title of the official:_____

Branch of government:_____

What is the article about?_____
_____
_____

When did this event happen?_____
_____
_____

Where did this event happen?_____
_____
_____

Why or how did this event happen?_____
_____
_____

©The Education Center, Inc.

Right On!

Familiarize students with the individual rights of people outlined in the first ten amendments to the Constitution.

Skill: Understanding the freedoms guaranteed by the Bill of Rights

Estimated Lesson Time: 45 minutes

Teacher Preparation:
1. Duplicate one copy of page 291.
2. Cut the copy of page 291 into ten separate amendment cards.

Materials:
1 copy of page 291
1 dictionary for each
   group of students
paper
scissors

Background Information:

After the adoption of the Constitution in 1789, some states refused to approve it unless a statement about the rights of the people was added. Delegates from every state, except Rhode Island, met to work on the Constitution and the Bill of Rights. The delegates to the Constitutional Convention in Philadelphia wanted to make sure that the personal rights of each citizen of the United States would be protected under the law.

The Bill of Rights is a list of rights of the American people, which the federal government is forbidden to take away. Even though these rights are protected by law, individuals must act responsibly. The first ten amendments guarantee individuals freedom of speech, the press, religion, petition, and assembly; freedom from unreasonable search and seizure; and the right to trial by jury. The Tenth Amendment also reserves for the states any powers not granted to the federal government.

Introducing The Lesson:

Have your students brainstorm a list of rights they have as American citizens. Record their responses on the board. Next ask students the following questions: "Where do you think these rights come from?", "Are they written down somewhere?", and "Are they ensured?" Lead students in a discussion about the purpose of the Constitution and the Bill of Rights. Then guide students through the steps below to help them understand what specific rights are guaranteed by the first ten amendments.

Steps:

1. Share with your students the Background Information on page 289.

2. Divide the class into ten groups. Give each group one amendment card from page 291, a sheet of notebook paper, and a dictionary.

3. Have one student from each group read aloud to the class his group's amendment card. Discuss with your students the difficult phrasing and vocabulary used in each amendment.

4. Next direct each group to use the dictionary to look up any unfamiliar words in its amendment. Then have the group rewrite the amendment on a sheet of paper using its own words. Have each group reread its amendment aloud to the rest of the class, pointing out which specific individual rights are outlined in the amendment.

5. Extend the lesson by having each student choose one amendment and write a paragraph explaining how the amendment affects his life today. Also have the student include in his paragraph how his life would be different if the amendment was not part of the Constitution.

Rights of American Citizens:

- the right to go to school

- the right to go in public places, such as the mall or a restaurant

- the right to have an opinion

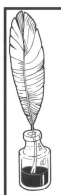

Amendment 1

Congress shall make no law respecting an establishment of religion, or prohibiting the free exercise thereof; or abridging the freedom of speech, or of the press; or the right of the people peaceably to assemble, and to petition the government for a redress of grievances.

Amendment 2

A well-regulated militia being necessary to the security of a free State, the right of the people to keep and bear arms shall not be infringed.

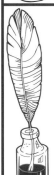

Amendment 3

No soldier shall, in time of peace, be quartered in any house without the consent of the owner; nor in time of war but in a manner to be prescribed by law.

Amendment 4

The right of the people to be secure in their persons, houses, papers, and effects, against unreasonable searches and seizures, shall not be violated, and no warrants shall issue but upon probable cause, supported by oath or affirmation, and particularly describing the place to be searched, and the persons or things to be seized.

Amendment 5

No person shall be held to answer for a capital or otherwise infamous crime, unless on a presentment or indictment of a grand jury, except in cases arising in the land or naval forces, or in the militia, when in actual service in time of war or public danger; nor shall any person be subject for the same offense to be twice put in jeopardy of life or limb; nor shall be compelled in any criminal case to be a witness against himself; nor be deprived of life, liberty, or property, without due process of law; nor shall private property be taken for public use, without just compensation.

Amendment 6

In all criminal prosecutions, the accused shall enjoy the right to a speedy and public trial, by an impartial jury of the State and district wherein the crime shall have been committed, which district shall have been previously ascertained by law, and to be informed of the nature and cause of the accusation; to be confronted with the witnesses against him; to have compulsory process for obtaining witnesses in his favor, and to have the assistance of counsel for his defense.

Amendment 7

In suits at common law, where the value in controversy shall exceed twenty dollars, the right of trial by jury shall be preserved, and no fact tried by a jury shall be otherwise reexamined in any court of the United States than according to the rules of the common law.

Amendment 8

Excessive bail shall not be required, nor excessive fines imposed, nor cruel and unusual punishments inflicted.

Amendment 9

The enumeration in the Constitution of certain rights shall not be construed to deny or disparage others retained by the people.

Amendment 10

The powers not delegated to the United States by the Constitution, nor prohibited by it to the States, are reserved to the States respectively, or to the people.

How To Extend The Lesson:

- Help students reinforce the skills of critical thinking and writing with this idea. Write each of the following issues on several index cards. Pair students and provide each pair with a card. Direct the pair to read the issue, then research to find out more about the topic. Next have the pair write a thoughtful answer to the question(s).

The First Amendment gives Americans the right to voice their views. Suppose a speaker talks to a crowd and they become angry over what he is saying—and try to stop his speech. When the police come, whose rights should they protect? Explain your answer.

During the 50 years following the adoption of the Constitution, all white men gained the right to vote. Changes in the law occurred slowly. Women could not vote until 1920. Why do you suppose it took so long for women to gain the right to vote?

Suppose a student, as a joke, yells "Fire!" in an auditorium filled with classmates. Many students panic and some are hurt trying to escape. Does the student who yelled have the right to express himself in this way? Why or why not? Can you think of other instances when it is fair to limit one's freedom of expression?

The Fifth Amendment gives every American the right to due process. This means that people must be treated fairly by the government. Suppose your parents own some property along a road that needs to be widened because it is dangerously narrow. Does the government have the right to use part of the property to build a safer road? Explain.

- Have your students put the first ten amendments to the Constitution not in writing, but in pictures! Provide each student with a 12" x 18" sheet of drawing paper and crayons or markers, and assign each one an amendment to research. Direct the student to fold her paper in half and label it as shown. On the left side of the paper, have her draw a picture showing a scene before the amendment. On the right side of the paper, have her draw a picture showing a scene after the amendment. Display the pictures on a bulletin board titled "What A Difference Amendments Make!"

Headin' West

Lace up your hiking boots and get ready to hit the trails to learn more about the West.

Skill: Identifying major geographic features found in the West

Estimated Lesson Time: 45 minutes

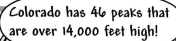
Colorado has 46 peaks that are over 14,000 feet high!

Teacher Preparation:
Duplicate one copy of page 295 for each student.

Materials:
1 copy of page 295 for each student
map of the United States and Canada
crayons or colored pencils

Background Information:

The western region of the United States is made up of two sections—the Mountain states and the Pacific states. Much of both of these areas is mountainous. Also found in the West are areas of deserts, plains, plateaus, dense forests, and dramatic ocean shore.

Wyoming, Montana, Idaho, Nevada, Utah, and Colorado make up the Mountain states. Together these six states cover almost one-fourth of the area of the 48 connected states. However, only 6 of every 100 people in the country live in this region. The Mountain states area is named for the rugged, majestic Rocky Mountains, one of the main geographic features of the region.

The Pacific states are California, Oregon, Washington, Alaska, and Hawaii. A large number of the country's fruits, nuts, vegetables, and wine grapes are grown in the fertile valleys of the Pacific states.

The West is a region of rapid growth. Only a few years ago, California passed New York to become the most populated state. Los Angeles now ranks as the second largest city in the country. The beautiful scenery and climate attract many people to the region.

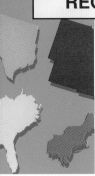
Introducing The Lesson:

Show your students a map of the United States. Ask a student volunteer to locate the states that make up the Western region of the United States *(Alaska, California, Colorado, Hawaii, Idaho, Montana, Nevada, Oregon, Utah, Washington, and Wyoming)*. Then explain to your students that they will be learning more about some geographic features of this region.

Steps:

1. Point out that the Western region is made up of two sections—the Mountain states and the Pacific states. Then explain that much of both of these areas is mountainous.

2. Further explain that the Rocky Mountains, the largest mountain system in the United States, is located in the Western region. Have a student volunteer locate on a large U.S. map the Western states that contain the Rocky Mountains *(Colorado, Utah, Wyoming, Idaho, Montana, Washington, and Alaska)*.

3. Tell students that in addition to the Rocky Mountains, the Western region is also the home of many other mountain ranges.

4. Provide each student with crayons or colored pencils, a map of the United States, and a copy of page 295 to learn more about the mountains of the Western states.

Way Out West

Wander way out West to learn about the type of landform that covers most of the Western region of the United States!

Directions: Study the map and map key. Then use a map of the United States to find and label each of the places listed below.

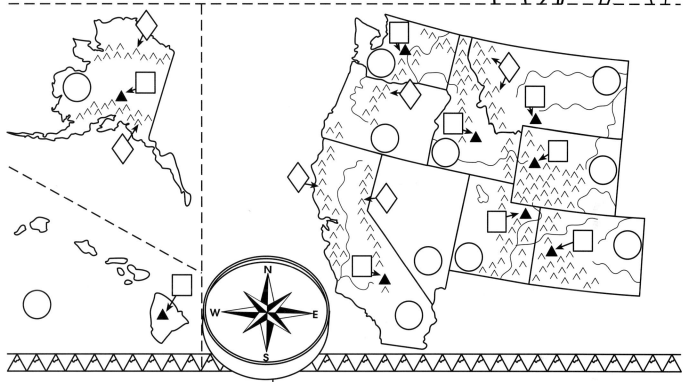

Map Key

▲ = mountain peak

∧∧∧ = mountain range

Western States:

① Alaska   ⑦ Nevada

② California   ⑧ Oregon

③ Colorado   ⑨ Utah

④ Hawaii   ⑩ Washington

⑤ Idaho   ⑪ Wyoming

⑥ Montana

Mountain Peaks:

12 Mt. Elbert, Colorado   17 Mt. Rainier, Washington

13 King's Peak, Utah   18 Mt. Whitney, California

14 Gannett Peak, Wyoming   19 Mt. McKinley, Alaska

15 Granite Peak, Montana   20 Mauna Kea, Hawaii

16 Borah Peak, Idaho

Mountain Ranges:

⟨21⟩ Rocky Mountains   ⟨24⟩ Cascade Range

⟨22⟩ Sierra Nevada   ⟨25⟩ Alaska Range

⟨23⟩ Brooks Range   ⟨26⟩ Coast Ranges

Lightly color the Mountain states brown and the Pacific states yellow.

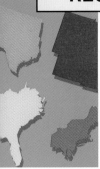

How To Extend The Lesson:

- Explain to students that many of the inhabitants of the state of Hawaii are descendants of the Polynesians, who were the first settlers of the Hawaiian Islands. Point out that descendants of the Polynesians are called Hawaiians. Explain that while most Hawaiians do speak English as their primary language, they also have their own language, which is derived from a 12-letter alphabet. Write the 12 letters of the Hawaiian alphabet on the board *(A, E, H, I, K, L, M, N, O, P, U, W).* Share some of the following Hawaiian words with your students; then have each child make his own Hawaiian dictionary that lists each word, its pronunciation and definition, and an illustration.

Word	Pronunciation	Definition	Word	Pronunciation	Definition
ae	eye	yes	lei	lay	wreath or garland
ai	AH ee	eat			
ala	AH lah	path; road	luau	LOO ow	feast
aloha	ah LOH hah	love; greetings; welcome; farewell	mahalo	mah HAH loh	thanks
			manu	MAH noo	bird
			mauna	MOW nah	mountain
aole	ah OH lay	no	mele	MEH lay or MEHL eh	song; chant
hale	HAH lay	house	moana	moh AH nah	ocean
hana	HAH nah	work	moopuna	moh oh POO nah	grandchild
hele mai	HAY lay MY	come here	nani	NAH nee	beautiful
hiamoe	hee ah MOY	sleep	nui	NOO ee	great; large
huhu	hoo HOO	angry	oe	OH ee	you
hula	HOO lah	dance	ohana	oh HAH nah	family
kai	KAH ee	the sea	pau	POW	finished; done
kane	KAH neh	man	pehea oe	pay HAY ah OY	How are you?
kaukau	KOW kow	food	pilikia	pee lee KEE ah	trouble
keiki	KAY kee	child	pua	POO ah	flower
kokua	koh KOO uh	help; cooperation	pupule	poo POO lay	crazy
lani	LAH nee	sky; heavenly	wahine	wah HEE nay	woman

History Of Potatoes
Foods Made From Potatoes
Parts Of The Potato Plant
Conditions Required For Growing Potatoes
Harvesting Potatoes
Interesting Potato Facts

- Share with students that the United States produces more than 400 million bags of potatoes annually. Point out that Idaho and Washington, two Western states, are the leading potato-producing states in the country. Then have your students research the topics at the left to find out more about the potato. Duplicate copies of a potato pattern; then provide each student with a supply of the copies on which to record his research findings. Staple the potato patterns together to form a mini booklet. Mount the completed booklets on a bulletin board titled "Look What We Dug Up In The Western States Region!"

Southwest Region Roundup

*Lasso some information on the Southwest region
with this ripsnortin' lesson!*

Skill: Researching key features of the states found in the Southwest

Estimated Lesson Time: 45 minutes

Teacher Preparation:
Duplicate one copy of page 299 for
each student.

Materials:
1 copy of page 299 for each student
one 9" x 12" sheet of construction
paper for each student
map of the United States
glue
scissors
crayons or colored pencils

Background Information:
The following states make up the Southwest region of the United States:
Arizona, New Mexico, Texas, and Oklahoma.

The Southwest covers a large area of the United States. Many ranches
and farms are located in this region's wide-open land areas. The region is also known
for its large deposits of petroleum and natural gas. During the 1900s fuel refineries
and chemical factories helped industrialize the area and brought a great deal of
urban growth. Many of the fastest growing cities of the United States are found in the
Southwest. These cities include Austin, El Paso, San Antonio, Dallas, and Phoenix.

The Southwest region has a diverse mixture of ethnic populations, including some
of the largest populations of Native Americans in the United States. Other ethnic
groups represented in the Southwest include Black Americans, Mexican Americans,
and people of European descent.

Introducing The Lesson:

Have a student volunteer come to the front of the room and locate Texas, New Mexico, Arizona, and Oklahoma on a map of the United States. Explain that these four states make up the Southwest region.

Steps:

1. Write the names of the four Southwestern states on the chalkboard.

2. Poll students to see if any have visited one of the Southwestern states. For each student who has visited a Southwestern state, place a check mark next to the name of the state.

3. Challenge students to brainstorm what they know about each of these states.

4. Write students' responses on the board under each state's name. Then point out the similarities in the list.

5. Explain that these states are grouped into the same region because they have similar climates, natural resources, and landforms.

6. Point out that while the states have those features in common, each state also has its own unique qualities.

7. Share the Background Information on page 297.

8. Point out that with the industrialization of the area, many cities in the region are some of the fastest growing in the United States. Then ask a student volunteer to locate Austin, El Paso, San Antonio, Dallas, and Phoenix on the map.

9. Provide each student with glue, scissors, crayons, a sheet of construction paper, and a copy of page 299 to learn more about the interesting characteristics that make the states of the Southwest unique.

A Southwestern Roundup

Saddle up your buckin' bronco and ride out on the range to round up interesting facts about the Southwestern states!

Directions: Read each clue below. Then cut out the clues and the state outlines. Divide a sheet of construction paper into four equal columns. Glue each state outline at the top of a column. Then glue each clue below the outline of the state it describes. Look in reference materials if you are unsure about which state a clue describes.

Arizona

New Mexico

Texas

Oklahoma

My state flower is the *saguaro,* or giant cactus.

My nickname is the Land of Enchantment.

My land area is larger than any state except Alaska.

In the 1800s the United States made most of my land into a huge Indian reservation.

My capital is Santa Fe.

My state bird is the scissor-tailed flycatcher.

My nickname is the Lone Star State because of the single star located on my flag.

Phoenix is my state capital.

My capital is Oklahoma City.

My capital is Austin.

The Grand Canyon, Petrified Forest, and Painted Desert are just a few of my tourist attractions.

In 1930, the planet Pluto was discovered from Lowell Observatory in Flagstaff, one of my cities.

The U.S. government opened my land to white settlement in the 1880s. I then became known as the Sooner State because many settlers arrived on my land before it was even open for settlement.

My state bird is the roadrunner.

Bonus Box: Add two additional facts in each state's column.

How To Extend The Lesson:

- Challenge your students to find out more about the Native Americans of the Southwest. Divide students into small groups. Assign each group a tribe from those listed on this page. Have each group research its assigned tribe to learn more about its shelter, food, clothing, religion, and arts and crafts. Then have each group build a village model for its tribe to represent its research findings. Have each group label its model and provide a written description of the significance of the items included. Display the completed village models in your school's media center under a sign titled "Native Americans Of The Southwest."

- Have your students find out more about the Southwestern states with the following letter-writing activity. Allow each student to choose a state; then instruct her to write the tourism board to request information on popular tourist attractions located within that state. As students receive responses from each organization, place the information in a basket for students to review during their free time.

Arizona Office of Tourism
1100 West Washington
Phoenix, AZ 85007

Texas Department of
Transportation
P.O. Box 5000
Austin, TX 78763

Oklahoma Department of
Tourism and Recreation
P.O. Box 60789
Oklahoma City, OK 73146

New Mexico
Department of Tourism
Lamy Building
491 Old Santa Fe Trail
Santa Fe, NM 87503

- Explain to students that the Grand Canyon, located in northwestern Arizona, is one of the seven natural wonders of the world. Point out that the Grand Canyon is an excellent example of the effects that water erosion can have on land over a period of millions of years. Divide students into groups of two or three. Have each group research the effects that water erosion by the Colorado River has had on the Grand Canyon. Have each group create a poster diagram of the Grand Canyon to outline the process of water erosion. Then have each group present its findings to the rest of the class. Conclude by challenging students to imagine what the Grand Canyon will look like in another six million years.

Pueblo
Apache
Navajo
Papago
Pima
Mogollon

Housing
Pueblo villages were made of houses of stone or adobe. The houses looked like apartment buildings and sometimes reached as high as four stories. Extended Pueblo families often lived in two or more connected houses.

Arts And Crafts
The Pueblo were excellent weavers of baskets and cotton to make clothing. They were also excellent pottery makers.

Mealtime In The Midwest

Belly up to the breakfast table to learn more about the major agricultural resources of the Midwest.

Skill: Identifying major agricultural products grown in the Midwest

Estimated Lesson Time: 45 minutes

Teacher Preparation:

1. Program a copy of page 303 with the number of activities you want students to complete and a due date. Then duplicate a copy of the page for each student.
2. Gather empty cereal boxes (one per student) for the activity on page 303.

Materials:

1 programmed copy of page 303 for each student
1 cereal box for each student
map of the United States
crayons or colored pencils
plain white paper
scissors
glue

Fun Facts:

- More hogs are raised in Iowa than in any other state.
- Kansas leads the United States in wheat production.
- Wisconsin is called "America's Dairyland" because it produces one-third of all cheese and one-fourth of all butter in the United States.

Background Information:

The following states make up the Midwest region of the United States: Illinois, Indiana, Iowa, Kansas, Michigan, Minnesota, Missouri, Nebraska, North Dakota, Ohio, South Dakota, Wisconsin.

The Midwest is a large area of mostly flat land that spans over much of the center of the United States. The region is known for its large stretches of fertile farmland. Farms located throughout the region produce large quantities of crops, such as wheat and corn, and raise dairy cows and other livestock.

Introducing The Lesson:

Ask students what they ate for breakfast; then write their responses on the board. Point out that the Midwest region of the United States is particularly well-known for its production of grains, such as corn and wheat, that are used to make cereal and many other foods. Circle the food items on the board that contain corn or wheat. Further explain that Battle Creek, Michigan, is called the "Cereal Bowl Of America" because it is the world's leading producer of breakfast cereal.

Steps:

1. Have a student volunteer come to the front of the classroom and locate each of the following states on a U.S. map: Illinois, Indiana, Iowa, Kansas, Michigan, Minnesota, Missouri, Nebraska, North Dakota, Ohio, South Dakota, and Wisconsin.

2. Point out that these are the states of the Midwest region.

3. Share with your students the Background Information and Fun Facts listed on page 301.

4. Have students list other foods that are made from corn and wheat. List these foods on the board. Explain that corn and wheat are just two of the many agricultural resources produced in the Midwestern states.

5. Explain that the Midwestern states produce enormous quantities of wheat, corn, hogs, and many other commodities. Then share with students the following lists of the top ten producers of specific agricultural products. Have students identify the Midwestern states from each list.

Hogs	Soybeans
1. Iowa	1. Illinois
2. Illinois	2. Iowa
3. North Carolina	3. Indiana
4. Minnesota	4. Ohio
5. Nebraska	5. Minnesota
6. Indiana	6. Missouri
7. Missouri	7. Arkansas
8. South Dakota	8. Nebraska
9. Ohio	9. Kansas
10. Kansas	10. Michigan

6. Ask students to imagine what would happen if all agricultural production from the Midwest region were to cease.

7. Provide each student with an empty cereal box, white paper, crayons, glue, scissors, and a programmed copy of page 303. Have the student complete the page as directed to learn more about the agricultural resources that make the Midwest a leader in farm production.

Making A Meal Out Of The Midwest

Serve up a spoonful of facts about the Midwest by following the directions below!

Directions: Cover an empty cereal box with white paper. Then decorate the box to represent the Midwest region. Complete ___ of the activities below before _____. Place your completed work inside of the cereal box.

1.
Iowa leads the United States in production of corn, producing about one-fifth of the national harvest. Look up other Midwestern states in an almanac to find out how much corn they produce annually. Then create a bar graph to show how other states in the Midwest compare to Iowa in the production of corn.

2.
Nine of the top ten hog producers in the United States are located in the Midwest. List all the food products you can think of that are produced from hogs. Then plan a menu for a day that includes at least one food product at each meal made from hogs.

3.
Many states in the Midwest grow wheat, including North Dakota, Kansas, South Dakota, and Minnesota. Wheat can be classified into two broad categories: winter wheat and spring wheat. Research to find out what characteristics are used to determine the classification of a particular wheat.

4.
Nine of the top ten soybean producers in the United States are located in the Midwest. In Ohio and Missouri, soybeans are the state's leading farm product. List at least 15 things soybeans are used for. Include both food and nonfood uses in your list.

5.
Nebraska was once considered to be part of the "Great American Desert." As a result of irrigation systems and scientific farming, Nebraska is now one of the leading farming states in the United States. Research how irrigation systems work. Then draw a diagram showing how an irrigation system carries water to farmland.

6.
Wisconsin is nicknamed "America's Dairyland" because it is one of the nation's leading dairy producers. One of the leading industries in Wisconsin is the manufacturing of milk into butter, cheese, and other dairy products. Wisconsin produces about one-third of the nation's cheese and one-fourth of its butter. Find out how ice cream, another popular dairy product, is made. Then write a how-to paragraph describing the process. Copy your completed paragraph on a piece of paper cut to look like an ice-cream cone.

7.
Find an advertisement from a local grocery store. Circle all the foods in the advertisement that are made from crops or livestock that are found in the Midwest region.

How To Extend The Lesson:

- Duplicate a picture of Mount Rushmore for each student. Have each student glue the picture of Mount Rushmore onto a sheet of paper, leaving room on either side. Explain to students that in 1927 Gutzon Borglum began work on the Mount Rushmore memorial on a granite cliff in the Black Hills of South Dakota. Explain to students that the carving shows the faces of George Washington, Thomas Jefferson, Theodore Roosevelt, and Abraham Lincoln. Tell students to imagine that they have been commissioned to add another face to the monument. Point out that, like the individuals already present on Mount Rushmore, the figure needs to have made a positive contribution to American society. Have each student draw her chosen person next to the other figures. Then have each student write a brief paragraph explaining why the person she chose is a worthy addition to Mount Rushmore.

- Students are sure to give the Midwest a stamp of approval after completing the following activity. Provide each student with 13 sheets of 4" x 5" white paper stapled together to make a booklet. Challenge the student to design and color a commemorative stamp featuring a tourist attraction for each of the 12 Midwestern states. Then have the student create a cover for his stamp series. Staple the completed booklets to a bulletin board titled "The Midwest Gets Our Stamp Of Approval!"

- Remind students that Battle Creek, Michigan, is nicknamed the "Cereal Bowl Of America" because of the large amounts of cereal produced there. Challenge each student to complete the following activities to learn more about one of Michigan's leading products.
  —Survey your classmates and friends to find out which cereals are their favorites. Create a pictograph to show the results.
  —Read the label on the backs of different cereal boxes to find out which cereal contains the highest levels of vitamins, minerals, and other nutrients.
  —Find out which cereal has the most sugar, fat, calories, and sodium per serving.
  —Find out where each type of cereal is manufactured.

Sightseeing Through The Southeast

Pack your bags for an exciting tour of scenic attractions found throughout the Southeast region of the United States.

Skill: Identifying tourist attractions located in the Southeast

Estimated Lesson Time: 45 minutes

Teacher Preparation:
1. Make a copy of page 307 for each student.
2. Gather an assortment of brochures advertising various tourist attractions found throughout the Southeastern states.

Materials:
1 copy of page 307 for each student
tourism brochures
map of the United States
reference materials

Background Information:
The following states make up the Southeast region of the United States: West Virginia, Virginia, Kentucky, Tennessee, North Carolina, South Carolina, Arkansas, Mississippi, Alabama, Georgia, Louisiana, and Florida.

Prior to the mid-1900s the Southeast's economy was based primarily on agriculture. Today agriculture is still important in the Southeast, but in recent decades other industries such as manufacturing and tourism have helped balance out the region's economy.

Annually, many tourists visit an assortment of popular tourist attractions located throughout the Southeastern states. Tourism is especially popular during the winter months, when the temperatures in much of this region remain mild. The money generated by the tourism industry is a major source of revenue for the region's economy.

Introducing The Lesson:

Divide your students into several groups based on their hair color. Explain that you have grouped the students based on a similar feature or characteristic. Further explain that the United States is divided into several *geographic regions* based on similarities between the states in those regions.

Steps:

1. On a U.S. map, point out the states located in the Southeast region. Write the names of those states on the chalkboard.

2. Ask students if they have ever visited any of the states listed. Make a check mark next to each state that someone in the class has visited.

3. Explain that the states located in the Southeast share similar features, such as geography, climate, economy, traditions, and history.

4. Tell students that the economy in the Southeast was at one time based primarily on agriculture. Point out that in recent years, other industries such as manufacturing and tourism have helped generate income and have contributed to the region's economy.

5. Point out that each state in this region has a wealth of tourist attractions that draw people from all over the country. Explain that the climate in the region is usually mild during the winter, which only adds to the popularity of vacationing in the area.

6. Provide each student with a copy of page 307 and a selection of tourism brochures or other reference materials. Have the student complete the page as directed to learn more about major tourist attractions in the Southeastern states.

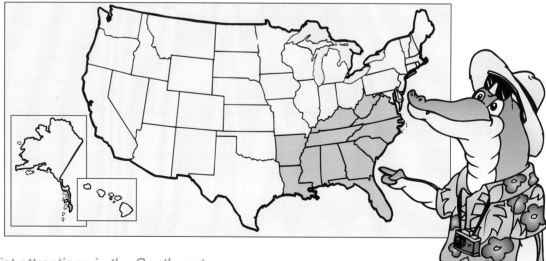

Sightseeing Through The Southeast

Hit some hot spots as you shuffle through the Southeast! Each postcard below shows a tourist attraction located in one of the 12 Southeastern states. On the line provided, write the name of the state in which the tourist attraction is located; then color each postcard.

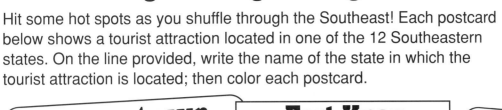

Jamestown Settlement

_____
_____

Fort Knox

_____
_____

The World of Coca-Cola®
Things go better with **Coke®**

_____

Cape Hatteras

_____

Fort Sumter

_____

Opryland USA

_____

Hot Springs National Park

_____

New River Gorge Bridge
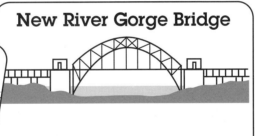
_____

U.S. Space and Rocket Center

_____

French Quarter

_____

Everglades National Park

_____

Natchez Pilgrimage

_____

Bonus Box: On the back of this page, write a sentence or two describing each tourist attraction mentioned above.

Clue 1: I lead the United States in the growth and manufacturing of tobacco.
Clue 2: Mount Mitchell is located within my borders. At over 1 1/4 miles above sea level, it is the highest peak in the eastern United States.
Clue 3: My nickname is "the Tar Heel State."
Question: What Southeastern state am I?
Answer: North Carolina
Jake, Annie, and Jamal

How To Extend The Lesson:

• Divide students into groups of two or three. Assign each group a specific state in the Southeast to research. Using the format shown, have each group come up with a series of three riddles for its state and write them on an index card along with the name of its state and the group members' names. Collect the index cards and shuffle them. Explain that students should not answer the riddles they have written. Then read each card aloud to the class. Award a point to each group who correctly answers a riddle.

• Guide your students in brainstorming the names of famous people from the Southeast, such as those shown on the list below. Write students' responses on the chalkboard. Next instruct each student to choose a person from the list to research. Have the student write a report about the person, including information such as birth and death dates, place of birth, description of achievements, and other interesting facts. Finally, have each student draw and color a portrait of his featured person; then mount the portraits on a bulletin board titled "Success In The Southeast."

Famous Southeasterners

Muhammad Ali	Francis Marion
Louis Armstrong	Margaret Mitchell
Pearl S. Buck	Edward R. Murrow
Kit Carson	Jesse Owens
Jimmy Carter	Dolly Parton
Jefferson Davis	Sidney Poitier
Ella Fitzgerald	Elvis Presley
Althea Gibson	Leontyne Price
Lillian Hellman	Walter Reed
Patrick Henry	Jackie Robinson
Helen Keller	Sequoya
Dr. Martin Luther King Jr.	Fran Tarkenton
Loretta Lynn	Booker T. Washington
General Douglas MacArthur	Tennessee Williams
Dolley Madison	Woodrow Wilson

• Explain to students that Kitty Hawk, North Carolina, is the location where Wilbur and Orville Wright, inventors and builders of the world's first successful airplane, made their first successful airplane flight. Point out that the Wright brothers chose Kitty Hawk as the sight of their experiment based on advice from the Weather Bureau. Explain that over the years the Wright brothers experimented with many designs before creating the one that worked. Challenge students to work in pairs to build a prototype airplane from paper and other common supplies found around the classroom or at home. Then have a competition to see which prototype airplane will fly the farthest. Award the winning pair with a certificate that reads "You've Got The 'Wright' Idea!"

Waterway Wonders

Expose your students to the waterway wonders of the Northeast with this thought-provoking lesson.

Skill: Identifying the major Northeastern waterways on a map and analyzing their importance to the region

Estimated Lesson Time: 1 hour

Teacher Preparation:
1. Make one copy of page 311 for each group of students.
2. Gather reference materials on the northeastern states.

Materials For Each Group Of Students:
1 copy of page 311
colored pencils
1 sheet of white poster board
reference materials
glue

Background Information:

The following states make up the Northeast region of the United States: Connecticut, Delaware, Maine, Maryland, Massachusetts, New Hampshire, New Jersey, New York, Pennsylvania, Rhode Island, and Vermont.

Water is a distinguishing characteristic and one of the most valuable resources of the Northeast. The Northeast has over 5,000 rivers and over 10,000 lakes, covering a total of 7,196 square miles.

Water is important to life in the region. Most people in the Northeast live on the coastal plain next to the Atlantic Ocean. Many of the region's major cities are located along the coast, harbors, and rivers. The rivers and lakes, carved by glaciers long ago, and the man-made canals allow large ships to carry goods and people throughout the region and out to the world.

The rivers also contribute to the quality of the farmland in the river valleys. The people, farms, industries, and large cities use vast amounts of the area's water. Water provides power to the region's homes and businesses through hydroelectric dams and plants.

Fishing and the processing of seafood are a major industry of the Northeast. The ocean, rivers, and lakes provide large quantities of food to the region and to the rest of the United States.

Introducing The Lesson:

Have students brainstorm types of waterways *(oceans, rivers, lakes, etc.)* and their uses *(food, drinking water, household use, farms, industries, recreation, power, transportation, etc.)*. Then inform your students that water is a major feature of the Northeast and is very important to life in the region.

Steps:

1. Share the Background Information on page 309 with your students.

2. Write the following categories on the board: transportation, food, recreation, industry, and agriculture. Discuss with students the meaning of each term.

3. Divide your class into five groups. Assign each group a different category listed on the board.

4. Give each group one copy of page 311 and the materials listed on page 309. Instruct each group to complete the page as directed. Then have the group write its assigned category name at the top of the sheet of poster board. Instruct the group to paste its completed map underneath the category name.

5. Next have each group research to find as many examples as possible that show how the various water ways (rivers, lakes, streams, the ocean, etc.) help support or enhance its category.

6. Then instruct each group to list the examples on the poster board underneath its map. Have the group illustrate, on the poster board, at least one listed example.

7. Finally have each group present its findings to the rest of the class. Post the completed posters around the classroom during your study of the Northeastern states.

FOOD
1. In New Jersey, huge clam beds extend from Barnegat Bay to Cape May.
2. New York has an annual fish catch valued at $55 million. Commercial fishing takes place in Long Island waters and in Lakes Erie and Ontario.
3. New Bedford, Massachusetts, accounts for half the scallops produced in the United States.
4. Valuable catches in the Chesapeake Bay of Maryland bring in bluefish, catfish, clams, and crabs.
5. Maine's annual lobster catch from the Atlantic is the biggest in the United States.
6. The annual fish catch of Rhode Island is valued at $85 million.

Waterways Of The Northeast

Directions: Identify each waterway listed below by placing the correct number in the appropriate box on the map. Then use the map key to help you correctly color each numbered box.

1. Lake Champlain	9. Lake Ontario	17. Allegheny River
2. Kennebec River	10. Lake Erie	18. Susquehanna River
3. Lake Winnipesaukee	11. The Finger Lakes	19. Penobscot Bay
4. Connecticut River	12. Niagara Falls	20. Atlantic Ocean
5. Delaware Bay	13. Boston Harbor	21. Massachusetts Bay
6. Chesapeake Bay	14. Hudson River	22. Potomac River
7. Narragansett Bay	15. New York State Barge Canal System	23. Penobscot River
8. Long Island Sound	16. Delaware River	24. Cape Cod Bay

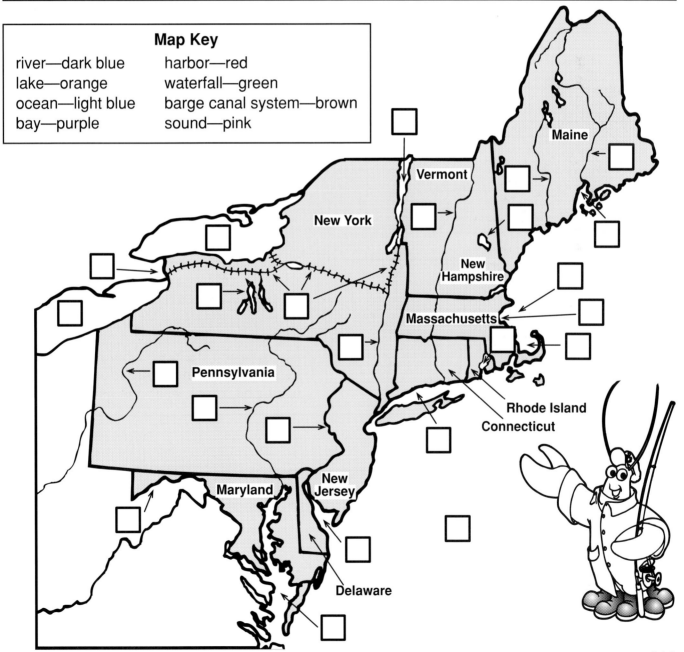

Map Key

river—dark blue harbor—red
lake—orange waterfall—green
ocean—light blue barge canal system—brown
bay—purple sound—pink

How To Extend The Lesson:

- Examine the population centers of the Northeast with this cooperative group math activity. Make one enlarged copy of the chart below. Cut the chart into separate strips, one for each Northeastern state. Divide the class into eleven groups and assign each group a Northeastern state. Give each group the appropriate strip of population data, a piece of poster paper, and markers. Instruct each group to make a colorful, labeled bar graph that accurately depicts the data. Display all the completed graphs; then have students compare and contrast the data. List their observations on the board. Ask students to predict how the findings would compare to other regions of the country. As a further challenge, have students research population data from other U.S. regions and compare it to that of the Northeastern states.

STATE	TOTAL 1990	CITY	CITY	CITY	CITY
Maine	1,233,223	Portland 64,143	Lewiston 39,757	Bangor 33,181	Auburn 24,309
New Hampshire	1,113,915	Manchester 99,567	Nashua 79,662	Concord 36,006	Rochester 26,630
Vermont	564,964	Burlington 39,127	Rutland 18,230	South Burlington 12,809	Bennington 9,532
Massachusetts	6,029,051	Boston 574,283	Worcester 169,759	Springfield 156,983	Lowell 103,439
Rhode Island	1,005,984	Providence 160,728	Warwick 85,427	Cranston 76,060	Pawtucket 72,644
Connecticut	3,295,669	Bridgeport 141,686	Hartford 139,739	New Haven 130,474	Waterbury 108,961
New York	18,044,505	New York City 7,322,564	Buffalo 328,123	Rochester 231,636	Yonkers 188,082
New Jersey	7,748,634	Newark 275,221	Jersey City 228,537	Paterson 140,891	Elizabeth 110,002
Pennsylvania	11,924,710	Philadelphia 1,585,577	Pittsburgh 369,879	Erie 108,718	Allentown 105,090
Delaware	668,696	Wilmington 71,529	Dover 27,630	Newark 25,098	Brookside 15,307
Maryland	4,798,622	Baltimore 736,014	Silver Spring 76,046	Columbia 75,883	Dundalk 65,800

©The Education Center, Inc. • *Ready-to-Go Lessons* • TEC1118

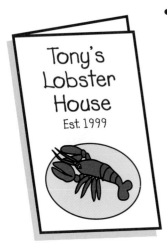

Tony's Lobster House
Est. 1999

- Use this activity to tempt your students' taste buds while teaching them about the agricultural products of the Northeast. Post a list of agricultural products produced in the Northeastern states: potatoes, eggs, milk, cranberries, apples, blueberries, raspberries, strawberries, grapes, peaches, cherries, mushrooms, tomatoes, lettuce, cabbage, snap beans, corn, hay, oats, peas, soybeans, lobsters, flounder, scallops, clams, squid, beef, pork, chicken, turkey, duck, maple syrup. Then divide your students into pairs. Give each pair a large sheet of white construction paper and markers. Tell the students that they are now the owners of a famous restaurant that specializes in food from the Northeast. Instruct each pair to select a name for its restaurant and create a menu of dishes prepared from Northeastern products. Have each pair present its menu to the rest of the class. As a further extension, have parent volunteers prepare some tasty dishes unique to the Northeastern states for the students to sample.

Answer Keys

Page 7

1. German shepherds, Chihuahuas, and basenjis have ears that are pointed and stand straight up.
2. Kara, do you believe that bloodhounds can follow scent trails more than four days old?
3. Guard hairs, fine hairs, and tactile hairs are the three basic types of hair in a dog's coat.
4. At the back of each eye, a dog has a mirrorlike structure that helps the animal see in dim light.
5. Unlike cats, dogs cannot retract their toenails.
6. The vet said, "Do not feed your dog any table scraps."
7. Charleton, do you want to go outside for a walk?
8. A dog's coat may consist of several colors, and members of the same breed may have different-colored coats.
9. Cocker spaniels, Labrador retrievers, poodles, and beagles have long, hanging ears.
10. Dogs often bury bones, or they may simply dig holes.
11. "Yes, the basenji is the only dog that cannot bark," remarked Tisha.
12. Bone chewing is natural for dogs, but it can cause broken teeth.
13. "The dog," John commented, "is an animal that has lived with people as a pet for more than 10,000 years!"
14. Yes, dogs can hear much better than people can.
15. Some dogs are born with long tails, but a veterinarian may dock (cut off) their tails shortly after birth.

Page 27
Complete sentences: 1, 5, 9, 13, 14
Fragments: 2, 3, 6, 11, 15
Run-on sentences: 4, 7, 8, 10, 12

Possible fragment and run-on sentence corrections:
2. The customer spilled his drink.
3. The new waiter did a fine job.
4. Alexis put a quarter in the jukebox, and she played her favorite song.
   Alexis put a quarter in the jukebox; she played her favorite song.
   Alexis put a quarter in the jukebox. She played her favorite song.
6. The chef prepared a fabulous dessert for Jessica.
7. Joseph likes green peppers on his pizza, and Joshua likes extra cheese.
   Joseph likes green peppers on his pizza; Joshua likes extra cheese.
   Joseph likes green peppers on his pizza. Joshua likes extra cheese.
8. Erin was really hungry, so she ordered an appetizer before her meal.
   Erin was really hungry; she ordered an appetizer before her meal.
   Erin was really hungry. She ordered an appetizer before her meal.
10. Ian paid for his food, and then he went to the movies.
    Ian paid for his food; then he went to the movies.
    Ian paid for his food. Then he went to the movies.
11. Thomas ate his food with his fork and knife.
12. Jeff couldn't decide what to eat, so he ordered a piece of pizza and a bowl of spaghetti.
    Jeff couldn't decide what to eat; he ordered a piece of pizza and a bowl of spaghetti.
    Jeff couldn't decide what to eat. He ordered a piece of pizza and a bowl of spaghetti.
15. The crazy cook tossed the pizza in the air.

Page 51

Answers may vary.
1. Shena is having a birthday party, and she is going to invite all her classmates.
2. Shena needs to decide where to have her birthday party soon, or she might not have enough time to mail the invitations.
3. Shena planned the party, and she sent the invitations to her classmates.
4. The party will be at Ice Castles, the only ice-skating rink in town.
5. The boys and girls planned on skating at the party.
6. The best skater in the class, David, will be at the party.
7. Jamie asked her parents if she could go to the party, but they won't let her go.
8. Greg listened to the music and skated with his friends.
9. Beverly Cleary, an author, sent a birthday card to Shena.
10. John played loud music at the party, and Tim went home with a headache from the music.
11. Shena had a great time at the party, and her guests had a great time, too.

Page 99

1. 17.8	8. 2.72
2. 36.8	9. 0.438
3. 10.08	10. 0.246
4. 63.0	11. 0.753
5. 4.92	12. 63.92
6. 20.61	13. 40.14
7. 13.734	14. 2.9283

Bonus Box: 0.246, 0.438, 0.753, 2.72, 2.9283, 4.92, 10.08, 13.734, 17.8, 20.61, 36.8, 40.14, 63.0, 63.92

Page 79

1. **Clue:** narrow arch
   Color: yellow
2. **Clues:** long, wooden, hammerlike stick used to hit the ball
   Color: blue
3. **Clues:** game/fast and dangerous
   Color: green
4. **Clues:** ball slightly smaller than a baseball
   Color: blue
5. **Clues:** to win the game/hitting it as hard as he could
   Color: green
6. **Clues:** continued for five minutes until/hit out of bounds
   Color: green
7. **Clue:** special breed
   Color: green
8. **Clue:** seven-minute periods
   Color: yellow
9. **Clue:** game played with bats and a ball
   Color: yellow
10. **Clue:** hit the ball
    Color: green

Page 83

Round 1
1. 65,875
2. 7,277
3. 38,685
4. 478,714
5. 8,850
6. 1,909,746

Round 2
1. 337,754
2. 6,204,292
3. 22,654
4. 651,516
5. 7,186
6. 1,104,369

Round 3
1. 241,859
2. 3,391,010
3. 59,567
4. 5,907
5. 29,325
6. 7,165,689

Page 87

2/3 − 1/2 = 1/6
1/6 + 1/3 = 1/2
1/2 + 1/3 = 5/6
5/6 − 1/3 = 1/2

Page 91

1. O	9. H
2. M	10. C
3. K	11. B
4. E	12. L
5. I	13. J
6. G	14. A
7. D	15. F
8. N	

Bonus Box: Answers will vary.

Page 108

Letter	# of acute angles	# of obtuse angles	# of right angles
A	3	2	0
E	0	0	4
F	0	0	3
H	0	0	4
I	0	0	4
K	2	2	0
L	0	0	1
M	3	0	0
N	2	0	0
T	0	0	2
V	1	0	0
W	3	0	0
X	2	2	0
Y	1	2	0
Z	2	0	0

Page 111

2. (crown)
4. (crown)
5. 2
6. 3
7. 4
8. 6

9.
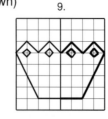

10.
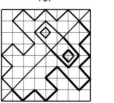

11.

Bonus Box: Answers will vary.

Page 115

1. 66
2. 121
3. 484
4. 747
5. 2,882
6. 7,117
7. 3,553
8. 7,337
9. 79,497

Bonus Box: Answers will vary.

Page 119

1. Rule: E; 2,000; ...400; 4,000; 500
2. Rule: F; 30, ...40, 49, 50
3. Rule: J; $1.50, ...$2.25, $2.50, $2.75
4. Rule: B; 100, ...101, 103, ...104
5. Rule: G; 5, ...60, 5, 55
6. Rule: C; 20; ...160; 320; ...1,280
7. Rule: H; 105, ...78, 60
8. Rule: D; 1,600; ...3,200; ...6,400
9. Rule: A; 22, ...3, ...55
10. Rule: I; 95, ...8, 91

Bonus Box: Answers will vary.

Page 123

1. 16 cm²
2. 7 cm²
3. 11 cm²
4. 11 cm²
5. 14 cm²
6. 15 cm²
7. 8 cm²
8. 10 cm²
9. 8 cm²
10. Minnie (Red)
11. Mikey and Mary (Blue)
12. Maury (Orange)
13. Marky (Yellow)
14. Malky and Mandy (Purple)
15. Molly and Melanie (Green)

Bonus Box: Answers will vary.

Page 127

Designs of Pizzas 1–5 will vary among the following five arrangements. The perimeter for each design is given.

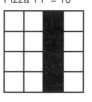
 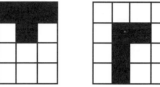

Pizza 1 P = 10 Pizza 2 P = 8 Pizza 3 P = 10 Pizza 4 P = 10 Pizza 5 P = 10

1. The selected pizza should be square in shape.
2. 8 feet
3. $16.00

Bonus Box: $24.00

Page 131

Order of answers will vary, and the length and width columns are interchangeable.

Design	Length	Width	Height
A	8	1	1
B	1	1	8
C	4	1	2
D	2	1	4
E	2	2	2
F	2	4	1

1. Answers will vary.
2. The volume of each wall design is 8 cubic units. Methods of calculating the volume will vary.

Bonus Box: Answers will vary.

Page 135

1. **Solution:** The singers and dancers will rehearse together three times in the first three weeks.

Day	1	2	3	4	5	6	7	8	9	10	11	12	13	14	15	16	17	18	19	20	21
Dancers		x			x			x			x			x			x			x	
Singers	x		x		x		x		x		x		x		x		x				

2. **Solution:** Two of the 15 costumes will have both pink and purple polka dots.

Costume	1	2	3	4	5	6	7	8	9	10	11	12	13	14	15
Pink			x			x			x			x			x
Purple		x		x		x		x		x		x		x	

3. **Solution:** Five sundaes had chocolate syrup and peanuts, and two sundaes had all three toppings.

Sundae	1	2	3	4	5	6	7	8	9	10	11	12	13	14	15
Chocolate Syrup			x			x			x			x			x
Whipped Cream				x			x			x					
Peanuts					x				x				x		

Sundae	16	17	18	19	20	21	22	23	24	25	26	27	28	29	30
Chocolate Syrup			x			x			x			x			x
Whipped Cream	x			x			x			x					
Peanuts		x				x				x					x

Bonus Box: Ten sundaes would have chocolate syrup and peanuts, and four sundaes would have all three toppings.

Page 139

1. Sam had 40 cards.
2. Callie had 17 dolls before her birthday.
3. Joe had 114 marbles on Monday.
4. Jaclyn had 25 rocks.

Bonus Box: 196 ÷ 4 = 49

Page 143

1. 3 blocks south, 7 blocks east; 10 blocks total

2. 6 strings

3. 16 total

4. 3 feet west, 8 feet south

5. next to the last (fourth in line)

6. 39 in all

7. 12 sides

8. 3 miles west

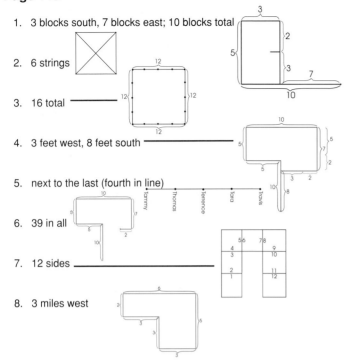

Bonus Box: Answers will vary.

Page 147

	pens	notebooks	pencils	bookbags	folders	3-ring binders	erasers
red	20	4	28	8	22	7	*
blue	35	11	16	6	14	4	*
total number	55	15	44	14	36	11	36

Bonus Box: Students' clues and chart entries will vary, but the sum of the red erasers and the blue erasers must add up to 36 erasers.

Page 151

1. Made $20. The "buyer" begins with $60. After buying the card for $30, he then has $30. If he then sells the card for $40, he has $70. If he buys the card for $50, he has $20. If he sells the card for $60, he has $80 left. Compare $80 with $60.
2. Moe is the youngest.
3. Fred finished the race in 4th place.
4. The students are sitting in the following order: Pam, Tam, Sam, and Cam. Also accept Cam, Sam, Tam, and Pam.
5. Sue's jersey is gold.
6. Each team will play six games in all. The four teams will play a total of 12 (not 24!) games.
7. There are 13 people in the movie line.
8. Three cars remain in the parking lot.

Bonus Box: Dan's album contains 42 photos.

Page 155

1. mystery, historical, adventure, science fiction; mystery, historical, science fiction, adventure; mystery, adventure, historical, science fiction; mystery, adventure, science fiction, historical; mystery, science fiction, historical, adventure; mystery, science fiction, adventure, historical;

2. banana/strawberry; banana/lemon; banana/lime; cherry/strawberry; cherry/lemon; cherry/lime; peach/strawberry; peach/lemon; peach/lime

3. white/pink; white/purple; white/yellow; white/blue; pink/purple; pink/yellow; pink/blue; purple/yellow; purple/blue; yellow/blue

4. peanut butter, carrots, juice; peanut butter, carrots, spring water; peanut butter, carrots, milk; peanut butter, bagels, juice; peanut butter, bagels, spring water; peanut butter, bagels, milk; carrots, bagels, juice; carrots, bagels, spring water; carrots, bagels, milk

5. 1 quarter, 3 dimes; 1 quarter, 2 dimes, 2 nickels; 1 quarter, 2 dimes, 1 nickel, 5 pennies; 1 quarter, 2 dimes, 10 pennies; 1 quarter, 1 dime, 4 nickels; 1 quarter, 1 dime, 3 nickels, 5 pennies; 1 quarter, 1 dime, 2 nickels, 10 pennies; 1 quarter, 6 nickels; 1 quarter, 5 nickels, 5 pennies; 1 quarter, 4 nickels, 10 pennies; 1 quarter, 5 nickels, 5 pennies; 3 dimes, 5 nickels; 3 dimes, 4 nickels, 5 pennies; 3 dimes, 3 nickels, 10 pennies; 2 dimes, 6 nickels, 5 pennies; 2 dimes, 5 nickels, 10 pennies

Bonus Box: Answers will vary.

Page 159

1. Tramal ordered lettuce on his hamburger.

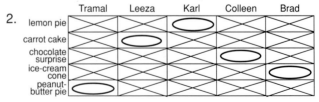

2. Karl had lemon pie for dessert.

Bonus Box: The total lunch bill was $28.75.

Page 175

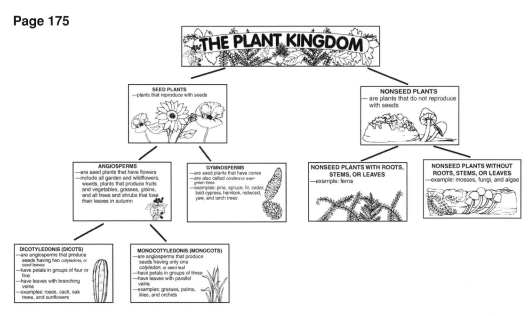

THE PLANT KINGDOM

SEED PLANTS
—plants that reproduce with seeds

NONSEED PLANTS
—are plants that do not reproduce with seeds

ANGIOSPERMS
—are seed plants that have flowers
—include all garden and wildflowers, weeds, plants that produce fruits and vegetables, grasses, grains, and all trees and shrubs that lose their leaves in autumn

GYMNOSPERMS
—are seed plants that have cones
—are also called *conifers* or *evergreen trees*
—examples: pine, spruce, fir, cedar, bald cypress, hemlock, redwood, yew, and larch trees

NONSEED PLANTS WITH ROOTS, STEMS, OR LEAVES
—example: ferns

NONSEED PLANTS WITHOUT ROOTS, STEMS, OR LEAVES
—example: mosses, fungi, and algae

DICOTYLEDONIS (DICOTS)
—are angiosperms that produce seeds having two *cotyledons*, or seed leaves
—have petals in groups of four or five
—have leaves with branching veins
—examples: roses, cacti, oak trees, and sunflowers

MONOCOTYLEDONIS (MONOCOTS)
—are angiosperms that produce seeds having only one *cotyledon*, or seed leaf
—have petals in groups of three
—have leaves with parallel veins
—examples: grasses, palms, lilies, and orchids

Page 179

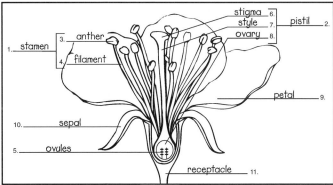

1. **stamen**—male reproductive part of a flower
2. **pistil**—female reproductive part of a flower
3. **anther**—produces pollen grains which develop sperm
4. **filament**—supports the anther
5. **ovules**—become the seeds when sperm cells fertilize the egg cells
6. **stigma**—sticky, pollen-receptive part of the pistil
7. **style**—the stalk of the pistil down which the pollen tube grows
8. **ovary**—contains the ovules and becomes the fruit
9. **petal**—colorful part of a flower used to attract insects and birds
10. **sepal**—protects the bud of a young flower
11. **receptacle**—reproductive parts of a plant are attached here

Page 183

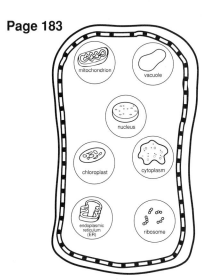

Bonus Box: Accept any reasonable drawing.

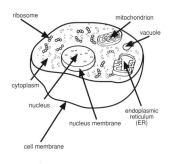

Page 187

Order of answers and interesting facts about animals will vary.

1. clam, invertebrate
2. turtle, vertebrate
3. amoeba, invertebrate
4. earthworm, invertebrate
5. dolphin, vertebrate
6. spider, invertebrate
7. cat, vertebrate
8. rabbit, vertebrate
9. jellyfish, invertebrate
10. starfish, invertebrate
11. crab, invertebrate
12. frog, vertebrate
13. fish, vertebrate
14. mouse, vertebrate
15. skunk, vertebrate

Page 191
Ocean
5. I cover about 70 percent of the earth's surface.
8. I have a variety of plants and animals that live at different depths.
17. I'm primarily salt water.
20. I include many species of fish and invertebrates.

Wetlands
12. I can be located near an ocean and contain salt water, or in forests and contain freshwater.
19. I provide homes for birds, fish, animals, and insects.
21. My areas contain permanent moisture: bogs, swamps, marshes, estuaries, ponds, lakes, and rivers.

Forest
6. I cover about 30 percent of the earth's land.
11. I provide homes for birds, insects, and animals, as well as sources of medicines.
13. I'm an area that helps absorb carbon dioxide, produce oxygen, and prevent erosion.
22. I contain tropical, temperate, coniferous, and deciduous trees.

Desert
3. I cover one-seventh of the earth's land surface, but because of environmental changes, that amount is increasing.
7. I receive less than ten inches of moisture a year.
14. I can be located in very cold or very warm climates.
18. Many plants and animals thrive in my hostile environment.

Tundra
4. My temperature range is from less than 0°C to never above 10°C.
15. The ground below my surface stays frozen all year.
16. I'm the name for the plains of the arctic circle.

Grassland
1. I'm a large expanse of land covered with tall grasses.
2. I'm also known as a *prairie* or *savanna*.
9. Most of my land in the United States has been plowed under and used for agricultural land.
10. I don't receive enough precipitation to support large trees.

Page 199

The scenes in each student's filmstrip should be pasted in the following order:

1. "Down The Food Tube"
2. Mouth
3. Pharynx
4. Esophagus
5. Stomach
6. Small Intestine
7. Large Intestine
8. "The End"

Page 203

1. physical change
2. chemical change
3. chemical change
4. physical change
5. physical change
6. physical change
7. chemical change
8. physical change
9. chemical change

Page 207

1. conduction
2. convection
3. radiation
4. radiation
5. conduction
6. convection
7. radiation
8. convection
9. radiation
10. convection
11. radiation
12. conduction

Bonus Box: Answers will vary.

Page 211

1. Some magnets are stronger than others.
2. Some larger magnets may have a stronger pulling force.
3. More paper clips will collect at the poles of the magnet because the magnetic field is strongest there.

Page 215

Students' answers may vary. Accept reasonable responses.

	Force	Reason
1.	friction	bike tires rubbing against road
2.	push	pushing the body into the air
3.	gravity	gravity causing movement downhill
4.	push	pushing the ball upward
5.	push	pushing the body upward
6.	pull	pulling back top of can
7.	push and pull	pushing up brush and pulling it down
8.	push and gravity	pushing up the seesaw and gravity bringing it down
9.	pull	pulling the drink into the mouth
10.	friction	body rubbing against the ground
11.	friction	tractor tires gripping the mud
12.	pull or push	pulling the door toward the body or pushing it away
13.	gravity	gravity pulling the body down the slide
14.	pull	pulling the nail out of the wall toward the body
15.	push	pushing the pedals of the boat to make it move

Page 227

Answers may vary. Possible answers include:

Grassland
- large crops of grain are grown here
- home to many grazing animals and burrowing animals

Tundra
- low-growing plants and flowers live for a few months
- only a few animals (arctic foxes, polar bears, wolves) stay through the winter

Coniferous Forest
- mostly evergreen trees (including cedar, pine, and redwood)
- migratory birds and moose, elk, and deer

Deciduous Forest
- mostly trees that shed their leaves each year
- many animals hibernate through the winter when the trees are bare

Savanna
- grasses and sparse clumps of trees
- lions, zebras, giraffes

Tropical Rain Forest
- has about 400 different kinds of trees
- parrots, monkeys, lizards, snakes

Desert
- cacti and yucca; plant life is scarce
- many animals are *nocturnal:* active only at night when it's cool

Chaparral
- drought-resistant evergreen shrubs
- lizards, rodents, rabbits, and their predators find shelter under the shrubs

Page 231

1. A temperate forest has the widest temperature range.
2. A tropical rain forest has the narrowest temperature range.
3. A tundra has the coldest temperatures. It is located far from the equator.
4. A tropical rain forest has the most precipitation in one year; a desert has the least precipitation.
5. If a city has very high temperatures and very little precipitation throughout the year, it most likely belongs to the desert region.
6. A taiga's temperature is about −10°C in the winter and about 17°C in the summer.
7. *Accept reasonable responses.*
   Tundra: very cold temperatures, little precipitation
   Taiga: cold temperatures, fair amount of precipitation
   Temperate forest: some cold temperatures, fairly high precipitation
   Tropical rain forest: warm temperatures, very high precipitation
   Grassland: warm temperatures, little precipitation
   Desert: very warm temperatures, very little precipitation
8. *Accept reasonable responses.* If the climate in a tropical rain forest changed to that of a tundra, most plants and animals would probably die. Some animals might migrate to a more suitable climate, while others may eventually adapt to the new climate.

Page 239

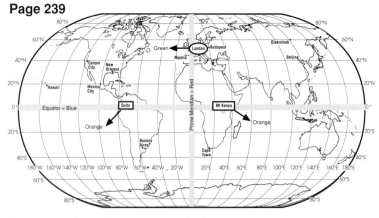

See map above for answers 1–4.

5. Madrid
6. 60°N latitude, 120°E longitude
7. Budapest, Cape Town
8. Mexico City

Bonus Box: Buenos Aires and New Orleans have similar climates. Both cities are approximately the same distance from the equator. London is located farther away from the equator and would have a much cooler climate.

Page 243

1. Oklahoma
2. Oregon
3. California
4. Montana
5. Nebraska
6. South Carolina
7. New York
8. Colorado
9. Mississippi
10. Utah
11. Pennsylvania, Delaware
12. Louisiana
13. Georgia
14. New Mexico
15. Oregon
16. Mississippi
17. North Dakota, South Dakota
18. Ohio
19. Massachusetts
20. Texas

Bonus Box: Missouri is bordered by eight states. They are Illinois, Kentucky, Tennessee, Arkansas, Oklahoma, Kansas, Nebraska, and Iowa.

Page 247

1. Missouri River
2. Mount Saint Helens
3. Niagara Falls
4. Mammoth–Flint Ridge Cave System (or Mammoth Cave)
5. Death Valley
6. Mississippi River
7. Rio Grande
8. Grand Canyon
9. Great Salt Lake
10. Rocky Mountains

Bonus Box: Superior, Michigan, Huron, Erie, and Ontario

Page 267

Union

States: California, Connecticut, Delaware, Illinois, Indiana, Iowa, Kansas, Kentucky, Maine, Maryland, Massachusetts, Michigan, Minnesota, Missouri, New Hampshire, New Jersey, New York, Ohio, Oregon, Pennsylvania, Rhode Island, Vermont, Wisconsin

President: Abraham Lincoln

Famous Generals: Ulysses S. Grant, William T. Sherman

Famous Battle Victories: Antietam, Chattanooga, Fair Oaks, Fort Donelson, Gettysburg, Nashville, Perryville, Shiloh

Causes Of The War: Your Side's Point Of View:

- opposed slavery
- felt they were fighting a war to free the slaves
- had a way of life based on factories and trade
- wanted higher taxes on European goods so Southerners would buy Northern products
- believed that the Union must be preserved above all else

Page 275

A.

1. Europe
2. Asia, Latin America
3. Latin America
4. 22%
5. Most immigrants came from Europe in the early 1900s. Today most immigrants are from Latin America and Asia.

B.

1. California, New York
2. Florida, New Jersey, Texas, and Illinois
3. 34 states
4. Answers will vary.

Page 283

Union—a political unit such as the 13 former colonies
justice—rights according to the law
domestic—originating from our own country
tranquility—a state of calmness
common—relating to the community at large
defense—protecting oneself
general—involving the whole
welfare—referring to good fortune, happiness, well-being, and prosperity
secure—guarantee
liberty—freedom
posterity—all future generations (offspring)
ordain—to establish by law
establish—to institute permanently by enactment or agreement

Your Version Of The Preamble
Answers will vary.

Americans want to work together. Everyone should be treated fairly. We want to get along with each other and defend ourselves. We want freedom for ourselves and our children. These are the reasons for writing the Constitution of the United States of America.

Page 295

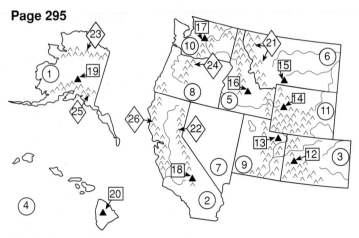

Confederacy

States: Alabama, Arkansas, Florida, Georgia, Louisiana, Mississippi, North Carolina, South Carolina, Tennessee, Texas, Virginia
President: Jefferson Davis
Famous Generals: Robert E. Lee, Stonewall Jackson
Famous Battle Victories: Chancellorsville, Chickamauga, Fredericksburg, Kennesaw Mountain, Seven Days
Causes Of The War: Your Side's Point Of View:
* favored slavery because it was needed to run the plantations
* felt they were fighting a second war of independence
* had a way of life based on small farms and plantations
* wanted lower taxes on goods so they could make better trades for European goods
* believed in states' rights

Page 299
New Mexico
* My nickname is the Land of Enchantment.
* My state bird is the roadrunner.
* My capital is Santa Fe.

Texas
* My land area is larger than any state except Alaska.
* My capital is Austin.
* My nickname is the Lone Star State because of the single star located on my flag.

Oklahoma
* My state bird is the scissor-tailed flycatcher.
* My capital is Oklahoma City.
* In the 1800s the United States made most of my land into a huge Indian reservation.
* The U.S. government opened my land to white settlement in the 1880s. I then became known as the Sooner State because many settlers arrived on my land before it was even open for settlement.

Arizona
* My state flower is the *saguaro,* or giant cactus.
* Phoenix is my state capital.
* The Grand Canyon, Petrified Forest, and Painted Desert are just a few of my tourist attractions.
* In 1930, the planet Pluto was discovered from Lowell Observatory in Flagstaff, one of my cities.

Page 307
Jamestown Settlement—Virginia
Fort Knox—Kentucky
The World of Coca-Cola®—Georgia
Cape Hatteras—North Carolina
Fort Sumter—South Carolina
Opryland USA—Tennessee
Hot Springs National Park—Arkansas

page 307 continued...
New River Gorge Bridge—West Virginia
U.S. Space and Rocket Center—Alabama
French Quarter—Louisiana
Everglades National Park—Florida
Natchez Pilgrimage—Mississippi

Bonus Box: Students' answers will vary. The following are acceptable responses:
* *Jamestown Settlement,* located less than a mile from the original Jamestown site, displays replicas of three ships that carried the first permanent English settlers to America. Also located at the tourist attraction is a model of Powhatan's lodge, the area's first fort.
* *Fort Knox,* sometimes called "the Home of Armor," is the site of the nation's gold depository and the Patton Museum of Cavalry and Armor.
* *The World of Coca-Cola®,* a museum honoring the famous soft drink, is located in Atlanta, Georgia.
* *Cape Hatteras* is located at the southeastern end of Hatteras Island, which is part of North Carolina's Outer Banks. Because many ships have been wrecked at Cape Hatteras by the treacherous seas, it has been nicknamed "the Graveyard of the Atlantic."
* Located in the harbor of Charleston, South Carolina, *Fort Sumter* is the place of the initial shot fired in the Civil War.
* *Opryland USA* is a musical show theme park and home of "The Grand Ole Opry," a famous, live country music radio show.
* Built around hot mineral springs, *Hot Springs National Park* is a health and pleasure resort nestled in the Ouachita Mountains of Arkansas.
* *The New River Gorge Bridge,* located near Fayetteville, West Virginia, is the world's longest steel arch span bridge. Its main span is 1,700 feet long.
* *The U.S. Space and Rocket Center* in Huntsville, Alabama, houses the world's largest collection of spacecraft, rockets, and other space-related exhibits.
* Top jazz musicians and the allure of an old European town are just two reasons that tourists flock to the *French Quarter,* New Orleans's historic district.
* *Everglades National Park* covers approximately 1.5 million acres of Florida's original Everglades, one of the most intriguing swamp areas in the world.
* Many tourists visit Mississippi during the spring or fall for the *Natchez Pilgrimage.* Visitors can travel back in time as they view some of the finest antebellum homes in the nation.

Page 311

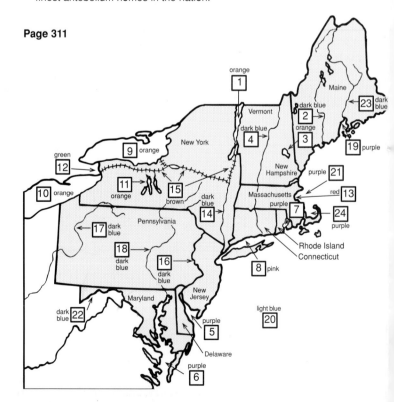